CRITICAL ESSAYS
ON ISRAELI SOCIAL ISSUES
AND SCHOLARSHIP

A PUBLICATION FROM *THE ASSOCIATION FOR ISRAEL STUDIES*

SUNY Series in Israeli Studies
Russell A. Stone, editor

Critical Essays on Israeli Social Issues and Scholarship

Books on Israel, Volume III

Edited by Russell A. Stone and Walter P. Zenner

State University of New York Press

Published by
State University of New York Press, Albany

© 1994 State University of New York

All rights reserved

Printed in the United States of America

No part of this book may be used or reproduced
in any manner whatsoever without written permission
except in the case of brief quotations embodied in
critical articles and reviews.

For information, address State University of New York Press,
State University Plaza, Albany, N.Y., 12246

Production by Marilyn P. Semerad
Marketing by Dana E. Yanulavich

Library of Congress Cataloging-in-Publication Data

Critical essays on Israeli social issues and scholarship / edited by
    Russell A. Stone and Walter P. Zenner.
        p.   cm. — (Books on Israel ; 3) (SUNY series in Israeli
studies)
    ISBN 0-7914-1959-2. — ISBN 0-7914-1960-6 (pbk.)
    1. Israel—Intellectual life—Book reviews. 2. Israel—Social
conditions—Book reviews.   I. Stone, Russell A., 1944– .
II. Zenner, Walter P.   III. Series.   IV. Series: SUNY series in
Israeli studies.
DS102.95.B66   1988 vol. 3
[DS113]
956.94 s—dc20
[956.9405]   93-39862
                                                                        CIP
            10 9 8 7 6 5 4 3 2 1

CONTENTS

Introduction
  Walter P. Zenner and Russell A. Stone 1

I. LITERATURE AND LANGUAGE

Rewriting the Holocaust:
An Israeli Case Study in the Sociology of the Novel
  Aviad E. Raz 9

Espionage and Cultural Mediation
  Walter P. Zenner 31

An Authentic Human Voice:
The Poetry of Amnon Shamosh
  Abraham Marthan 43

On *The Schizoid Nature of Modern Hebrew*
  Shmuel Bolozky 63

II. CULTURE AND SOCIETY:
Gender, Ethnicity, Community

Does Gender Matter?
  Madeleine Tress 89

Studies on Ethnicity
  Walter F. Weiker 107

The Search for Israeliness: Toward an Anthropology
of the Contemporary Mainstream
  James Armstrong 121

III. SOCIAL ANALYSIS

From Apparatus to Populus:
The Political Sociology of Yonathan Shapiro
 Uri Ram 137

Governing in a Turbulent National Policy Environment
 Giora Goldberg and Efraim Ben-Zadok 161

IV. HISTORY AND POLITICS

The Significance of Israeli Historical Revisionism
 Jerome Slater 179

The Utopian Crisis of the Israeli State
 Yagil Levy and Yoav Peled 201

The Arab-Israeli Conflict and the Victory of Otherness
 Ilan Peleg 227

The Intercommunal Dimension
in the Arab-Israeli Conflict: The Intifada
 Efraim Inbar 245

List of Contributors 265

INTRODUCTION

Walter P. Zenner and Russell A. Stone

This volume of critical essays is part of a series that comments on issues within Israeli culture, literature, politics, scholarship, and society. The series is sponsored by the Association for Israel Studies, which was founded in 1985 by scholars from several disciplines to provide a framework for the discussion of all aspects of Israeli society. This association was formed to provide a place where the study of Israel from widely differing perspectives could be presented. In this structure there would be room for scholars with a wide range of differing opinions, but who could agree on the importance of academic discourse. The three volumes published so far in this series reflect at least some of this divergence of opinion. Obviously the views expressed in each chapter are solely those of the author. They do not represent the outlook of the association, of SUNY Press, or of the editors.

The authors in this volume were called upon to identify a series of recently published books, or one book of importance to their field of inquiry. Then, they were requested to shape a critical essay which was to be based upon consideration of the book(s), but which would reach beyond the scope of a usual book review, or even a review essay. They were to use the work(s) as an opportunity to comment upon the state of scholarship, or the state of society in the subject area in question. The result is the collection of essays in this volume, which is divided into four sections, Literature and Language, Culture and Society, Social Analysis, and History and Politics. Many of the works are related to the essays in the earlier volumes in the series.[1]

I. Literature and Language

The essays on literature generally follow those in earlier volumes, which related literary works to changes in national ideology and political discourse (Divine in volume 1, Katriel, Shenhar, and Jacobson in volume 2). Those essays were primarily concerned with the decay of secular Zionism, the turn away from a view of Israel as a utopia, and the increased attraction of life abroad. In the present volume, other themes are considered. Raz shows how Israeli authors have changed their treatment of the Holocaust since the Second World War and how they have increasingly identified with the victims. This has accompanied other changes in Israeli national ideology.

Zenner and Marthan deal with a single author, Amnon Shamosh. Zenner, like Raz, analyzes literary works sociologically. Both Zenner and Marthan look at Shamosh in relationship to Shamosh's search for his ethnic roots. One looks primarily at a single work by the author, while the other looks at his corpus of poetry and relates it to a more general consideration of the Sephardic tradition.

Bolozky's chapter is the first essay on linguistics for this series. His essay deals with the work of Paul Wexler, who has proposed a provocative thesis that both Yiddish and modern Hebrew are intrinsically based on an extinct Slavic language, rather than classifying them in the usual manner as Germanic and Semitic languages respectively. Bolozky analyzes this thesis in a straightforward fashion on purely linguistic grounds. While the chapter may appear technical, it is not difficult to follow, especially for those who know modern Hebrew. The technical linguistic meaning of classification and affiliation is, of course, based on intra-disciplinary consideration. Still, propositions like those of Wexler have potentially social ramifications in terms of how peoples view themselves in relationship to other nations, ethnic groups, etc.

II. Culture and Society

The chapters in the second section continue some of the themes discussed in the first section, since they also deal with Israeli Jewish self-image and the foundations of communal cohesion. Tress's chapter is the first one in this series dealing with the important topic of gender. In a highly critical manner it shows how the status of women in Israeli society is related to security policy. Tress's theoretical orientation is derived from current "post-modernist" paradigms in the social sciences, as are the authors dealt with by Armstrong.

Weiker's chapter on ethnicity utilizes a more traditional social scientific orientation. His chapter reviews theories of ethnicity as they have been applied to Israel and thus continues a discussion begun by Zenner (volume 1). This chapter is particularly concerned with relationships between different Jewish origin-groups. Although class has not been at the fore of the analyses of stratification in Israel, several of the social scientists discussed by Weiker have analyzed the relations between European and Middle Eastern Jews in Israel as those between distinct classes.

While this topic was foremost on the agenda of anthropologists studying Israel before 1980, it has been replaced by other interests of late. Armstrong's review of works on the "mainstream" gives attention to one such trend. These works deal with the manner in which political ideology and nationalism have been internalized by Jewish Israelis, particularly but not solely those of Ashkenazic background. The works in this section can be seen as reviewing how the sociology of Israel reflects general interests in race, class, and gender.

III. Social Analysis

The chapters by Ram and Ben-Zadok and Goldberg deal with the analyses of the Israeli polity by two political analysts.

One is the sociologist, Yonathan Shapiro, who broke away from the structural-functional paradigm of Eisenstadt (discussed by Lustick in volume 1). He is considered one of the chief proponents of conflict-sociology in Israel. Yehezkel Dror has been a practitioner of social policy analysis and has served as a government advisor. His criticism comes from within the Israeli political establishment. In fact, his analyses are in the form of memoranda to the prime minister. Shapiro, unlike the historical revisionists, unequivocally accepts the legitimacy of the state and its underlying ideology.

IV. History and Politics

The final section is dominated by a discussion of Israeli historical revisionism which has questioned the previous dominant interpretation of Israel's conflict with the Palestinians. The former paradigm saw the Yishuv and Israel as reacting defensively against the Arabs and did not question the Zionist claims to the land. The revisionists, discussed by Slater (also see chapters by Peretz and Heydemann in previous volumes), question both premises. Levy and Peled seek to extend revisionist interpretation to the Six Day War. They also extend the discussion of Israeli sociological thought, which we find in the previous sections.

Peleg deals with social psychological concomitants of the Arab-Israeli conflict. He finds this in the view of both Arabs and Israelis that their enemies are totally "Other." This demonization is particularly symbolized by the Israeli identification of Palestinians with "terrorism" and the Arab image of Jews as "Zionists." This process of stereotyping is not unidimensional and may go through various phases, as Rejwan (in volume 1) showed with regard to Arab analyses of the rise of Israel (also see Peretz in volume 1). Peleg, however, sees this demonization reaching its apex in right wing extremism within contemporary Israel.

Inbar, in the final chapter in this volume, discusses the Intifada as an intercommunal struggle. He sees it as one dimension of the conflict between Israel and the Arabs. He tries to give us a balance sheet on the costs to both Israelis and Palestinians. He also gives us a sense of both divergence and convergence between Palestinian and Israeli commentators on the Intifada.

Note

1. See Ian S. Lustick, ed., *Books on Israel*, vol. 1, (Albany, N.Y.: SUNY Press, 1988); and Ian. S. Lustick and Barry Rubin, eds., *Critical Essays on Israeli Society, Politics, and Culture: Books on Israel*, vol. 2, (Albany, N.Y.: SUNY Press, 1991).

Part I

Literature
and
Language

Rewriting the Holocaust: An Israeli Case Study in the Sociology of the Novel

Aviad E. Raz

Omer Bartov, *Border Patrol*, (in Hebrew) Tel Aviv: Hakibbutz Hame'uchad, 1988.

Dorit Peleg, *Una*, (in Hebrew) Tel Aviv: Hakibbutz Hame'uchad, 1988.

> *"In each and every generation, everyone must see himself as if he were destroying Hitler"*
> —Efraim Sidon, *Fighting and Killing.**

Two recently published novels by young Israeli authors, Dorit Peleg's *Una* and Omer Bartov's *Border Patrol* (both published by Hakibbutz Hame'uchad, 1988), are the starting point of the following inquiry. Both contain large sections concerning the life of a Jew during the Holocaust, as seen and portrayed through the eyes of a contemporary Israeli. This portrayal makes no claim for historical accuracy, as opposed to an altogether different, and ever more frequent, literary genre of the Holocaust—the testimony—

---

*Sidon, E. "Fighting and Killing." in *Fighting and Killing without End: Political Poetry in the Lebanon War*, edited with an afterword by Hannan Hever and Moshe Ron, (Tel Aviv: Hakibbutz Hame'uchad 1984), p. 124.

to be later contrasted with these novels. As such, it is portraying the contemporary Israeli rather than the Holocaust Jew.

This chapter, therefore, will attempt to place these novels in their social context. The argument underpinning this task is that in the act of writing, the novelist (the playwright, the poet) is trying to "make sense of our lives."[1]. The parallels evident in the two novels can thus be cautiously compared with, and perhaps shed light on, trends common to "our lives" in contemporary Israeli society.

The social context in question encompasses the whole gamut of Israeli culture's complex relations to the Holocaust, and in particular to the image of the Holocaust Jew. More specifically, the novels in question can serve to illustrate the process of social construction of the image of the "Holocaust Jew." I argue that the construction of such an image can be seen to alternate between two opposites: the stereotype of "lamb to slaughter," on the one hand, and the "rebel" on the other. This alternation is much more reflective of Israeli collective identity than of historical data. The depiction of the "Holocaust Jew" in Israeli literature can thus represent changes in the evolving collective identity of Israeli society. The two novels in point will serve here to illustrate such a change.

I. The Holocaust in Israeli Eyes: A Brief History of Ideological Typification

The impact of the Holocaust on the Jewish state, from its very inception (considered internationally, though not necessarily nationally, as an aftermath of the Holocaust) to its gradual formulation of identity, cannot be overlooked. Yet this impact has received only scant and partial attention, relative to its significance, and only recently have empirical studies of psychosocial effects of the Holocaust been systematically carried out.[2] Due partly to the sheer enormity of events, partly to the great proportion of Holocaust survivors in Israel (nearly one-half the population in 1948), and partly to the central negative place of the Holocaust in Zionist ideology as the ultimate consequence of Jewish vulnerability in the Diaspora, images of the Sho'ah have become key symbols preceding any attempt to fashion an Israeli identity.[3] Indeed, the Sho'ah has begun not only to figure retroactively pre-Sho'ah catastrophes, it has also become a standard by which all post-Holocaust calamities are measured.[4] The following concise description of the various phases in the typification of the Holocaust is a sketchy attempt deserving a much lengthier elaboration, yet it should provide us with the broad perspective needed for the ensuing discussion.

The Israeli Yishuv (pre-state community) reactions to the Holocaust reflected to a large extent a sense of resentment, and rejection, of the behavior of the Jewish victims. These, according to the widely held belief, passively accepted their fate, subscribing to the "traditional line of conduct" of Jews in the Diaspora.[5] This negative stance was combined with the socialist-Zionists' ideological rejection of the Jewish Diaspora, and ideas of militarism and state sovereignty turned into a way of life in newly formed Israel.[6] In a kibbutz Haggada for Passover written just after the Holocaust, it is argued that "not only Hitler is responsible for the death of the six millions—but all of us—and first and foremost these six millions. Had they known that a Jew has power too, they would not have all gone as lambs to slaughter."[7]

Without any attempt to assess the historical factuality of the metaphor of "lamb to slaughter," it is argued here that its actual acceptance was a result of its relevance to the predominant ideological trends in Israeli society. A very partial yet representative list of examples concerning the use of "lamb to slaughter" in Israeli society should make the case clearer. The metaphor of "lamb to slaughter" was not directed to the Holocaust alone; it was the cumulative conception of what was considered the Jews' passive acceptance of their own victimization, from the crusades of the Middle Ages to Kishinev's pogroms. Originally a biblical metaphor (Isaiah 53:7) it was to become first a metonymy and then a slogan. In prayers of Kaddish dedicated to the victims of the Holocaust, the Israeli ministry of education has included the words "lamb to slaughter." As early as June 22, 1944, when everyone already knew what went on in Auschwitz, the Israeli newspaper related to the socialist movement, *Davar*, asked in its first page: "Why don't Hungarian Jews defend themselves?" An Israeli paratrooper returning from Hungary in 1945 reports that in Tel Aviv he was repeatedly asked, "why didn't the Jews rebel? why did they go as lambs to slaughter?"[9] It was around this period that the popular nickname "soap" was invented and used widely in reference to Holocaust survivors.[10] Ben-Gurion, in an interview with the *New York Times* (December 18, 1960) before the Eichmann Trial, justified the trial as "proving to Israel's younger generation that Israelis are not like lambs to be taken to slaughter, but a nation able to fight back."[11]

Along with the image of "lamb to slaughter" there existed another, opposite image: the Jew as rebel. It was articulated, for example, in the naming of the national memorial day for the Holocaust as being also "in memory of the ghetto uprisings," or the naming of the Yad va-Shem Institute as the "Memorial Agency for the Holocaust and Heroism." However, this formal reference only attests to the dominance of the other metaphor. Indeed, the metaphor of the rebellious Holocaust Jew could not have served as an equivalent to the "lamb to slaughter." Even if there was a small number of Jewish rebels, they were all defeated by the Nazis, and their rebellion was a priori futile. It is interesting to note that early Israeli educational texts replaced the word "Jews" by "Hebrews" (*Ivrim*) and "sons of Israel" when referring to the rebels.[12] This pair of archetypical opposites, the "lamb to slaughter" and "the rebel," will later form the basis for discussing the common narrative of the two novels.

The image of the Holocaust Jew as a "lamb to slaughter," with all its problematics, has become legitimized through the militaristic ethos of Israeli society and the ideological negation of historic 'Jewish passivity.' This sense of resentment has its perhaps most extreme expression in the Ben-

Gurion doctrine of state sovereignty, which rejects the exile and the Holocaust as irrelevant to the Israeli reality. To Ben-Gurion, the Holocaust was something which "happened to the diaspora Jews because they were diaspora Jews," and "antisemitism, the Dreyfus trial, Jewish persecutions in Rumania . . . are for us events from foreign history and sad memories of diaspora Jews, but not a spiritual experience nor life facts of instructive value."[13]

Liebman and Don-Yehiah, in their account of the transformation of civil religion in Israel, describe how its new form after 1967 redefined the Holocaust as the ultimate expression of the evil intents of the Gentiles and their everlasting hatred of Jews.[14] The Holocaust was molded as a constant reminder of "what happened and can happen anew." Thus, in a memorial ceremony to the Holocaust held in 1976, Golda Meir said that "the Holocaust of each and every Jew has become the collective Holocaust for the state of Israel,"[15] and Gideon Hausner, former prosecutor in the Eichmann Trial in 1960 stated that "the Holocaust and the rebels are still part of our reality".[16] A major popularizer of this viewpoint was Menachem Begin who, in the middle of the Lebanon War, during the siege on Beirut, described Ya'ser Arafat as a "Hitler hiding [from Israeli soldiers] in a bunker."[17]

Thus, whereas the selective attitude of Ben-Gurion's "state sovereignty" dismissed the Holocaust as irrelevant to Israeli reality and encouraged the rejection and silencing directed toward the Holocaust survivors and their experience, Begin's interpretation redefined it as a national integrating factor and a locus of Jewish solidarity.

However, it was only in the third stage, and with the third generation, that Israeli society has reconsidered the Holocaust in terms of individual suffering. Instead of the all-embracing generalizations of a "memorial day for the six million," the year 1990 saw the memorial project called "everyone has a name," in which people were invited to read, through a loudspeaker, the names of Holocaust victims at various sites erected throughout the country. Nothing is perhaps more illustrative of the change in Israelis' perceptions of the Holocaust than the new custom of "youth delegations" sent to concentration camps in Germany and Poland. For a description of one of these journeys, portrayed as a political pilgrimage of "oneness"—as well as a journey to confront xenophobia—see Segev.[18]

II. The Holocaust in Israeli Literature: Writing the Unspeakable

The meaning and use of the Holocaust as a literary theme have been widely studied, not surprisingly mostly by Jewish authors, from various political, sociological, and philosophical, as well as literary, perspectives.[19] In the case of individual writers such as Sylvia Plath, Edmond Jabes, Primo Levi or Elie Wiesel, no study of their work is complete without reference to the Holocaust. It was the Holocaust that also created a new genre of literary testimony, with its own distinct poetics.[20]

Yaoz,[21] in her study of the Holocaust in Hebrew literature, considers the perspective of the "other planet" as a key to the poetic task of attempting to express the inhuman horror of the Holocaust. This literary attempt to grasp the uncommunicable, poetically self-defeating as it might be, is nevertheless functional in framing the otherwise incomprehensible into a textual, and hence intelligible, structure.[22] The metaphor of "the other planet" is taken from Ka-Tzetnik (Yechiel Dinur) novels,[23] in which the poetic drive of the writing is "to prove" that the Holocaust is an aberration, a rupture of history. Without addressing the intricate task of classifying the whole of Israeli Holocaust literature, a brief glance at the titles chosen for Ka-Tzetnik's novels, along with those of books by other Israeli authors, should serve to demonstrate the common denominators of this "other planet" genre, which emphasizes the uniqueness of the Holocaust by repeating several motives that have been turned into metonymys. This list of titles contains, for example, *Star Eternal* and *Sunrise over Hell*

(Ka-Tzetnik); *Not of This Time, Not of This Place* and *Bells and Trains* (Yehuda Amichai); *The Burning Bush* (Aharon Meged); *Children of the Shadows* (Ben-Zion Tomer); *Smoke* and *Night Train* (Aharon Appelfeld); *Night Chariot* and *The World's Vacuum* (Itamar Ya'oz-Kest).

The "other planet" genre, which has until recently dominated the literary scene, is perhaps the other side of rejection and silencing which characterized the first phase of typifying the Holocaust in Israel. By overemphasizing the absence of a proper language for describing the Holocaust, it unconsciously encourages its obscuration, and furthermore its silencing, by those who do not share that language. By claiming the incomparable uniqueness of the Holocaust, it unintentionally prepares the ground for rejecting it as an aberration, a mutation, a kind of transcendental monstrosity. In short, by withdrawing ever more persuasively into a private planet and a private language, it serves to widen the distance between "their Holocaust" and "our life." Other novels exploited more indirect, subtle approaches. Avoiding the actual "horror time" of the Holocaust itself, they focused on historical periods either preceding or following it. Thus, one of the most prominent novels written in Hebrew under the influence of the Holocaust, *Saul and Johanna* (*Sha'ul ve'Yohanna*), by Naomi Frenkel, describes Jewish life in Germany before the destruction. Another famous novel, David Grossman's *Look Under: Love*, focuses on the Holocaust's impact on both its survivors and their children now in Israel. Rather than emphasizing the trans-historical nature of the Holocaust, Frenkel's trilogy seeks to express its precedents by drawing a historical panorama of the decline of the Weimar Republic. Other novels belonging to this historical genre are, for example, *Amidst the Living and the Dead* (Yonat and Alexander Sand) which focuses on one class in a Polish *gymnasium* during the thirties; *Lead Soldiers* (Uri Orlev); and Ka-Tzetnik's chronicle-type novels, for instance *Salamander*. Thomas Mann's *Buddenbrooks* is another, well-known example of this genre.

Grossman's novel (*Look Under: Love*), written thirty years after the Holocaust, was the first to deal directly with the experience of Holocaust survivors vis-à-vis its conception by Israel's second generation. In effect, the "real" protagonists of the novel are the Israeli children of Holocaust survivors (the so-called "second generation"). The novel revolves around their attempt to embark from silence into speech. In it the narrator, an Israeli child named Momik, the son of Holocaust survivors, imagines the Holocaust to be a monster lurking in the darkness of the family house's locked cellar. Another novel belonging to the same category as Grossman's is, for example, *Adam Resurrected* (by Yoram Kaniuk), in which the protagonist, a Holocaust survivor now living in Israel, is forced into an asylum by his relatives.

The types, or genres, of Israeli Holocaust literature that I have in mind, then, can be generally classified into four categories. They include, first, the "other planet" type and the testimonies (personal autobiographies), which can be written only by Holocaust survivors; second, the historical, and third the accommodation and confrontation types, both characterizing the attempt of the "second generation" to come to terms with the Holocaust; and, finally, the manipulation type, to which I shall now turn. The linkage between these four literary types and their counterparts in Israeli symbolic and ideological conceptions of the Holocaust will be discussed in the ensuing conclusion.

III. The Case of Literary Manipulation: *Una* and *Border Patrol*

Several reasons exist for discussing these two novels together. They are the latest additions to the fast-growing corpus of Israeli Holocaust literature. Although belonging to different literary genres (*Una* is a psychological, stream-of-consciousness novel, *Border Patrol* is a thriller), both share a parallel narrative in which a young contemporary Jew is mysteriously drawn back to the Holocaust, witnessing it anew through the eyes of a Jewish person who lived under Nazi occupation during World War II. The two authors share high socioeconomic backgrounds. Both are Ashkenazi intellectuals working in the academy, neither claim political orientation, and neither are children of Holocaust survivors. Thus, their social identity, briefly illustrated as it is, represents the central concensus of Israeli society. One of them is male, the other female, and their "Holocaust Jews" are respectively male and female. The differences in gender present themselves in the writing, yet the parallels I discuss loom even larger in this light.

Let me now turn to a brief textual comparison of the novels, starting with a concise description of the plots, which will then lead to a detailed analysis of two specific excerpts. Bartov's narrator and protagonist is a young Israeli scholar who comes to Germany to research some unknown details of the Nazi regime. During his work in the archives he comes across a report written by an S.S. officer, commander of a special unit (*Einsatzkommando*) whose function is to exterminate Jews in conquered areas. He is thereafter consumed by vivid hallucinations, which culminate in the observation of an imaginary fight between the Nazi officer (Georg Hasse) and a Jewish woodcutter (Jacob Himmel).

Peleg's narrator and protagonist, in contrast, is a little girl living in a village under Nazi occupation, watching every night, together with all the villagers, how her Jewish mother fights with a Polish woman. This little girl is in fact dreamt of by the "real" protagonist, a grown-up Jewish woman living in contemporary New York. Several clues hint that she is in fact an Israeli expatriate. Both the Jewish woman in New York and the Israeli scholar in Germany are "dreaming about" the Holocaust, reconstructing certain episodes in it and living them through the eyes of a Holocaust Jew, to whom they find themselves strangely attracted. This Jew is perhaps the great-grandfather or great-grandmother they were told about long ago, when they were children. However, this reconstruction claims no commitment to historical facts; rather, it manipulates them according to a different scheme.

The transitions between "real" time (i.e., the present of the narrator) and "dream time" (i.e., the present of the Holocaust Jew) constitute the compositional structure of the plot. A parallel use of moving in time as an organizing principle is found in Amichai's Holocaust novel which bears the telling title *Not of This Time, Not of This Place*.[24] His novel is built on a deliberate entangling of diachronic and synchronic time systems. In one time system the narrator, Yoel, is living in Jerusalem in the 1950s, and in the other he finds himself in post-Holocaust Germany, where he is said to be "like that hero, Odysseus, who ventured down into Hell, so that the demons might be revealed to him" (p. 133). In Bartov's and Peleg's novels, the transition in time, accompanied by a transition in dramatis personae, also functions as a rite of transition, in which the contemporary person recaptures his sense of identity through becoming one with the spirit of his ancestor.[25] This sense of identity, however, is too fragile and momentary to last long. It exists only during the rite of transition. This means that in order to sustain it, the narrator must forever remain in the liminal state of his subjective consciousness. Indeed, the two novels conclude with an abstract stream of consciousness in which time, place, and dramatis personae all chaotically diffuse with no sign of possible order.

Focusing on the unique characteristics of that ancestor, namely the "Holocaust Jew" that the authors have chosen to reconstruct, I would now like to address the fight scenes in each of the two novels. Each scene holds a central function both in the novel's plot and in its narrative structure. In *Border Patrol*, this scene is found at the end of the novel, and provides a culmination and a catharsis for the whole plot; in *Una*, it stands at the beginning, providing a setting and a motivation for the protagonist's quest for self-identity. A comparison of the actual excerpts might be illuminating:

He went out of the woods, and easily identified the man lying on the moist leafy couch. Stopping a few steps from him, he tapped his heels and introduced himself: "S.S. Hauptsturmführer Georg Hasse, Einsatzcommando commandant." . . . His black uniform fit tightly to his strong body. The badge of death skull glittered on the right lapel of his collar, . . . his clear eyes were reflecting beams of the setting sun.

Jacob looked a while at the young officer, then got up heavily. "Jacob Himmel, woodcutter, at your service," he said in Yiddish. "I have been looking for you for a long time," said Hasse. "I was waiting for you, because I knew you would come," said Jacob Himmel.

The sun touched the trees, and a cold wind began to blow. Leaves were turning round in the clearing and Yiftach no longer knew where he was, because he was now seeing simultaneously the road junction and the two men in the middle of it, the many towns lying around, the lines of tanks and trucks and soldiers, the smoke and the fires. Despite all this he remained in the clearing, beside the two men. Now he knew they would fight until death. ("The Fight," p. 126, from *Border Patrol*)

For the sixth time, father Anton's cry terrified us . . . his black priest robe pulling him down to the sawdust floor, anchoring him to the ground . . . six times, when that coil of snakes, tangled in the sawdust, the coil that was two women. They were a heavy Jewish woman who used to read sacred books of heretics by the window in the evenings, and beautiful Zelka whose image was seen in the woods when she was strolling through the forest, of whom the very earth would reflect her unbearably pretty face; when that coil of snakes became petrified in that last moment just before the end, before expiring, before the climax, and you could hear the silence solidifying, turning hard as steel—then it was broken by father Anton's cry . . . six times it postponed the end, but now, we knew, it wouldn't. Because the necessity is stronger than the cry, stronger than the refusal, stronger than the will, and tonight it will be decided. ("The Battle," p. 11, from *Una*)

Both scenes portray a duel to the death between two opponents: Nazi and Jew. The chapters' titles attest to their ritualistic contents: "the battle" and "the fight." The dramatic settings, located in a sort of dream time that is really out of time or place, suggest a myth of an eternal return, where the two opponents represent two extremes, two worlds that cannot reside together. Accordingly, the persons fighting are essentially archetypes, metonymically standing for Nazi and Jew.[26] The Holocaust Jew, in whom we are interested, undergoes a dramatic transformation. Whereas usually portrayed in Israeli culture as passive, powerless, a "lamb to slaughter" (and in Jewish culture, also as martyr), here we find someone who rebels, fights back, and finally defeats the Nazi in a bare-handed face-to-face confrontation.

The common narrative underpinning both texts (that of the contemporary Israeli's quest for identity, which inevitably brings him, and her, to the Holocaust) reaffirms the previously discussed significance of the Holocaust as a key symbol preceding any attempt to fashion a modern Israeli or Jewish identity. As we gradually move away from the historical events of the Holocaust, it becomes inaccessible to us except in textual forms. "Writing about" the Holocaust then necessarily passes through its prior textualization, its narrativization in what Jameson calls the political unconscious.[27] It is in this context that the startlingly similar formulation of the image of the Holocaust Jew poses itself and asks to be explained. I suggest that the explanation does not lie solely "inside" the plot. It also has to be reconstructed as a symptom whose cause is another order of phenomenon. The prominent function that this parallel formulation holds in both novels presumably reflects the preoccupation of three Israeli generations with that symbol. Moreover, the complete transformation of the Jew from a "lamb to slaughter" into the opposite archetypical "warrior" or "rebel" demands further explanation.

Among its many reapplications to unrelated events, the Holocaust Jew has become, among other examples, the trope for suffering Russians (in Yevtushenko's poetry), for poets (for Paul Celan), for psychic pain (for Sylvia Plath), and for Palestinian refugees (for Israeli poets). The case in point, however, is different, since the novelists did not replicate the archetype of the Holocaust Jew, but transformed it. This transformation can make sense within the narrative structure of the novel, since it is this rebellious quality of the ancestor that gives meaning to the quest and restores his/her offspring's identity. Artificially manipulated and lacking credibility as it does, it is still functional. But how are we to account for that transformation sociologically? Here the discussion is open for hypotheses. A possible clue is that all the cases of "replication" indicated above emanate from a primarily *Jewish* archetype of the Holocaust Jew, reflecting victimization, suffering, and martyrdom. In contrast, the unique archetypical characteristics of the Holocaust Jew in the two novels suggest a reversal from a primarily *Israeli* conception of that archetype—the concept of "lamb to slaughter." Perhaps it is here, in the denial of the conception of "lamb to slaughter," that we should look for the answer.

IV. Discussion

A case study in the sociology of the novel, this inquiry has proceeded in two directions, literary and sociological, picking up examples and explanations of both kinds as it progressed. I shall first attempt to introduce some order into the puzzle, organizing the two domains into one matrix. For this purpose, let me define three principles, or axes, around which transformations occur.

Within the historical-sociological sphere, there are two axes of transformation:

1. Personal distance from the Holocaust: the diminishing contact with Holocaust survivors living in Israel, or any other authentic Holocaust text, for that matter. This contact grows weaker as time decreases the number of living survivors. As survivors pass away, the genre of testimony also dies out; and, literary works dealing with the problematic confrontation with the Holocaust experience

(whether by survivors themselves, in the form of "the other planet" genre, or by second-generation Israelis who confront their upbringing) are also gradually disappearing.
2. Social distance from the Holocaust: the spreading of various ideologies (militarism, state sovereignity, socialist-Zionism, national-religious) in Israeli society, which interpret the Holocaust in a certain manner and define its key symbols (among these, "lamb to slaughter" is the most relevant to this study).

The space unfolded by these two axes of transformation grows in direct relation to the passage of time. As the distance from the Holocaust grows, the degrees of freedom expand. In this respect, the Holocaust is like the center of a crack in a mirror.

Whereas the sociological axes provide the larger context for the emergence of the genres identified here, the literary-aesthetic parameters denote their syntax. Here we find the third principle of transformation: the transformation of genres. This syntax is made up of two categories: the representative and the expressive. According to Scholes and Kellog,[28] the representative tends to replicate reality, whereas the expressive brings up only certain aspects of it, and reorganizes them on a higher level. The representative is metonymical (standing as part to a whole), self-contained, and tending to mimesis, whereas the expressive is metaphorical (links different worlds), open-ended, and tends to metaphysics. This distinction is also echoed in James's[29] notions of the historical and the trans-historical, where the former contains a well-constructed set of spatio-temporal events and historical facts, striving for completeness and authenticity of description, and the latter avoids historical facts and relies on an inner logic, in a manner parallel to myths, dreams, and madness.

Figure 1 illustrates the isomorphism between literature and society within these axes of transformation. The alternation of literary genres follows the aesthetic transformations, and moves from the representative (historic) to the expressive (trans-historic). These aesthetic axes themselves are contained within a broader, social frame of reference, which includes the diminishing contact with Holocaust survivors on the one hand and the spreading of ideologies on the other. The diagram thus provides a general framework through which the relations among different genres (testimony, documentary, fiction) as well as symbols ("lamb to slaughter" vs. "the rebel") can be defined.

It can be seen that within a short distance from the Holocaust, the texts tend to be representative and historical (testimonies); where ideology enters the scene and increases the social distance, we find a representative text which is also trans-historical ("lamb to slaughter"); trans-historical novels which are also representative (the "other planet" type) as well as novels of the historical and expressive type (e.g. Frenkel's *Saul and Johanna*) then follow. When time further increases the personal distance, second- (e.g. Grossman's *Look Under: Love*) and third-generation (e.g. the novels discussed here) literature appear. They are both expressive and trans-historical.

The model of cumulative evolution shown in figure 1 expects a geometrical increase in the possible alternatives and the actual variability of the texts. Contrary to this forecast, therefore, it is odd to encounter the startling parallelism between the two novels in point.

Possible explanations can be traced in three directions. First, it can be seen as a coincidence: a perfectly logical explanation, but not much to write about. Second, neomarxism might be invoked to explain the phenomenon as an ideology which has become internalized, an anti–lamb-to-slaughter symptom. Let me discuss this option further. Neomarxism is concerned with literature as a social institution, an objective demonstration of the articulation of traditional values and of emergent values which, in turn, reflect the power structure of society and the challenges to it. Explored as a socially symbolic act,[30] the texts in point present a logical step forward in the interpretation of dominant ideology. For if, as argued, the criticism concerning the negativity

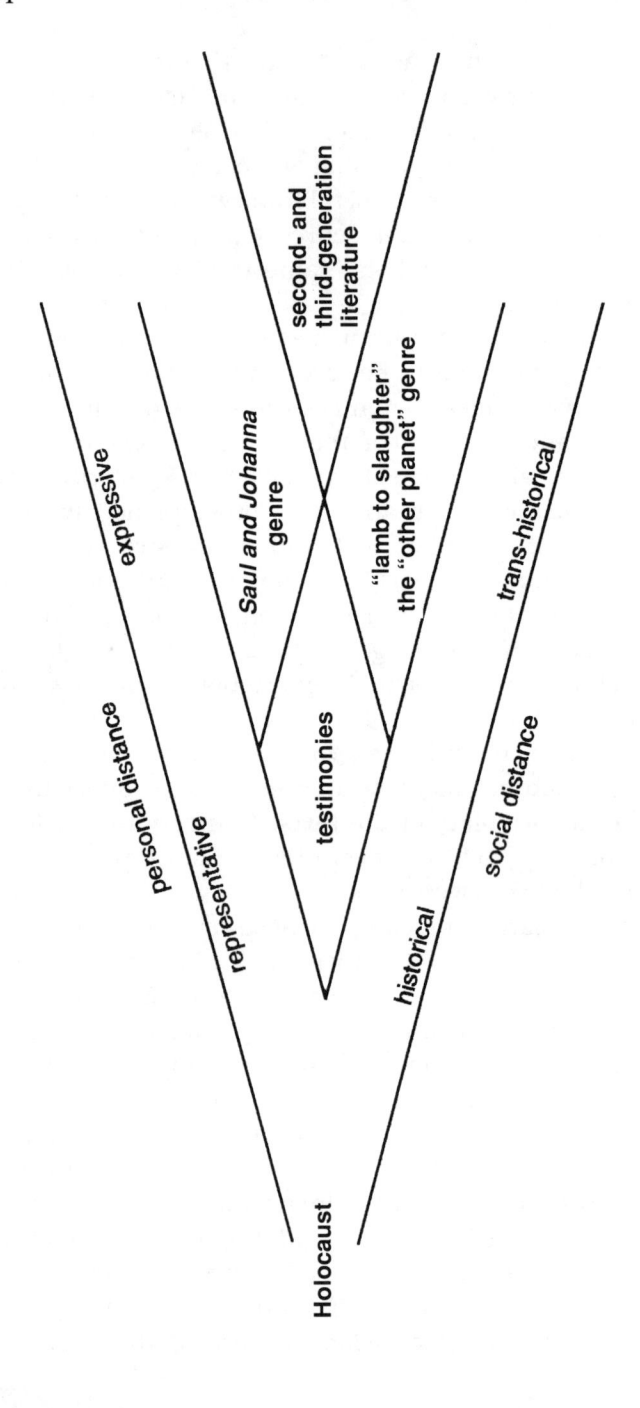

Figure 1. A "Time Scale" Typology of Holocaust Tropes and Literary Genres

and passivity of "lamb to slaughter" have been long legitimized and reinforced by the dominant socialist-Zionist and militaristic ideology, and reproduced through the education system, then the literary transformation of that metaphor into a positive, active Jewish rebel is the final victory of that ideology.

However, such a strictly neomarxist interpretation would seem oversimplistic to many. Moreover, the fact that other novels written by the same authors are completely incongruent with that interpretation, and the fact that both authors hold different political opinions than those attributed to them by that interpretation, render it somewhat equivocal. These novels are not a parallel case to *Robinson Crusoe* or *Tarzan*, and their authors do not adhere to a certain doctrine they wish to articulate. A more subtle, structural approach is needed.

My argument is, first, that the Holocaust has reached a new stage in its role as a literary subject. Previously documented, represented, and expressed in various (trans-) historical fashions, it now lends itself to extreme manipulation. Evidently, any of these poetic vehicles is manipulative to a certain extent. However, *Una* and *Border Patrol* not only contain some sort of manipulation, but fictional manipulation constitutes their very meaning. In their replacement of fact for fiction and history for narrative, they present a novel concerned not with the experience of the Holocaust, its survivors or their children, but with the Israeli third-generation Sabra alone. This Israeli has come to terms with the Holocaust through second- (and third-) hand texts of mass communication such as television, movies, books (most popularly, Anne Frank's diary), and memorial ceremonies at school. A study shows that Ashkenazi pupils indicate they learned something from talking with their parents and from history classes, however these two sources were not very influential.[31] What is remembered of the Holocaust, then, depends on the texts now giving it form. It is startling to notice that both *Una* and *Border Patrol* contain no survivors (only Holocaust Jews and Sabras); nor does the word *"Sho'ah"* appear in them.[32] Their titles also suggest a novel approach, compared with the metonymic categories of titles discussed in section 2.

Furthermore, the two novels share a manipulative presentation of the Holocaust Jew, a presentation seen through third-generation Israeli eyes. The reformulation of the Holocaust Jew as a rebel attests to the denial of the opposite metaphor—the lamb to slaughter. Irresistibly attracted to their Jewish Holocaust ancestors as a kind of haunting enigma containing the key to their identity, these authors have reshaped them to befit their quest. Thus, as the search for identity became a pilgrimage, the object of that search had to be archetypically transformed. The logic of the narrative implies that had it been the Sabra who was hypothetically to find himself entrapped in the Holocaust—as indeed happens in these novels—then he would not have chosen to go as lamb to slaughter, but rather have chosen the active, militaristic line of conduct—as indeed is the case in the two novels.

Lucien Goldmann once posed two questions which, he wrote, contain the whole substance of the sociology of literature: Why was this book written? and Why is it still read?[33] This case study attempted to address the first question. The second—which necessitates a temporal perspective—remains beyond our current reach. It awaits further elaboration and expansion, through the structural framework defined here, in the future. The issue, therefore, remains open-ended. Far from presuming a decisive and strict reply to the questions it raises, this analysis has striven to set those questions in a general context, invoking the unique conditions pertinent to the Israeli scene under which literature can be seen to provide, as it always does, a symbolic structure within which people can make sense of, and come to terms with, their past and present history.

Notes

1. Kermode, F., "Literary Fiction and Reality," in *The Sense of an Ending*, by Kermode, (New York: Oxford University Press), 1967, pp. 127–152.

2. Bar-On, D. and O. Sela. "The Psychosocial Effects of the Holocaust in Third and Second Generation Israel," (Ben-Gurion University, Dept. of Behavioral Sciences, 1991) (in Hebrew).

3. Young, J. E., *Writing and Rewriting the Holocaust: Narrative and the Consequences of Interpretation*, (Bloomington: Indiana University Press, 1988).

4. This is true world-wide. It is intriguing to notice that the massacre of nearly one and half million Armenians by the Turks between 1915 and 1923 has come recently to be known as the "Armenian holocaust." Thus, the Armenian massacre is called after an event that postdates it by twenty-five years.

5. Porat, D., *Leadership in Conflict*. (Tel Aviv: Am-Oved, 1986) (in Hebrew). Liebman, C., and E. Don-Yehiah, *Civil Religion in Israel*, (Berkeley: University of California Press, 1983).

6. Ben-Eliezer, Uri, "Militarism, Status and Politics." Unpublished PhD thesis, (Tel Aviv University, 1988).

7. Reich, A., "Changes and Developments in the Passover Haggadot of the Kibbutz Movement." Unpublished PhD diss. (Austin: University of Texas, 1972) p. 393.

8. Segev, T., *The Seventh Million*. (London: Maxwell-Macmillan, 1991) p. 453.

9. Palgi, Yoel, *Ru'ach Gdola Ba'ah (A Great Wind is Coming)*. (Tel Aviv: Am-Oved, 1978) (in Hebrew), p. 243.

10. Segev, T., *The Seventh Million*. (London: Maxwell-Macmillan, 1991) p. 167; Firer, R. *Agents of Morality*. (Tel Aviv: Hakibbutz Hame'uchad, 1989) (in Hebrew), p. 53.

11. Ben-Gurion, D., "The Eichmann Case as Seen by Ben-Gurion." *New York Times Magazine*, Dec. 18, 1960, pp. 1 ff.

12. Firer, R., *Agents of Morality*. (Tel Aviv: Hakibbutz Hame'uchad, 1989) (in Hebrew).

13. Ben-Gurion, D., "Concepts and Values." In *Hazut (Visions)*, by Ben-Gurion. (Tel Aviv: Mapai publications, 1957) (in Hebrew).

14. Liebman, C., and E. Don-Yehiah, *Civil Religion in Israel*. (Berkeley: University of California Press, 1983).

15. *Ma'ariv* (newspaper). April 27, 1976. Tel Aviv (in Hebrew).

16. Ibid.

17. *Ye'diot Acharonot* (newspaper). August 4, 1982. Tel Aviv (in Hebrew).

18. Segev, T., *The Seventh Million*. (London: Maxwell-Macmillan, 1991) pp. 451–469.

19. See Young, J. E., *Writing and Rewriting the Holocaust: Narrative and the Consequences of Interpretation*. (Bloomington: Indiana University Press, 1988); Langer, L. L., *The Holocaust and the Literary Imagination*. (New Haven and London: Yale University Press, 1975); Rosenfeld, A., *A Double Dying: Reflections on Holocaust Literature*. (Bloomington: Indiana University Press, 1980); and Steiner, G., *Language and Silence: Essays on Language, Literature, and the Inhuman*. (New York: Atheneum, 1967).

20. Such a poetic is characterized, for instance, by the following problematic: on the one hand, the survivor-scribe's claim to have produced an authentic text which enriches the already-existing "library" of testimonies lies in incorporating himself and his unique experience into the text, thus making it a "text of identity." On the other hand, in order to make his testimony seem true, he has to simultaneously efface himself from the text (Young 1988, op. cit.).

21. Yaoz, H., *The Holocaust in Hebrew Literature*. (Tel Aviv: Eked, 1980) (in Hebrew).

22. The paradoxical quality inherent in the poetics of "the other planet" can be located in the unresolved tension between metaphor and metonymy. "There are no metaphors for Auschwitz," writes Alvin Rosenfeld (1980, op. cit, p. 180), "just as Auschwitz is not a metaphor for anything else . . . why is this the case? because the flames were real flames, the ashes only ashes, the smoke always and only smoke." Thus, the "other planet" literature is at once both metaphorical (metaphysical, expressive, trans-historical) and literal (metonymic, representative, historical).

23. For example, Ka-Tzetnik 135633 (Yechiel Dinur), *Star Eternal*, translated by Nina Dinur. (New York: Arbor House, 1971).

24. Amichai, Yehuda, *Not of This Time, Not of This Place*, translated by Shlomo Katz. (New York: Harper and Row, 1968).

25. A brief etymological analysis of the opponents' names in *Border Patrol* might be relevant: *Hasse* can refer in German either to *Hass*, "hatred"—or, in contrast, to *Hase, Hare* (figuratively, "coward"); whereas *Himmel* is "heaven." In both cases, the reference is archetypal. In addition, the title of the other novel—which is also the title of the protagonist—*Una*, is a non-name either standing for "the one" (as in the Latin stem) or simply "woman" (as in Japanese).

26. This phenomenon is of course well known to anthropologists, and has been reported from places as disparate as the Aborigines' Australia and the Huichols' Mexico. One might argue that in the novels' case, this ancestor is "fictitious"; however, isn't this always the case?

27. Jameson, Frederic, *The Political Unconscious*. (London: Methuen, 1981).

28. Scholes, R., and R. Kellog, *The Nature of Narrative*. (New York: Oxford University Press, 1966).

29. James, Henry, *The Art of Fiction*. (London: Charles Somber's Sons, 1962).

30. Jameson, Frederic, *The Political Unconscious*. (London: Methuen, 1981).

31. Prego, Uri, *Measuring Holocaust Awareness in Israeli Pupils*. Research on the Holocaust, III, (Tel Aviv: Hakibbutz Hame'uchad, 1984) (in Hebrew).

32. The words *sho'ah* and *churban* carry a definite sense of divine retribution (alluding to their biblical meaning—see for instance Isa. 6:11, 10:3, 47:11). Interestingly, the word "holocaust" is etymologically derived from the Greek *holokauston*, which literally means "whole burnt," and refers in the Septuagint specifically to sacrifice by fire, standing for the Hebrew term for sacrificial offering, *ola*.

33. Goldmann, Lucien, *Pour Une Sociologie du Roman*. (Paris: Idées, 1965) p. 23.

Espionage and Cultural Mediation

Walter P. Zenner

Amnon Shamosh, *Arazim* (*Cedars of Lebanon*), Tel Aviv: Massada, Ltd., 1990.

When we speak about the meeting of cultures, we usually think about individuals who represent differences between two distinct social systems and who learn traits and patterns from the "other" culture. The spy, however, must stand between two cultures surreptitiously. I recall a World War II film about American spies who had to learn to eat in a European fashion, holding the knife in the left hand and the fork in the right in order to pass as Frenchmen after parachuting into Nazi-occupied France. The central irony of Amnon Shamosh's 1990 novel, *Arazim*, deals with this kind of ambiguity. In this case, the spies have been subjected to a double acculturation process. They are Middle Eastern Jewish immigrants to Israel who have been taught by Europeans who wanted them to rid themselves of their "Oriental" ways. However, as Israeli agents, the spies must now return to an Arab world which they had left behind.

The author of this novel has made the movement across cultural boundaries a major theme in his fiction, as it was in his own life. Amnon Shamosh was born in Aleppo in 1929 and immigrated to Eretz Yisrael as a child.[1] He became a member of Kibbutz Ma'ayan Baruch at its founding in the late 1940s; he has continued to live there. He turned to writing in the late 1960s. Shamosh has published novels, poems, short stories, and nonfiction. Much of his writing is centered around the portrayal of Aleppine Jewry in Aleppo, the metropolis of North Syria, and in the various countries to which they have immigrated. The Aleppian Jews constantly mediate between cultures. He points out that even in their everyday language, words from Arabic, Hebrew, French, and Spanish are strung together in single intelligible sentences. In describing their lives in Syria, the Americas, and Israel, he shows how they preserved their identity while at the same time adapting to a variety of settings.

While the fate of Aleppine (North Syrian) Jewry is a central theme, Shamosh is more than an ethnic author. In fact, the dilemmas of the kibbutz as it has changed from a revolutionary experiment into an agribusiness represents a strong motif in his work. The loss of collective ideals, the disenchantment with socialism, defection of kibbutz youth, the loss of a clear vision by members of communes, the kibbutz as a Jewish community without a synagogue, and similar topics can be found in his stories. They play a role in *Arazim*, too.

Ethnic themes serve both as a counterpoint to his concern with the kibbutz and as a critique of the way in which Israeli society in general has absorbed immigrants. He is particularly critical of the way in which the Diaspora culture was devalued in Israel, especially with regard to the rich cultures of the Middle East. In his fiction, he uses a historical perspective on the conflict between dominant Euro-Zionist culture and that of Middle Eastern Jews which extends from the 1930s to the present.

In this chapter, we will see how Shamosh weaves the motif of the spy as a traveler across cultural boundaries together with threads from the motif of the upbringing of Middle Eastern Jews on the kibbutz in *Arazim*. This will be shown through reference to two novels by Shamosh: to a chapter in *Michel Ezra Safra and Sons* (1978) devoted to the espionage career of one of the characters, and to *Arazim*, which was published in 1990. While the intelligence agents in the earlier novel work after the establishment of the State, and the latter work at the time of its creation, Shamosh takes a critical stand towards espionage in both works.

Avrum Safra as Spy

In his best-known novel, *Michel Ezra Safra and Sons* (1978), Amnon Shamosh briefly deals with Israeli espionage.[2] This novel traces a single Aleppo Jewish family's history from the late 1930s to the late 1970s and from Syria to France, Israel, and the Americas.

In chapter 31 Shamosh depicts the spying career of one of Michel Ezra Safra's sons, Albert/Avrum. Avrum is the most "Zionist" character in the book. He is the son who most clearly rebels against his father by joining a youth movement and becoming a kibbutznik. The chapter begins with the patriarch, Michel Ezra, comparing the Jews with the Druzes. Unlike the Jews, the Druzes are agriculturalists and fighters. They appear to blend in with their neighbors, but they manage to live their own inner lives without arousing those of other religions. Michel Ezra, who opposes Albert's Zionism, believes that the Jews will never succeed in living in harmony with their neighbors. Michel Ezra uses the example of the Druzes to throw cold water on Albert's enthusiasm for the Zionists. The introduction of the Druze example in a chapter which will deal with espionage is strange, but perhaps the Druze, who are known to hide their private religious beliefs, serve as an example to spies, who also must not arouse the suspicions of their hosts.

Then the scene of the chapter changes to the 1950s, the difficult period of consolidation after the attainment of Israeli independence. Albert, now known as Avrum, lives on a kibbutz. He is recruited by "them," the intelligence services, for a mission abroad. Young Arabic speakers are being mobilized to infiltrate the neighboring countries. Avrum is first given a course in intelligence, but then he is sent home to await further instructions. He experiences relief and disappointment.

He feels that his efforts in the course were wasted, though Shamosh comments through Avrum, "what is this waste compared to the waste in the procurement of weapons?"[3]

When Avrum is sent abroad, his cover is that of a Syrian millionaire who has made his fortune in South America. He goes first to South America and then to meetings with high governmental officials in Syria and Lebanon. He also comes face to face with the son of a powerful Aleppine notable who knew his father well. At the end of this chapter, he finds out that this man had recognized him, but had not blown his cover. As his father had suggested, Avrum had ultimately failed in his mission because he did not blend in.

This story has parallels to one of the most famous episodes in Arab-Israeli espionage, the Eli Kohen case. Eli Kohen was an Israeli spy, born in Egypt, who infiltrated into Damascus. His cover was that of an Arab who had made his fortune in South America. Kohen provided valuable intelligence on Syria before he was exposed and hung as a spy in the 1960s. Incidentally, at that time the Egyptians sent to Israel a spy, Kaburak Yacobian, whose experiences parallel those of Kohen. He was an Armenian, whose background was also "laundered" in Latin America and who passed as an Egyptian Jew of Turkish background when he was sent to Israel.[4] Thus both Arab and Israeli intelligence agencies used overseas communities to establish covers. The various Levantine diasporas were sources for the cadres of many intelligence agencies. People who have lived in communities like interwar Cairo or Beirut are able to pass through the borders which separate Israel from its neighbors with the greatest of ease. While Israelis have long feared "Levantinization," they have needed those who came from the cosmopolitan centers of the Middle East, where many Jews learned to speak Arabic and French fluently to serve as diplomats and undercover agents.

While *Michel Ezra Safra and Sons* contains many incidents in which both Ashkenazim and Sephardim display their ethnocentrism, this chapter does not focus on ethnic relations among Jews. The chapter does, however, give an equivocal account of the often-praised espionage exploits of the Mossad. In the context of the novel, the need for this chapter is not clear. Perhaps the author felt that in telling the story of Syrian Jews since the 1940s, he should include the contributions made by Syrian and other Arabic-speaking Jews to Israeli intelligence. Their knowledge of their former home-countries gave invaluable assistance to the Zionist cause, but they were often denied recognition for it. This chapter was one way of putting the spotlight on this contribution.

Israelis in Lebanon—1948

Arazim takes up this theme. The 1990 novel is dedicated "to the good comrades from the Arab Department of the Palmach who were active in Syria and Lebanon and to the memory of those who went out and never returned" (p. iii). It explicitly serves to underline the important role played by the Middle Eastern Jewish spies who served Israel.

Arazim is a historical novel about Israeli agents in Lebanon in a period which coincides with the establishment of the State. It is not, however, a traditional spy novel. Rather it is an account of the initial experiences of a small group of Jews of Middle Eastern background, both immigrants and Sabras, as they learn to be spies. It shows how these callow youths were sent to collect intelligence and carry out sabotage operations during the War for Independence.

The protagonist, Abu Salim, and his companion, Mirro, are sent to Beirut on the eve of the war. They pose as Palestinian Muslim refugees. For cover, they purchase a grocery store. Through much of the novel, they are shown as bored and disappointed that they are missing the battles going on in Eretz Yisrael. One of the protagonists laments that spying is basically a very boring activity (*Arazim*, p. 89). Shamosh here portrays the initial amateurishness of early Israeli espionage and the mundane activities that accompany secret operations. It is something which many spy novels allude to, but few portray.

Shamosh does have didactic motives in writing this novel, as he does in much of his fiction. In addition to showing that

Syrian Jews are an integral part of the Israeli mosaic, the novel permits the author to give voice to his doubts about Israel's ability to adapt to its neighbors and the complex web of ties that made the older Levantine mosaic last for a long time. For instance, Hassan, the Syrian who does not expose Avrum, is the son of a powerful patron of Avrum's father. In the relationship between the two fathers one found arrogance and importunity, but also loyalty.

In *Arazim*, Shamosh brings out this theme through the main characters. Spies in Arab countries were often recruited from among Jews of Middle Eastern background because they had the necessary characteristics to pass, even though they had also been subjected to "Euro-Sabra" socialization. The theme has importance here. The Middle Easterners are recruited as spies precisely because they know the culture of the enemy, yet this culture is devalued within Israel.

The novel brings forth the irony of this paradox. Together the two main characters discuss and evaluate their experiences on the kibbutz, where both received their education. Abu Salim is a native of Syria while Mirro is a son of Syrian immigrants to Egypt. They both reminisce about their kibbutz mother, Fania. Fania was the key figure who cared for the "Syrian youths" when they arrived on the kibbutz. She was a strong, dedicated woman.

Their other counselor, Yokel, was not really very forceful. He was involved with his music and he felt very hurt when the Syrians received his lessons in Western classical music with indifference. To himself, but never aloud, he thought of them as Levantines, inferior half-breeds. It was Fania, however, who sought most energetically to remove the stigma of the Orient from them. They accepted, yet resented her efforts.

The process of transforming Syrian and other Middle Easterners into Sabras on the kibbutz was dealt with by Shamosh in another work, "Ben Mesheq," a short story which appeared in 1980.[5] The protagonist in this story, like Abu Salim, is part of a group of Syrian children who are brought to a kibbutz. The various children are separated on the basis of age, with the older children going to one kibbutz and the younger to another. The protagonist is given a kibbutz mother who is unlike his own mother. From the start, when she assumes that all children like cocoa, she forces European ways on her Syrian charge. Over time, the Syrians become accepted as if they were kibbutz natives. Hence the ironic title, "Ben Mesheq" ("son of the farm"), which is the term used for those native to the kibbutz whose parents are full members. The early trauma, however, never leaves. At one point, when another contingent of Syrian children is brought to the kibbutz, the protagonist asks a child his family name. When the child insists that it is the clearly Ashkenazic name of Orenstein, he takes this as a sign of premature assimilationism. Later he finds out that there was indeed such a family in Aleppo. Toward the end, when he and his (biological) father start, but never finish, a conversation about the difficulties of childhood, he realizes how alienated he is from his parents and his heritage.

Shamosh underwent such acculturation, albeit in a milder fashion, in Tel Aviv and thus realizes that European Jews were also forcibly transformed.[6] What was different in their cases was the fact that since radical Zionist-socialists were themselves Europeans, the culture which they tried to create was both consciously and unconsciously modeled on European ideas and tastes.

In the Arab Department of the Palmach, however, Abu Salim and Mirro had to relearn how to act like Arabs. They are called by Arab names. They must penetrate Muslim Arab society. For instance, they are sent in disguise to Arab areas in Palestine, like the mosque at Ramleh, to see if they will pass muster. The unit itself is called the *jaami'ah*, the Arabic term for university. There appears to be a perverse pride in reversing the Europeanization which they have undergone and reacquiring the Arab culture which they were forced to abandon.[7]

This paradox is one which Shamosh has explored before in his work. In some stories, like "Naim's Lessons," Middle Eastern Jews devalue their own culture, in part because of the education they have received in European schools like those of the Alliance.[8] They only learn to treasure their background because of a European's interest. But in general the negative stance of Israelis towards Diaspora Judaism, especially that of the Middle East, comes through. Shamosh shows this in his recollections of going to school in Tel Aviv in the 1930s.[9] Middle Eastern youth raised in Israel, and even in big cities like Cairo and Aleppo, were encouraged to forget their "Oriental" ways.

In fact, despite the demand that those selected for espionage must learn Islamic customs and model themselves on Arabs in a wide variety of ways, the intelligence services reflect the state which they serve. For instance, Iser Harel, who was the first director of Shin Bet, the internal Israeli security agency under Prime Minister Ben-Gurion, found Middle Eastern Jews useful as agents, but he generally appointed Europeans to executive positions in the agency. He mistrusted "professional Orientalists" as well as Ashkenazim who had "too much" contact with Arabs.[10]

The Experience of Spying

In the book *Arazim*, Shamosh portrays the daily experience of these spies. To begin with, they are employed by novices and they themselves are new to the game. The organization for which they work is engaged in a war, but they are outside the main theater of action. The novel takes place when the fighting between Israel and its enemies was at its height. While Lebanon was involved briefly in fighting Israel, it was a minor player at this time. Beirut, however, was the destination of many Palestinian refugees. When Abu Salim and Mirro arrive in Beirut posing as Palestinian Muslim refugees, they must protect their cover. One way in which they do this is by leaving the hotel and avoiding camps for refugees. Instead, they rent an apartment and buy a grocery store. As Palestinian refugees, they face the prejudices of Lebanese who are quite ambivalent toward these "fellow-Arabs" who have landed on their doorsteps. This prefigures the later hostility of the Lebanese against the Palestinians.

The two spies also must establish contact with their superiors in Israel. It takes them some time to do this. Meanwhile they spend much time waiting and talking to each other in the store. It is in the chapters set during this early period that they reminisce about their kibbutz experiences.

Shamosh emphasizes the fact that these spies are inexperienced young men barely past adolescence. They are lonely, and they seek sexual fulfillment. Abu Salim, going against all that he has learned, persuades Mirro to accompany him on a trip to Aleppo, to visit Abu Salim's mother. This is an extremely dangerous journey, since it involves crossing borders in time of war. Their documents might be spotted as forgeries and Abu Salim could easily blow his cover. Yet his homesickness is so intense that he feels he must see his mother again.

Both Abu Salim and Mirro break rules because of their sexual needs. Mirro goes to a house of prostitution, of which Beirut has many. Abu Salim becomes involved with a Maronite girl, whom he eventually marries. The two establish radio contact with Israel. Two comrades are sent to augment their team. They are asked to perform some acts of sabotage.

The four spies disagree and fight. One quarrel occurs when another of the four tries to seduce Margo, Abu Salim's girlfriend. Eventually Abu Salim marries Margo and the central command orders him to leave Lebanon. They go to Paris where he reveals to her his true identity. Margo is outraged when she discovers Abu Salim's deception, for she understands that she will be completely cut off from her family. The circumstances, however, give her few options. She must adopt a new identity and accompany Abu Salim to Israel under the name Margalit.

Shamosh's focus on the living conditions of spying and on the inevitable betrayals of friendship and love makes us realize the human costs of espionage. While Shamosh does not take the cynical view towards espionage which we find in the works of John LeCarre or Len Deighton, the episode in which Abu Salim reveals his true identity to Margo certainly is suggestive of some scenes in LeCarre's work.

The Lebanese Quagmire

Within the novel set in 1948 and 1949, Shamosh comments on what followed in the wake of those years in Lebanon. He makes his heroes face the anti-Palestinian prejudice of the Syrian and Lebanese hosts of the new refugees. This suggests the tensions which will lead to the tragic events of the 1970s and 1980s. He has a Maronite priest tell Abu Salim, whom the priest believes to be a Palestinian Muslim, about the situation of the Maronites. The viewpoint here is not that of Zionists. Many Zionists projected their own ideology onto that of Lebanese Christians. They saw Lebanon as a Christian Israel and the Lebanese Christians as a nation facing genocidal Muslim neighbors.

The Maronite priest instead sees the coexistence with Muslims as inevitable. While the Maronites are too proud, he says, to accept the second-class status of *dhimmis* (protected subjects; in a modern state, second-class citizens), they will also not do anything to endanger themselves by entering an alliance against the Arab world. They are bound to the Arab world, just as they are also part of European Christendom. They have always lived in these two worlds.

Uncle François, the monk, is fearful of people like Pierre Gemayel, the leader of the Phalangists. This was one of the parties with which the Israelis would become allied during the Lebanese civil war. Uncle François relates that Gemayel has started forming a private army, as have other Lebanese political leaders. As he points out, Gemayel was sympathetic to the Axis Powers during the Second World War (a hint that Israel is seeking alliances with some strange bedfellows). François is also afraid of the many colonels in Lebanon and elsewhere. The balance is a delicate one, which can be easily upset. In many ways, it parallels the views of Michel Ezra

Safra, who saw the Ashkenazic Zionists as a threat to the existence of Jews in Syria. Both Uncle François and Michel Ezra Safra represent the traditional minority elites of Southwest Asia, minorities which had survived by accommodation. Modern nationalists and significant outsiders threatened these arrangements, like bulls in a china shop.

This chapter on the Maronites can be seen as a commentary on the failure of Israeli policy toward Lebanon in the 1980s, a policy which Shamosh observed closely from his kibbutz on the border. In various other passages, especially toward the end of the novel, he relates such foreboding. When the Maronite monk points to the pro-fascist inclinations of the Phalangists, he is commenting on future Israeli allies.

Shamosh is here writing about the colossal misunderstanding of the Maronites by the Israelis. During the Israeli invasion of Lebanon, the Israeli government expected the Phalangists to attack the Palestine Liberation Organization in West Beirut, which the Phalange did not do. On the other hand, even hardened Israeli veterans were shocked by the Sabra and Shatila massacres, committed before their eyes by Phalangist units. They found to their surprise that even a Phalangist-led Lebanese government was reluctant to sign a peace treaty with Israel, because this entailed the breaking of ties with other Arab countries. Shamosh's Uncle François is seen as warning the Israelis against projecting their self-image onto the Lebanese. It is part of the book's warning that Israel must show greater sensitivity to the fabric of social relations of its neighbors. Ironically, the reader in the 1990s knows that the advice of those most knowledgeable about Lebanon was ignored by policymakers in Jerusalem when they decided to invade Lebanon in 1982.[11] Many of the efforts of Abu Salim's counterparts had been in vain.

When Abu Salim arrives in Haifa from Beirut, he notes the similarity between these two ports nestled against the mountains. Haifa in 1948, however, was a city which was partly destroyed by war and in which the coexistence between Jews and Arabs had resulted in bloodshed and flight, a fate which he feared for Beirut.

A message of this novel for Israel is that while the Ashkenazic elites have often disdained the Levantine culture, it has needed those who bear this tradition. Thus a novel which is a tribute to some of Israel's unsung heroes is also a commentary on Israeli domestic and foreign policies.

Notes

1. "A Family in Aleppo" (Jerusalem: Center for Programming, Department of Development and Services, World Zionist Organization), a radio talk. For a more complete analysis of these various themes in Shamosh's fiction, see Walter P. Zenner, "Aleppo and the Kibbutz in the Fiction of Amnon Shamosh," *Shofar* 6 (Spring 1988); pp. 25–35 (West Lafayette, Ind.).

2. A. Shamosh, *Michel Ezra Safra Uvanav* (Ramat Gan, Massada, 1978).

3. Ibid., p. 190.

4. Ian Black and Benny Morris, *Israel's Secret Wars: A History of Israel's Intelligence Services* (New York; Grove Weidenfeld, 1990), pp. 144, 227–29.

5. A. Shamosh, "Ben Mesheq," in *Kibbutz Hu Kibbutz Hu Kibbutz* (Ramat Gan, Massada, 1980), pp. 36–45.

6. "A Family in Aleppo."

7. See Black and Morris, *Israel's Secret Wars*, pp. 35–44, for another view of the "Arab Platoon." Black and Morris's evaluation is less sympathetic than Shamosh's. This may reflect the view of the Arab Platoon's superiors, but it also fits in the somewhat cynical tone of Black and Morris's book.

8. "Shi'urim shel Naim," in *Ahoti HaKallah* (Ramat Gan, Massada, 1974), pp. 147–60. For an English translation, see *My Sister, the Bride* (Ramat Gan, Massada, 1979), pp. 172–92. Many of Shamosh's stories have appeared in English in various English-language Jewish periodicals, most notably *Midstream*, *The Jewish Spectator*, and *Moment*.

9. See "A Family in Aleppo" and Zenner, "Aleppo," p. 26.

10. Black and Morris, *Israel's Secret Wars*, p. 138.

11. Black and Morris, *Israel's Secret Wars*, pp. 371–90.

An Authentic Human Voice: The Poetry of Amnon Shamosh

Abraham Marthan

Amnon Shamosh, *Spanish Diwan* (Poems), (in Hebrew), Ramat-Gan: Massada, 1981.

Amnon Shamosh, *Upon a Harp with a Solemn Sound* (Poems), (in Hebrew), Tel-Aviv: Sifriat HaPoalim, 1984.

I. Preliminary: The Sephardim and Modernity

The present situation prevailing between Ashkenazim and Sephardim in Israel is expressed sometimes in terms of tradition vs. modernity, East vs. West, European vs. Oriental, modern vs. pre-modern, secular vs. religious, or suchlike pairs of opposites. The relationship then is articulated in cultural, geographic, communal, or ethnic distinctions.

What is the source of this difference? Ashkenazi Jewry, as is well known, has been engaged since about the mid-eighteenth century, first in Western Europe and later in Eastern Europe, in the twin process of Modernization and Emancipation. Later, when Emancipation proved to be an illusory goal, especially in Eastern Europe, a significant and highly determined segment of this Jewry poured its energies into what is called Auto-emancipation or National Revival, resulting in the modern Zionist movement, and culminating in the establishment of a national sovereign state—the present State of Israel.

What was happening meanwhile among the Sephardim at the same time? (By "Sephardim" here we mean, specifically, those Jews in the Middle East and the former Turkish provinces, for Western Sephardim were part and parcel of European culture since the Renaissance.)

We have to remember that the tradition of secular knowledge, or the knowledge of Man, or Rationalism, never really died among the Sephardim wherever they were. It was well established since the time of Maimonides, and harks all the way back to patterns developed during the Spanish Golden Age. The aims of the early German Haskalah as we know, were rather modest. The manifesto "Words of Peace and Truth" written by N. H.Wessely in 1781, and regarded as the starting point for this movement, advocated a curriculum based on study of the Hebrew language and Bible as a prerequisite for Talmudic study, and study of secular and useful branches of human knowledge, such as arithmetic, geography, and such. (This curriculum itself may have been based on the educational curriculum of Etz-Hayim Sephardic School of Amsterdam, where Wessely's family had settled.) Now, it was always the practice among Sephardim to have a thorough grounding in the Hebrew language and Bible before studying Talmud. A modicum of secular, or "worldly" knowledge, *Derekh Eretz*, was always expected of the traditional Talmid Hacham, according to lines set by Maimonides. Therefore Sephardim really did not need a movement or special permission either to study the Bible or secular studies, against which there was no prohibition, either official or unofficial.

When modernity came, with the advent of European settlers and commercial enterprise, these influences were quietly absorbed for the most part. There was no equivalent to shocks that rocked European Jewry and split communities and individuals. The Sephardim were touched by modernity at about the same time as the Jews of Central Europe, certainly no later than the Jews of Eastern Europe. Napoleon's invasion of Egypt (1798) is a turning point. Arabic history marks the onset of the European impact at this time. The higher classes, as is true of European Jews, were exposed much earlier, due to their wider commercial contacts.

The first Alliance Israelite Universelle School was founded in Morocco the same year that it was founded in Russia (1860). Unlike in Eastern Europe, however, these schools encountered very little resistance. On the contrary, they were welcomed throughout the Sephardic diaspora. The official rabbinate took up its cause and received its emissaries with respect and encouragement. What is amazing actually is how little resistance there was. The official rabbis of North Africa, for example, sent their own children to the Alliance schools.

The impression that Sephardim for the most part were only exposed to modernity upon their arrival in Israel is, of course, totally false. The communities of North Africa, Egypt, Turkey, and the Balkans were exposed to Western culture, languages, and technology at about the same time as Eastern European Jews.

Whence then is the difference? The fundamental difference is that Sephardim went *directly* from tradition to European education *without* the mediating epoch of Haskalah or Hebraic/Jewish secularism. This is the major difference. For it is not a difference of chronology or degree, but of *kind*. When we say that Ashkenazim are "European" it is true only in this sense: that in the space of several generations, they have succeeded in accomplishing what Europeans have been trying to do since the Renaissance. They forged a new Jewish identity on the basis of nationality, rather than religion. They made it possible, for those who wish it, to identify as Jewish on a basis other than religious. This is something Sephardim have never done *collectively*. This is the most outstanding achievement of Ashkenazi Jewry in modern times, whether one likes it or not. It goes beyond any individual achievement of an Einstein or Freud, because it was the collective achievement of European Jewry. Interestingly, Jewish secularism, as an ideology, did not originate in Western Europe, among the more assimilated and emancipated Jewries, but precisely among the Eastern European Jews of traditional background. The theoretical foundation of the secular Jewish ethos were provided by ex-Yeshiva boys, such as Ahad-Haam, Berdichevsky and Bialik, making it possible for one to be both Jewish and secular at once. There was just no Sephardic Ahad-Haam! Not that there was no Sephardi intellectual equal to him in European culture, intellect, or originality. Someone like Elija Benamozegh (1822–1900) is at least his equal in these respects. But the latter remained wholly *within the religious tradition.*

When Sephardim made contact with European culture, they made it directly and without the mediating stage of Hebrew or Jewish secularism. Equally important, they made their contacts as individuals, not collectively. Even when they established communal schools to teach secular subjects, these schools taught secular subjects, but they were *not* secular schools. There was no Jewish secular ideology, expressed in collective communal terms and institutions.

Contacts with and exposure to Western culture on the part of Sephardim has been both broad and deep. Only this fact can explain that the leading literary critic in the world today is a North African Jew, Jacques Derrida, born in Algeria. A leading contemporary French poet is an Egyptian Jew, Edmund Jabes. There have been Sephardi Nobel Prize winners in literature (Canetti) and in the sciences (Baruj Benazzeraf). But this individual achievement does not help the Sephardim vis-à-vis the Ashkenazim, any more than the achievements of a Freud or an Einstein helped European Jews, for the struggle is a communal one, one between groups, not one-to-one, the achievements of one individual against another. Proportionate to their number in the total world Jewish population, individual Sephardim have probably contributed as much to modern Western culture as did their Ashkenazi brethren.

The fact is, however, that Sephardim stood collectively outside of Jewish secularism—the hallmark of the "Founding

Fathers" of the State—and did not as such play a role in the process of the formation of this Jewish secularism. (The process is just now taking place in Israel.) Even when Sephardim practice a seemingly secular way of life, it is only *de facto*. There has not been a collective Sephardi secular Jewish ethos. It may come about, it may not. For Sephardim distinguish between being *modernized*, mostly relating to technique and externals, and being *secularized*, which is an inner ideological transformation.

In this respect, current Sephardi writing in Israel presents an interesting phenomenon. While individually the writers may not pursue a traditional way of life, their attitude to tradition is that of respect and even empathy. Amnon Shamosh's writing is of such character. Other Sephardi writers would place this positive attitude to tradition as the most distinctive trait of Sephardim and what sets them apart from the majority of Israeli Ashkenazim and from the dominant Israeli ethos. This also may prevent many of them from being regarded as "mainstream," for modern Hebrew letters bear the indelible stamp of secularism, as set by "canonical" writers such as Bialik, Berdichevsky, and Brenner. Secularism is indeed the official religion of the contemporary Hebrew literary "republic."

II. The Emergence of Sephardi Writing in the Seventies

In the 1960s a new kind of writing emerged in Israel, what has become known as the New Wave of Israeli fiction, represented by such authors as A. B. Yehoshua and Amos Oz, among others, who rebelled both against the style and the themes of the preceding literary generation known as the Palmach Generation or the Generation of the War of Independence.

In the 1970s, a newer wave washed ashore. This time it was a wave of Sephardi writers, both in prose and poetry. The seventies witnessed an outburst of creative energies among Sephardi writers. New names seemed to emerge out of nowhere: Erez Bitton, Shalom Razabi, Shimon Balas, Sami

Michael, and Amnon Shamosh. Shamosh first made his mark in prose, then began publishing his poetry in the 1980s.

III. Amnon Shamosh—The Lives of the Author

Amnon Shamosh was born in Aleppo in 1929, to Reina Cabasso and Moshe Shamosh. The mother traced her descent to the Ben-Yahya family of Andalusia, Spain, and the father to a family which never left the Middle East. Amnon was the youngest of eight children in a family which included six brothers and two sisters. His father was a silversmith-embroiderer who specialized in the making of curtains for the Holy Ark. He died quite young in Aleppo—when Amnon was seven years of age—after some years of illness and having experienced the indignity of seeing his noble profession made obsolete and replaced by machines. Following immigration patterns customary among Syrian Jews, two of the brothers left for Mexico, before our author was born, to scout new territory for the family's livelihood. The rest migrated to Palestine in 1938, when Amnon was a child of nine; his eldest brother Isaac had been promised and obtained a job teaching Arabic literature at the Hebrew University.

The mother was educated in the Alliance school, but her education was interrupted at age fifteen due to her marriage. She continued, however, to educate herself and read endlessly in French. At home, Amnon was to write later, they spoke Arabic, wrote French, and prayed in Hebrew. Circumstances were comfortable enough; typically middle class, the family was sufficiently well provided for to afford an Armenian nurse and to move to Jumiliyeh (a European-style quarter of Aleppo), living in a private home, with a balcony and a porch. In his parents' home he experienced, he says, a true encounter of diverse cultures, of East and West, of Hebrew, Arabic, and French culture. Father had two sets of clothing, one European and the other Middle Eastern, depending on the occasion and the company. Mother always dressed in the European fashion, with dresses she sewed herself according to the latest catalogs from Paris. She wore a coat and a hat à la mode, and many gold bracelets on her arms, adding Near

Eastern accents to her appearance. She also used perfumes and rouge that were imported from France. At home they played records of Edith Piaf and Maurice Chevalier as well as of the popular Egyptian singers Abdul-Wahab and Umm Kulthum.

Amnon Shamosh thinks that he inherited his intellectual curiosity from his mother who loved to read. She read with a magnifying glass and loved to tell stories (about that later). His artistic bent he attributes to his father, who did delicate work with threads of gold and silver, and which the poet immortalized in his poem "Curtain." His own openness and tolerance of cultural differences and influences he attributes to the ambience in his parents' home in which East and West dwelt together peacefully.

In the Palestine of the time, he lived in Tel Aviv at the house of his second brother Joseph, an editor of an Arabic paper of the Histadrut, and attended Bialik (elementary) School. Afterwards he enrolled in the Herzeliah Gymnasium, became a member of the youth movement, and upon graduation in 1946 joined the underground, serving in the Palmach. He was one of the original founders of Kibbutz Ma'ayan Baruch in the Upper Galilee, on the Syrian-Lebanese border. He remains there to this day, and has served successively as a shepherd, youth counsellor, kibbutz secretary, school teacher, and principal. He undertook various missions abroad, including one to find the missing pages of the Aleppo Codex, the *Kether*.

He acquired his higher education at the Midrasha Beit-Berl, and graduated from the Hebrew University. He first tried out his hand in writing several children's books, the first of which came out in 1966. But his mature literary career began in earnest comparatively late, in the 1970s, when the author was past forty, with a collection of short stories called *Ahoti Kallah (My Sister the Bride*, 1974). It was rejected by the Worker's Publishing House (Sifriat Ha Poalim), and it was published by a private company, Massada, with the encouragement of its editor, Amir Gilboa. His greatest fame rests on his novel *Michel Ezra Safra and Sons*, published in 1978, and serialized on Israeli television for seven weeks, ultimately winning the Israel Television's Harp of David prize.[1]

He himself enumerates the sources, or the founts, of his inspiration and creativity: parents' home, Aleppo, Agnon, Sholom Aleichem, Sephardic poetry, and Ma'ayan Baruch.

In his autobiographical sketch which he called *Opto-Biography*, from "optic," he defines his world and the way he looks at the world. At age nine in the elementary school he was prescribed glasses: he "put . . . Israeli glasses on his Eastern eyes."[2] Then came bifocals, then the kibbutz outlook. Thus he sees the world with "triple lenses": the basic Eastern eyes, Israeli, and finally kibbutz, lenses (his Socialist education). All this is in addition to that which he sees in his dreams, i.e., the vision of the creative artist which we suppose to be the fourth dimension of his world.[3]

IV. Amnon Shamosh—The Poetry

Amnon Shamosh has published to date two volumes of poetry: *Spanish Diwan*, (Massada, 1981), and *Upon a Harp with a Solemn Sound* (Sifriat Poalim, 1984). His first poetic collection, *Spanish Diwan*, contains many interesting experiments in which he tried to emulate the poetics and the high elegance of the Hebrew poetry of the medieval Spanish period. *Diwan* is the name given by Sephardic poets to their collection of secular verse. It means an official register.

In many places in his writings and public lectures, Shamosh confesses his love and admiration for the Hebrew poetry of the Spanish Golden Age, which he imbibed at home, sung to the tunes of secular Middle Eastern music. Later on he was to study this poetry at the Herzeliah Gymnasium with the teacher-poet David Shimoni and at the Hebrew University with Dan Pagis. He regards this poetry as the apex, the very height of the Hebrew creative genius, anytime, any place. But he expresses disappointment that his teachers, who did so well in analysis of genres, forms, and patterns, treated this poetry surgically as a museum piece, as something exotic and ornamental, without a relevance to the present. They treated it coldly, analytically, as one would a specimen in the laboratory, without love or affection. But even if love and affection were present, it was the sort of love one has for grandma, a beloved and favored figure, in a remote and abstract way, not like love for a woman of flesh and blood, with whom one might have a real, vital contact.

He was amazed and disappointed that someone like the late Dan Pagis, who really established the code of Medieval Hebrew Poetics with such thoroughness and painstaking research and imagination, shows no affinity at all to this poetry in his own verse—neither in form nor in content. This, he said, he set to correct. In his first book he experimented with writing in the genres, metrics, and rhyme schemes of medieval Spanish poetry, trying to articulate contemporary topics in archaic forms, and using a variety of medieval devices such as alliteration and assonance, homonyms, play on words, allusion to Biblical texts, the mosaic style, double meanings, etc. This attempt too, was rebuffed by Sifriat Poalim as obsolete. And here again it was Massada Publishing House and its enthusiastic editor, Amir Gilboa, who came to the rescue. Actually, the collection contains three *diwans*—the Spanish *diwan*, a French *diwan* (fruit of a visit to Paris, written in the modern idiom and in free verse, in the contemporary fashion *comme il faut)*, and an Israeli *diwan*—reflecting Israeli experience and environment.

This last section closes with the poem "Vidduy Hagadol," "The Great Confession." This seems to me the heart of the book; it also provides a clue to the poet's inner world.

The Great Confession

My mother,
used to come visiting
every
summer

Her eyes tired of reading
her past
weighing heavily
she would tell stories
and tell

What did she recount
and what she did not
her voice melodious
like the lute
and palms of her hands explaining
her bracelets resounding
gold to gold
like those winged sayings
in her mouth
over which time had no dominion
and I
all of me
an ear that was tightly sealed.

Occupied
in getting the Kibbutz out
of the mire
to move things forward
and who
(well, really)
has time
for Mother

A curtain
between the voice of her yesterdays
and the ear intent
on the noise of the collective and its projects
she tells—
of Ben Zeruyah
and the powers of the amulet
and I shake my head
as if listening

One summer she did not come
and in the winter
she departed
the world
and the troubles
that are bound in the bond of life

The spring passed
summer expired
and in the autumn
my hand began to inscribe
stories

I read
and I found
the world
of Mother
A culture of life
that departed to its world
perhaps
my ear was blocked
but my heart awake
and perhaps
the words
permeated
in some other way

I wanted
to tell my stories
in the ear
of Mother

I sought
to hear more and more
from her
but Mother
who used to be
every summer
with me
(across that partition)
was—
and is no more.[4]
    (Kibbutz Ma'ayan Baruch, Yom Kippur Eve 1980)

    We have already mentioned the fondness of the author's mother for reading and telling stories. In "The Great Confession" the poet expresses mea culpa on a great opportunity that he missed in turning a deaf ear to his mother's stories. The mother represented another world. Though festive, colorful, and musical, it seemed to be static, irrelevant, and remote, while the son was dynamic and moving forward (or so he saw himself), occupied in everyday, practical affairs. After her departure the son begins to reconsider. He realizes what he missed. At the same time it dawns on him how much he owes her. As her words permeated him in some mysterious way he also begins to write stories—a talent perhaps he inherited from her. Now he wants to tell her *his* stories. But now she is no more to hear what he has to tell. Yet, she lives—in her son's stories.

The latter volume, *Upon a Harp with a Solemn Sound*, is much more conventional in technique, i.e., more modern in its poetic language and forms. The author seems to have abandoned the experiment with medieval patterns, after perhaps having exhausted the possibilities of these forms.

The book opens with a poem called "Anna and I," comparing the author's experience with that of Anne Frank, who was born the same year as our author. This discovery dawned on him when he visited her house in Amsterdam, accompanied by his own daughter, who was then Anne's age when she was taken away. She wrote a diary, he wrote a diary; she wrote from left to right, he wrote from right to left; hers was preserved, his is lost. Who is to say then which one of them has truly survived?

This is typical of the spirit of the whole book and could be said to be typical of his entire oeuvre, whether in prose or poetry. And that is to find analogies of Jewish experience, whether it be of the East or the West, Ashkenazi or Sephardi, Israel or the Diaspora. He is imbued with a strong sense of Jewish unity of the pre-Emancipation variety. In this he harks back to an earlier tradition of Hebrew letters, before the great scramble for "civil rights" and the eagerness of Jews to identify with their countries of citizenship, rather than with their historical brethren, wherever they are. Another trait of this book, and his work in general, is its humanistic temper, which almost gives it an old-fashioned ring, more akin to the poetry of the pre-state than to the current scene. One does not find the skepticism, the cynicism, and the fashionable, sometimes even pseudo, sophistication that characterize some current Hebrew poetry. Many of his poems vibrate with moral ardor, rare in the poetry of the present. For instance he has a poem called "Ani Ma'ashim," a play on the expression "Ani-Ma'amin," and also reminiscent of Emile Zola's famous "J'accuse." In this poem he pours scathing wrath on the Syrian regime which is holding hostage four hundred young Jewish women, who will never be able to bear or raise families. But he is even-handed in his moral indignation, for he has even more scathing words for the perpetrators of the Sabra and Shatila massacres. The poem "Upon the Slaughter" is constructed on the pattern of Bialik's famous poem on the Kishineff Pogrom. Except now the victims are non-Jews.

But however sharp is his moral stance, there is always his saving humor that takes the edge off his rage. This is due in a large measure to his deft exploitation of the wonderful potentialities inherent in the Hebrew language, its associative power and multiple layers of meaning, which he mines with great skill. His is a poetry that cares. It is also a poetry that laughs.

The poem "Curtain" in this book is dedicated to his father who, as mentioned before, derived his livelihood from making curtains for the Holy Ark. It is a poem of delicate weave in which the poet pays tribute to the legacy he inherited from both of his parents—a legacy of both beauty and holiness.

Curtain

My mother loved the beauty of words
that joined together
my father loved
the letters
that issued from his hands

Mother's words
a thread of grace

>a thread of loving-kindness
>run through them
>binding them into a self-contained melody
>Father's letters
>symbols that he loved
>threads of silver
>with threads of
>gold
>upon
>curtains
>of a synagogue
>
>My father left
>no silver
>no gold
>only
>the tip of a thread
>and swarms of
>letters
>
>May this poem to him
>be
>something of a curtain
>draped
>magnificently.[5]

One further word needs to be said about Shamosh's language. He has the keenest ear of anyone writing Hebrew at the present time, for the most delicate of nuances of the language. It can be stated with certainty that he writes the most *beautiful* Hebrew today. His language is rich, resonant, distinguished for its musicality, and sparkling like Joseph's "coat of many colors." He seeks harmony and pleasantness in the effects of the sounds he creates, rather than jarring discord. He also seeks to create a palpable sensation of fragrance through mere use of words. In general, the element of playfulness is very strong in his use of language, which is elegant and multifaceted and often elevates the discourse above the immediate issue at hand. This is what primarily invests his writing, whether in prose or poetry, with its aesthetic dimension. In so doing, he has perpetuated his ancestral heritage of combining holiness, in this case moral concerns, with beauty.

V. Prose Pieces: The Sephardim and Israeli Society

On many occasions, Shamosh expressed himself regarding the Sephardim and their situation in Israeli society. He sees three areas in which Sephardim can make a distinct contribution to Israeli society: the areas of family life, tolerance, and Arab-Jewish relations.

1. In the realm of family and its place in the scale of value: Sephardim have close family ties; they hold family values to be the supreme focus and center of social stability. Sephardim can serve as example of the very necessity for the existence of the family, and the need for its unity. In the modern Western world in which the family as institution is deteriorating, this is a very positive contribution. He cites the researches of Peres and Katz which claim that "the increase of the proportion of oriental Jews in the Israeli population plays a role in the growing tendency towards family stability in Israeli society."[6]
2. Another area in which the Sephardim can contribute is tolerance, acceptance of differences and lack of fanaticism. For Sephardim, according to Shamosh, are disciples of the Maimonidean "Golden Mean," and shun religious, political, and ideological fanaticism.

   He gives examples which show how Sephardim display both family values and tolerance, and how Ashkenazi society (including that society with which he is most identified and to whose basic *Weltanschauung* he is still attached, kibbutz society) can violate both, giving a single example of each: In the fifties the kibbutz displayed both fanaticism and disregard for family values—when families broke up and husbands separated from wives over ideological differences. On the other hand, he gives an example of his own mother, who adhered strictly to Jewish dietary laws,

but nevertheless was tolerant of other people's practices. Once upon a visit to her son's kibbutz they were served some pizza, but the cheese contained a piece of sausage. The son was confounded, did not know what to do. However, the mother nonchalantly said, "Oh, a piece of meat fell into the dish!" She removed it, and proceeded with the eating of her portion, as if nothing had happened. Thus she preserved family unity and accord, which she cherished, and showed tolerance towards the practices of others: "It [the forbidden meat] she avoided—but to us she drew closer," was her son's observation.[7]
3. The third area where the Sephardim can contribute is the area of Arab-Jewish relations. The Sephardim have millennial experience of living among Arabs and are familiar with their culture. They can facilitate contacts with Arab neighbors and help the process of understanding in the region. He cites an example: When the Camp David Accords were signed with Egypt, Israel sent an ambassador who was totally foreign to the culture and tastes of the host country. He was a fine and capable fellow, to be sure, but not one likely to appreciate the music of Umm Kulthum.[8]

VI. H. N. Bialik: On the Renaissance of the Sephardim

In the spring of 1927, Hayim Nahman Bialik gave an address to the Association of the Pioneers of the East—a group of Young Sephardim in Jerusalem—which he called a "talk," rather than a "lecture." This is the gist of what he said: He did not think that it was a disaster that the people of Israel are divided into "tribes." It has been that way since time immemorial, witness the "twelve tribes of Ancient Israel." He offered the model of the fruit tree: it is healthy for the tree to be multi-branched, provided that it has in common many roots underneath—a system of subterranean veins that nourish it—also that it pulses with one heart and one soul.

He said that in the last ten years he was working on medieval Sephardic poetry and he marveled at the genius and achievement of it. Up to the time of the Sephardim, he said, Jewish intellectual creativity was anonymous and collective: the Bible, the Talmud, the Midrash, the Piyuttim (liturgical poetry). With the Sephardim great individuals begin to emerge, whose creative work bears their individual stamp, such as Alfasi, Saadia, and Maimonides, etc.

He assigned the Sephardim then present three tasks:

1. It is the duty of the Sephardim to collect their dispersed treasures—their classic texts from the Middle Ages. Each tribe is responsible for the collection and gathering of its inheritance.
2. In the field of education, they must set up schools for themselves, where they will teach their own literary classics, wisdom, legends, customs, and folklore. The school system in general will share the basic legacy of Jewish sources, but each tribe must maintain its own distinctive brand of education, its own cultural coloration.
3. They must also start doing what Ashkenazim have already been doing: collecting their traditions, customs, folklore and folkways, and try to preserve them. In their case, the task is even much more urgent than among Ashkenazim due to their greater dispersion. He concluded by saying that if Sephardim wish to join the Ashkenazim in marriage, they must bring a "dowry"—the distinctive products of their own soul, spiritual gifts, that assure healthy and fruitful marriage and accrue to the benefit of the offspring.[9]

Upon the conclusion of Bialik's talk pandemonium broke out. He was accused, particularly by the young Sephardim in the audience, of advocating tribalization, fragmentation, segregation. Especially problematic was his advocacy of separate educational institutions for Sephardim, where they would study their own curriculum, their own distinctive texts. Bialik tried to explain, clarify, even mollify; he claimed that he was "misunderstood." But he did not retreat from his basic position. He pleaded for cultural pluralism that would enrich everyone. He returned to the organic model—now it was the human body that he used to illustrate his point. Every organ is differentiated as to function. As far as distinctive education and distinctive educational agenda for the Sephardim were concerned, he returned to the point with even greater vehemence: "I want to tell you that I do not understand, how they teach Sephardim from text books of Ashkenazim."[10]

He asserted that if Sephardim persisted in fostering their distinctive style and created according to their special genius they might come to prevail in other areas of cultural life—in spite of their being in the minority—as they have prevailed over the majority in the matter of pronunciation. Even in America, he says in illustrating his point, they have succumbed to the Havara Saphardit. He concluded his talk with the exclamation: If you will it is not a legend.[11]

VII. Conclusion

I would like to suggest that what Amnon Shamosh is doing is carrying out the task enunciated by Bialik, heeding his advice, knowingly or unknowingly. In the poem "The Great Confession," for example, we see a true marriage of East and West; we sense the sights and sounds of the East in the gold bracelet, the music of the "lute," the bodily movements, the stories, the legends. All this Oriental material is integrated in a modern poem, using Western devices and techniques—ambivalence and ambiguity, irony, open forms, free verse, occasional rhyme, lack of punctuation, allusions, tension, double meanings, etc. The poem fulfills the demand of Bialik that Sephardim bring a dowry of their own to the wedding. The very poem can be a metaphor for the seemingly paradoxical stance enunciated by Bialik, of differentiation as prerequisite to union—by the creation of a remarkable artifact that manages to achieve at once the hoped for cultural fusion, attaining both integration and integrity.

Notes

This is a somewhat expanded version of a paper given at the Association for Israel Studies Conference, held at Barnard College on June 9–10, 1991.

Both of the translations of Amnon Shamosh's poems "The Great Confession" and "Curtain" that appear in the course of this chapter, are the work of the present writer.

1. For the most comprehensive treatment in English of Amnon Shamosh's fiction see Walter P. Zenner, "Aleppo the Kibbutz in the Fiction of Amnon Shamosh," *Shofar* 6 (Spring 1988). The article does not only contain detailed discussions of individual narratives, but offers valuable insights on the nature of Shamosh's work as a whole.

2. *From the Source* (Jerusalem: Carta, 1988), p. 27.

3. The data on Amnon Shamosh's life, family background, and Israeli experience are based for the most part on his prose pieces collected in *Kibbutz Is a Kibbutz Is a Kibbutz* (Ramat Gan: Massada, 1980) and especially in *From the Source*.

4. *Spanish Diwan*, p. 88.

5. *Upon a Harp with a Solemn Sound*, p. 21.

6. "Hebrew literature between East and West," *From the Source*, p. 56.

7. Ibid., pp. 55–56.

8. Ibid., pp. 56–57.

9. H. N. Bialik, "The Renaissance of the Sephardim," *Addresses*, Vol. 1 (Tel Aviv: Dvir, 1935), pp. 110–116.

10. Ibid., p. 117.

11. Ibid., p. 119.

Bibliography of Amnon Shamosh (in Hebrew)

Spanish Diwan (poems), Ramat-Gan: Massada, 1981.

Upon a Harp with a Solemn Sound (poems), Tel Aviv: Sifriat Ha Poalim, 1984.

Kibbutz Is a Kibbutz Is a Kibbutz, Ramat Gan: Massada, 1980.

From the Source—Talks and Articles, Jerusalem: Carta Publishers, 1988.

On *The Schizoid Nature of Modern Hebrew*

Shmuel Bolozky

Paul Wexler, *The Schizoid Nature of Modern Hebrew: A Slavic Language in Search of a Semitic Past*, Volume 4 in *Mediterranean Language and Culture Monograph Series*, edited by A. Borg, S. Somekh and P. Wexler, Wiesbaden: Otto Harrassowitz, 1990.

The monograph's central argument is that Modern Hebrew (MH) is a Slavic language. Wexler claims that Yiddish was originally a dialect of the Sorbian subgroup of the Slavic language family (located in the southern corner of former East Germany), and that the supposed Germanic origin of this Judeo-Sorbian dialect is a misconception due to wholesale adoption of a Germanic lexicon for the language. In other words, Yiddish is Judeo-Sorbian, disguised with Germanic vocabulary. Similarly, he argues, the "revivers" of MH as a spoken language were native speakers of Yiddish, who applied the Hebrew lexicon in toto to essentially Yiddish structure—a process made easy by the large number of Hebrew items (at least 15 percent, some through the mediation of Aramaic) already incorporated in Yiddish. So, if MH is essentially Yiddish, and Yiddish essentially Judeo-Sorbian, then MH is—genetically—a Slavic language.

According to Wexler, this type of major lexical shift was not an isolated phenomenon in the history of Ashkenazic Jewry. Thus, from the sixteenth or seventeenth century, Yiddish cryptolects have had a major component of Hebrew vocabulary. In fact, up to 85 percent of the vocabulary of the Yiddish cryptolect used by Swiss horse dealers is of Hebrew origin! In scribal Yiddish, used between the sixteenth and nineteenth centuries primarily for recording testimonies in court cases, Hebrew words and phrases constituted about 50 percent of the lexicon. The author also feels that it was no accident that Ludwik Zamenhof came from the same region (Byelorussia) and grew up with the same tradition as Ben-Yehuda. While Ben-Yehuda and friends followed the tradition of wholesale lexical borrowing by transplanting masses of Hebrew vocabulary unto Yiddish, Zamenhof implanted an essentially Latinate lexicon onto a Slavic base in introducing Esperanto.

Wexler does not believe in the possibility of truly "reviving" a spoken norm for an unspoken language of liturgy and literature. No language that lost its spoken function has ever been revived, e.g. Akkadian, Latin, Classical Greek, Egyptian. Modern Hebrew (MH) is not a direct reincarnation of either Biblical Hebrew (BH) or Mishnaic Hebrew (MSH), and certainly not of Medieval Hebrew (MDH), and its first speakers did not learn it from an earlier generation of native speakers, but sort of reconstructed it from what they knew, or thought they knew, about earlier phases of the language. Even the evidence of continued Hebrew speech that has been documented for generations, among special groups, at some Jewish schools, and primarily in contact between members of Jewish communities of different liturgical traditions, cannot be considered the base from which MH sprang (although it may have served as an example to Ben-Yehuda and others that it (reviving) *can* be done).

Although the author refers to the notion of revival as a "hoax," he does not mean that it was intended as such. "Revivers" like Ben-Yehuda, though proficient in etymological and philological analysis, were linguistically naïve; they believed that by reintroducing the Hebrew lexicon, as well as Hebrew inflectional paradigms and a few basic syntactic phenomena, they were also reviving the linguistic structure of Hebrew as a whole. Concentrating on words, they were unaware of the degree to which they were applying them onto their own underlying Yiddish structure. However, identifying MH as direct heir of earlier phases of the language, particularly BH (MSH being too close to recent rabbinic traditions, from which the social Zionists wished to distance themselves), had powerful political motivation.

The unbroken link between contemporary Jews and their ancestors in Palestine some eighteen centuries ago required direct lineage from BH/MSH to MH, to emphasize the claim to the land and the right of the Jews to return to their ancestral home. Clearly, this was by no means unique to the Jewish people; the language component is an essential element in any national or ethnic movement, as is the appeal of a glorious past, when that language was the vehicle of a culture of importance. Furthermore, the revival concept was, and still is, strongly supported by educators, language planners, and normative grammarians, who perpetuate the belief in "correct" Hebrew that is based solely on written historical sources.

Wexler's claim may be analyzed diachronically as well as synchronically. This reviewer is by no means qualified to evaluate the historical-genetic argument, or the validity of the migration pattern required by Wexler's assumption. For Wexler's theory to work, it is essential that the migration of Yiddish-speaking Jewry within the German orbit be from east to west rather than vice versa; it is not clear how much evidence there is to substantiate such a claim. Furthermore, as strong as the linguistic evidence for a "hidden Slavic standard" for MH may be, it does not automatically follow, as Wexler claims, that its near-absence in the lexicon (due to re-lexification) and the knowledge that MH was "revived" as a spoken language a century ago allow us to identify the Slavic hidden standard as native rather than borrowed (p. 74). Nevertheless, one can weigh linguistic evidence which, though not constituting *direct* evidence for the diachronic hypothesis, might still be regarded as being compatible with it, or interpreted as indirect support for it.

Synchronically and typologically, the claim can only be judged by the degree to which the various components of the grammar are compatible with the basic principles of Semitic language structure. Wexler states that "Modern Hebrew is *'genetically Slavic, with a strong tendency to be(come) typologically Semitic'*" (p. 102 italics added for emphasis). In other words, he admits that MH *may* be *typologically* Semitic, at least in part. In the opinion of this reviewer, the degree of Yiddish structure preserved in MH is significant, but not distinct enough to qualify the language as only *partly* Semitic from a typological point of view. In particular, it is difficult to characterize MH typologically as anything but Semitic insofar as morphology is concerned. If typological classification is deemed just as important as genetic origin, then MH *is* essentially Semitic.

The author produces linguistic evidence for Slavic origin of MH, some of which is quite convincing. There is not enough of it, though. One can begin with the areas of phonology and phonetics. The sound system of MH is significantly different from that of a typical Semitic language, and can be claimed to be closer to that of Yiddish, or European sound structure in general. In itself, however, this cannot be used as evidence for Yiddish, or Slavic, origin of MH, and indeed Wexler does not resort to this type of argument. As pointed out in Goldenberg (1981), the phonological system is usually the least likely to maintain the characteristics of the proto-language,[1] and the most likely to be affected by adjacent languages, regardless of whether they are genetically related or not.[2] On the other hand, the loss of gemination (e.g. *dibber* > *diber,* etc.) in MH is a more likely inheritance from Yiddish, since degemination is a hallmark of Ashkenazi pronunciation of Hebrew.

Another argument for Wexler's position, a rather strong one, is phonotactic: the existence in MH of consonant clusters which Semitic languages generally try to avoid. Thus, in BH, potential consonant clusters were avoided in initial position, usually through the intervention of a schwa where an initial consonant cluster would be expected, as in *d^evårim*[3] "things," *k^etuvim* "written, ms. pl." (the schwa prevented the formation of *dvårim* etc. by antepretonic vowel reduction from underlying /*davår+im*/). When the initial consonant was low, a shorter variant of the original vowel fulfilled a similar function. Modern Hebrew maintains the modern counterpart of that short vowel (e.g. BH /'ašır+im/ "rich, m. pl." > 'ăšir+im > MH *aširim*; BH /ḥadåš+im/ "new, m. pl." > ḥădåš+im > MH *xadašim*), but the schwa itself, or rather its *e*-counterpart, is generally deleted, as in *dvarim*, *ktuvim*. The rule is blocked only when the resulting cluster would have violated the sonority hierarchy, with difficult-to-pronounce clusters like #*mk*, #*yl*, #*lv*, etc., in words like *mekomot* "places," *yeladim* "children," *levanim* "white, ms. pl." Yiddish *also* deletes the same schwas in its Hebrew words, as in *tfile* "prayer," *gdóylim* "big, ms. pl," *króyvim* "relatives" *šxéynim* "neighbors, ms.," *skéynim* "old, ms. pl." The only difference is that the deletion is extended to clusters with initial *x*, which *are* allowed in Slavic, i.e. to *xsídim* "Hassids" vs. Hebrew *xasidim*; *xšad* "suspicion" vs. Hebrew *xašad*.[4] Although this phenomenon can be attributed to Slavic substratum effect, it may also be used to support the claim for a direct genetic relationship between MH and Yiddish.

Wexler also claims that the severely reduced productivity of the spirantization phenomenon in MH is inherited from Yiddish. Thus, MH has *be#kita* "in a class" (instead of *be#xita*), *be#polin* "in Poland" (instead of *be#folin*), *be#berlin* "in Berlin" (instead of *be#verlin*), following Yiddish norms; it may preserve spirantization in items of BH origin, as in *lixvod* "in honor of," *lefaxot* "at least" (Yiddish *lepóxes*, though), but not in *le#kavod* "to honor (N)," *le#paxot* "to less," nor in most post-Mishnaic forms. Even if the explanation lies in the degree of collocability and binding, the fact remains that in the less frozen items, the spirantization rule is suppressed, following the Yiddish model.[5]

Naturally, Wexler also cites non-final stress of MH personal and place names, which is clearly of Yiddish origin, as in *šmúel, dína, ríšon, rexóvot*.

The most obvious area of Yiddish-in-Modern-Hebrew are vocabulary items and borrowing translations. The well known *kúmzic* "outdoor get-together and meal, usually around fire," *nébex* "poor, unable to take care of self," *špric* "squirt," *švic* "sweat; bragging" etc. are irrelevant here; these are straightforward borrowings. There are, however, semantic doublets in MH, where a Hebrew word coexists alongside the very same word found as a Hebraism in Yiddish, with certain semantic distinctions, as in

(1)   *kley zémer* "musical instruments"   *klézmer* "musician (who plays East European Jewish music)"

mikve "pool of water"   *míkve* "ritual bath"
taxlit "purpose, point"   *táxles* "the issue at hand"
náxat "comfort"   *náxes* "pleasure from children"

xevra "group, society"   *xévre* "the gang"
briya/birya "creature"   *bérye* "active and strong woman"

bitaxon "safety, security"   *bitóxn* "trust in God"
melamed "teach (pres. part.)"   *melámed* "*xéder* teacher"
maške "drink"   *máške* "alcoholic drink"

The very retention of Yiddish Hebraisms in the lexicon, side-by-side with BH or MSH items, fits nicely with a model that assumes a Yiddish base for MH, onto which a Hebrew vocabulary has been transplanted—otherwise, why borrow Hebrew words from Yiddish, with their specific Yiddishized meanings, when the same ones already exist natively? It makes more sense to assume that the Yiddishized elements were already there, and that the "Hebrew Hebrew" ones were borrowed.

Loan translations, including phrases and expressions—of the colloquial *ata coxek miméni* "you are laughing 'from' me" type, instead of *ata coxek li* "you are laughing at me," which corresponds to Yiddish *du laxst fun mir*—also abound.[6] However, loan translations are quite common across languages, and thus do not constitute a strong argument for Wexler's claim (and indeed he does not use them as evidence.) More significant, perhaps, is the fact that most adverbs, adverbial phrases, and conjunctions in Yiddish are Hebraisms[7] (or Aramaisms) that are also employed in MH, like *dávka* "in spite ... ," *ádraba* "on the contrary," *afílu* "even," *bekicur* "in short," *beikar* "primarily," *pašut* "simply," *halevay* "I wish ... ," *lehax(')is* "to spite." Grammatical elements such as these are usually inherited, not borrowed.[8]

The syntactic claims are harder to evaluate: firstly, because syntactic structure does change—in fact, according to Kutcher[9], there is no living Semitic language whose word order has not changed from that of its parent language; secondly, Wexler's syntactic arguments draw from only very basic phenomena, virtually ignoring complex sentence structure involving subordinate clauses, etc.; thirdly, many MH syntactic structures have parallels in both Yiddish and MSH, i.e. it is impossible to tell whether they were inherited from Yiddish, or constitute reintroduction of MSH processes. Here is one illustration. The use of the resumptive (or "retrospective") pronoun in relative clauses, as in *aséfer šekaráti bo/oto* "the book that I read ([in] it)"[10] as a variant of *aséfer šekaráti* "the book that I read" may be related to Yiddish *dos bux vos ix hob im geléynt*. However, although BH does not leave resumptive pronouns in object relative clauses, MSH occasionally does,[11] as in *śådɛ šɛqqᵉṣårúah goyim* "a field which Gentiles have reaped (it)," or *'ăvånim šɛzzi'za'tån hammahăreyšå* "stones which the plough has moved (them)." Since this phenomenon is found *both* in MSH and in Yiddish, on whom is the burden of proof?

A similar argument can be made regarding another apparent syntactic relationship: the tendency in MH to replace dependency constructions which mark possession, e.g. *sifri* "my book," by analytic structures involving *šel* "of" (e.g. *haséfer šeli* "the book mine = my book") parallels possessive structures in Yiddish, e.g. *mayn bux*. The same natural shift from synthetic to analytic constructions had already applied, however, in MSH, is found in all Slavic languages and many other European ones, and is even found in the colloquial dialects of Arabic, which replace synthetic structures involving inalienable possession with analytic ones containing *tábaʻ* "of," as in *kitābī* "my book" developing into *'alkitāb tábaʻī* "the book my = my book." This is probably why Wexler does not actually invoke this commonly raised argument for the impact of Yiddish on MH.

What Wexler does attribute to Yiddish in this connection is the colloquial variety of *definite smixut* (dependency) constructions. Colloquially, *báal habáit* "the landlord" (literally "the owner of the house") is replaced by *abáal báit*, i.e. the definite article *#(h)a+* precedes the whole construction instead of the second noun only. According to Wexler, this is a Yiddish feature maintained in MH, since in Yiddish such Hebraisms are always preceded by the definite article: *der balebos* "the landlord." Similarly, *ktav hayad* "the manuscript" becomes *aktav yad*, as it is in Yiddish, *der ksav yad*; *bet hadin* "the court" turns into *abet din* (see Yiddish *dos béyzdn*), etc. It is also obvious, however, that the shift of *#(h)a* to the front of the whole construction reflects the speaker's conception of it as a single unit, and would have probably happened even without the intermediacy of Yiddish—as it does, for instance, in the colloquial dialects of Arabic.[12]

Another point concerns definiteness and word-order. Hebrew subject-verb order is shifted to verb-subject when the subject is indefinite, as in *ayéled higía* "the child arrived" vs. *higía yéled* "arrived a child = a child arrived." Wexler attributes this distribution to Yiddish *der yíngl iz ongekúmen* vs. *es iz ongekúmen a yíngl*. Actually, for many native speakers of Yiddish, both *iz gekúmen a yíngl* and *a yíngl iz gekúmen* are equally acceptable, whereas in Hebrew, **yéled higía* is unacceptable (unless the subject is contrastively stressed). Still, the existence of verb-subject order in MH sentences with indefinite subjects has a parallel in Yiddish. However, this phenomenon is by no means unique to Yiddish and Hebrew (or Slavic): there is a tendency across languages[13] for the (indefinite) noun in presentational sentences to follow the verb, so as to place it in a less topical position and thus give it more prominence.

An additional syntactic feature: the order of a proper name and the noun in apposition to it. Biblical Hebrew and MSH require proper name first: *yeša'yåhu hannåvi* "Isaiah the prophet," *dåwid hamme̊lex* "David the King"; in MH, the order is often reversed (*anavi yešaayáu, amélex david*), reflecting parallel structures in Yiddish and other European languages.[14]

Yiddish and other European language elements are reflected in the use of the copula in structures like *habáit hu gadol* "the house is big," in addition to *habáit gadol* "the house big = the house is big." In BH and in MSH one finds either *habbáyit gådol* "the house big = the house is big," or *habbáyit gådol hu* "the house big is"/*gådol hu habbáyit* "big is the house," but not *habbáyit hu gådol*.[15]

Wexler also argues that MH *morphology* is Slavic-through-Yiddish. In some cases the connection is obvious, e.g. the diminutive/affectionate suffixes +*nik*, +*čik*, as in

(2) *kibúcnik* "kibbutz member"   *mošávnik* "moshav member"
    mapáynik "member of the Mapai party"
    the *katánčik* "very small"   *xabúbčik* "little dear"

These are relatively minor, though. A more substantial argument may be drawn from Blanc.[16] Hebrew seems to have inherited from Yiddish some aspect-type distinctions. There are cases in Yiddish where the plain verb has imperfect reference, while the prefixed one refers to perfect action denoting transition from one state to the one denoted by the plain verb, e.g. *šlofn* "sleep" vs. *áynšlofn* "fall asleep." The same aspectual difference is conveyed in a number of *pa'al-nif'al* or *pa'al-hitpa'el* pairs, all of which have Yiddish equivalents: *yašav* "be sitting"—*hityašev* "sit down" (see *zicn/[avek] zicn zix*); *šaxav* "be lying down"—*niškav* "lie down" (*lign/[avek] leygn zix*); *amad* "stand"—*neemad* "stand up, come to a halt" (*šteyn/[avek] šteln zix, ópšteln zix*); *zaxar* "remember"—*nizkar* "recall" (*gedénken/dermónen zix*). It is noted in Kutcher,[17] however (and to an extent by Blanc himself), that there were some BH precedents, such as BH *påḥad* "be afraid"—*nivhal* "become frightened" (though not same root), and MSH *zåxur 'ani* "I remember"—*'ani nizkår* "I recall." The phenomenon is certainly more systematic in Yiddish, though. The inherited aspect argument can be extended beyond the realm of morphology: *ix šrayb* "I write" denotes a plain action; *ix gib a šrayb* "I 'give a writing'" refers to an instantaneous or abrupt variety. Modern Hebrew *noten kfica* "'give a jump' = go and be right back" or *noten cilcul* "'give a ring'" thus go back to *gib a šprung* and *gib a klung*, respectively.

Wexler's main argument in the morphological domain is drawn from general observations regarding the verb system. He argues that the verbal derivation system was becoming unproductive in BH and in MSH, that MH continues this tendency, and that in the Hebrew component of Yiddish, the system of discontinuous verb patterns (*binyanim*) absorbed a strong Slavic influence, which has remained intact in MH. The reputed seven *binyanim* of MH already represent a reduced system, which lost the internal passive of *pa'al*, the *hitpā'el* counterpart of *hitpa'el* (a pair reflected in separate *tafá"ala* and *'iftá'ala* in Arabic?).

In MH, only four *binyanim* are truly productive: *pi'el*, *hif'il*, *nif'al*, *hitpa'el*; the first two are accompanied by their less productive passive equivalents, *pu'al* and *huf'al*. Loss of vocalic length difference as well as gemination contributed to increased opacity and breakdown of the *binyan* system. The decline in the productivity of *pa'al* (*qal*) began in BH, and has been gradually progressing, owing to the relative semantic opacity of *pa'al*, its inability to accommodate more than three root consonants, its relative paradigmatic complexity, the absence of a truly corresponding passive, etc. Wexler claims that the decreased productivity of the *binyanim* in general, as well as the weakening of semantic correlates of particular *binyanim*, reflects a tendency in Slavic and Yiddish for conjugations with particular affixes which are devoid of semantic functions (e.g. the Yiddish infinitival endings +*e(n)*, *enen* or *even*). In fact, he goes as far as to say that in MH the *binyan* system is being restructured in the direction of the Slavic practice of deriving compound verbs linearly by suffixation—that *hit+*, for instance, becomes a linear device for deriving new denominative verbs by mere prefixation, without reference to a root or a discontinuous consonant-vowel pattern.

As support for this claim he cites *hitxaver* "became friends (with)"—clearly derived from *xaver* "friend"—alongside *hitxaber* "joined," and the Yiddish use of the reflexive pronoun in translation equivalents: *xávern zix* "be associated with." The same claim may be made for the *hi+* of *hif'il* in *hišpric* "squirted" and *hišvic* "sweated; bragged." Although on the face of it, this appears to be Wexler's strongest claim, it is in fact this area of word-formation which *clearly* characterizes MH as a Semitic language. Wexler could argue that this is a consequence of wholesale lexical borrowing from earlier stages of the language, and thus does not constitute an *innate* component of MH. Still, synchronically, the morphology of MH is characteristically Semitic. Typical word-formation in Semitic is discontinuous, consisting of extraction of a sequence of consonants from an existing word (sometimes referred to as "root"), and reapplying it onto a fixed canonical pattern of consonants and vowels to form a new lexical item. This is the *only* way to form verbs. Although *hitxaver* "became friends (with)" happens to look like a linear sequence of *hit+ xaver* "friend," it has to fit into a canonical *hit+CaCeC* pattern, which is still done by extracting the consonant sequence *xvr* from *xaver* and reapplying it onto the canonical pattern *hit+CaCeC* (cf. *hištabec* "found its rubric" vs. *hištavec* "got a heart attack," the latter originating from *šavac* "heart attack"). Also, most recent denominative verbs are not in *hitpa'el* but in *pi'el*, a discontinuous pattern which is *not* characterized by a special derivational prefix.

Although in the total Hebrew lexicon there is little correlation between *binyan* and meaning, frequent everyday items do exhibit considerable form-to-meaning correlation, which is further reinforced in productivity tests. Thus, it can be shown that in recent word-formation, as well as when productive innovation cannot be avoided[18] (see Bolozky 1978, 1982, 1986a), speakers first distinguish between "focus on the patient" and "focus on the agent." If the focus is on the patient (be it reflexive, inchoative [i.e. "become . . . "], ingressive, reciprocal, etc.), *hitpa'el* is chosen:

(3) **Recent:** *hitazréax* "became a citizen" *hitpager* "died"
hitgamed "became very small" *hitmameš* "became real"
hitrakez "concentrated" *hitpalmes* "debated"
hizdayen "copulated"

Potential: *hištaref* "became a sheriff"
hitsnobeb/histaneb/histnobeb/hitsnabeb/histnabeb "became a snob"
histalen "became an armchair revolutionary"
hitmarkses/hitmarkes "became a Marxist"

If the focus is on the agent, true causatives would still tend to be realized in *hif'il*, as in

(4) **Recent:** *himxiš* "made real" *hitpil* "desalinated"
hincíax "eternalized" *himxiz* "made into a play"
hifnim "internalized" *hikvič* "squeezed (child speech)"

Potential: *higmid* "made (something/somebody) small"
hišrif "made (somebody) sheriff"
hisnib "made (somebody) snobbish"
hislin "made (somebody) into an armchair revolutionary"

But all other agentives, which make for the majority of innovations, would opt for *pi'el*:

(5) **Recent:** *biyel* "put stamp (on envelope)" *siveg* "assorted"
  bilef "lied" *viset* "regulated"
  nitev "marked route" *xiyeg* "dialed"
  flirtet "flirted" *fikses* "sent by fax"
  Potential: *širef* "behaved like a sheriff"
  pinel "covered with panels"
  isfelt "covered with asphalt"
  pitent/pitnet "registered as patent"
  sportet/spirtet/sipret "engaged in sports"
  keres "fitted with a hook"

Derivation of nouns is not as rigorously constrained as verb-formation is; new nouns may be formed linearly *as well as* discontinuously. It is from the area of noun-formation that Wexler's claim could receive its strongest support: if linear formation can be shown to be expanding *at the expense* of discontinuous derivation, then it could be argued that MH is indeed losing its Semitic character. However, it can be shown that while linear derivation of nouns is indeed on the increase, it has been operating *alongside* root-pattern derivation, with *both* strategies maintaining their productivity and reinforcing each other.[19] Even in this respect, MH is not less Semitic than a language like Arabic.

Many illustrations from the MH noun system can be introduced to prove that non-linear word-formation continues to be (very) productive. In this context, only one case will be discussed—one which Wexler also uses: nouns ending with the agentive suffix +*an*, like *kablan* "contractor." The use of this pattern as an illustration is particularly appropriate, since it allows both discontinuous *and* linear derivation, e.g. *kabl+an* "contractor" (constituting a realization of the discontinuous *CaCC+an* pattern) vs. *alxut+an* "wireless operator" (linearly derived from *alxut* "wireless" +*an*), and the choice of device is not affected by semantic considerations. Usually, transparent relationship with an existing verb form results in *CaCC+an* realization, whereas linear *N+an* preserves the transparency of the source noun or adjective—but not necessarily so.

Wexler believes that the expanded popularity of nouns with *+an* in MH is due to its common use in the Hebrew component of Yiddish. In fact, he points out that Yiddish uses it not only for nouns, as in *gázlen* "robber," *kábren* "undertaker," *bádxen* "joker," but also to derive new verbs from other stems. Thus, *badak* "check, examine" *+an* agentive + *+en* infinitive yields Yiddish *bádkenen*, *katvan* "writer, typist" (actually non-existent in Yiddish by itself) becomes Yiddish *kásfenen* "write = author (V)," *leycan* "joker" (Yiddish *leycn*) yields Yiddish *lécenen* "joke around." Slavic verbal derivation requires a linking suffix before the infinitive ending, and Wexler attributes the choice of *+an* to similarity with the Upper Sorbian verbal noun suffix *+nye*.

Essentially, both *CaCC+an* and *N+an* started in MSH:[20]

(6) CaCC+an *forms by origin*
    Biblical   3   [00.48 percent]
    Mishnaic   108   [17.48 percent]
    Medieval[21] 75   [12.14 percent]
    Modern   432   [69.90 percent]

    Total: 618   [100.00 percent]

    N+an forms by origin
    Biblical   —
    Mishnaic   44   [13.46 percent]
    Medieval   7   [2.14 percent]
    Modern   276   [84.40 percent]

    Total: 327   [100.00 percent]

Although the percentage of linear *N+an* innovations in MH is very high, there were significant precedents for it in MSH, and in spite of the fact that MH *CaCC+an* cases are "only" about 70 percent, their sheer number is overwhelming. In other words, both devices have coexisted from MSH, and are *very* productive in MH. There is no reason to believe that linear derivation is actually replacing discontinuous word-formation under the impact of European languages—or a "hidden Slavic standard."

Below are some instances of *CaCC+an* and *N+an* (even for MSH, gemination is not marked):

(7) Some CaCC+aa *innovations*
MSH *baṭlån* "idler, loafer"   *dabrån* "talkative, verbose"
     šaqrån "liar"   *gazlån* "robber"
     qablån "contractor"   *qamṣån* "miser"
MDH *'axlån* "glutton"   *badḥån* "joker"
     qabrån "gravedigger"   *lamdån* "learned man, scholar"
     šadxån "matchmaker"   *salḥån* "forgiving, lenient"
MH   *asfan* "collector"   *badran* "entertainer"
     rakdan "dancer"   *rašlan* "negligent, slovenly"
     baxyan "weeper, crybaby"   *bazbezan* "spendthrift"

(8) Some N+an *innovations*
MSH *dod+ån* "cousin"   /'eymat+ån/ > 'eymtån "terrorist"
     leyṣ+ån "mocker, jester"   *reyq+ån* "empty, vain"
     /*kotev+ån*/ > *kotvån* "scribe" *duvš+ån* "honey cake"
MDH *miṣr+ån* "neighbor"   /*śimḥa+ån*/ > *śimḥån* "a happy person"
     /*soléaḥ+ån*/ > *solḥån* "forgiving, lenient"
     /*ga'ăvat+ån*/ > *ga'avtån* "boastful, haughty"
MH   *roš+an* "tadpole"   *cor+an* "silicon"
     egrof+an "boxer"   *yevu+an* "importer"
     maxšir+an "tool operator"   *matir+an* "permissive"

The *CaCC+an* forms below are clearly related to existing *pa'al* or *pi'el* stems, as indicated by the difference in stop/fricative realization (*p*, *b* and *k* are maintained in *pi'el*-related forms; their respective variants, *f*, *v* and *x*, point to relationship with *pa'al* verbs):

(9) CaCC+an *forms, related to* pa'al *and* pi'el *bases*

Form	Gloss	Rel. Pa'al	Rel. Pi'el
dabran	talkative, verbose		daber
kabcan	beggar, pauper		kabec
kablan	contractor		kabel
šabšan	one who makes errors		šabeš
tapsan	climber, alpinist		tapes
vakxan	polemist		(hit)vakéax
axlan	glutton	axal	
baxyan	weeper, crybaby	baxa	
kafcan	jumper; sand flea	kafac	
safdan	mourner	safad	
savlan	patient, long-suffering	saval	
navran	field mouse; rodent	navar	

The relationships are further supported by the very existence, or relative frequency, of related stems. Thus, when no related verb exists, realization would occur in one pattern and never in the other: non-existent **sibel* accounts for *savlan* rather than **sablan*, **šabaš* accounts for *šabšan* rather than **šavšan*, etc. In other cases, the alternative option is marginally acceptable to the extent that a related verb can be shown to exist as an infrequent item. Thus, only *kablan* "contractor" is attested since *kibel* "received" is so much more frequent than literary *kaval* "complained," and only *axlan* "glutton" is attested because *axal* "ate" is so more frequent than literary *ikel* "consumed." Marginally, speakers do understand what potential forms like ??*kavlan* "chronic complainer" (from literary *kaval* "complained"), or ??*aklan* "corrosive" (from literary *ikel* "consumed") would mean had they been attested. Their knowledge of the meaning of such potential forms also emphasizes how productive the process is.

One might be tempted, then, to try to derive such forms from their related verbal stems in a simple linear fashion, followed by stem-vowel elision: /daber+an/ > dabran, /axal+an/ > axlan, etc.

Though quite possible, this type of *linear* derivation is not very probable, particularly not in MH. In general, agentive nouns formed from verbs are derived from the *benoni* (the present tense or the present participle); in most cases, the same form is used for both, as in

(10)   *ofe* "bake, baker"   *yored* "go down, emigrant from Israel"
       šomer "guard, guard"   *šoxet* "slaughter, ritual slaughterer"
       menahel "direct, director"   *meamen* "train, trainer"
       mefakéax "inspect, inspector"   *metofef* "drum, drummer"
       malxin "compose music, composer"   *marce* "lecture, lecturer"
       mazkir "remind, secretary"   *maškif* "observe, observer"

Agentives related to *hitpa'el* and to *hif'il* stems with +*an* are *also* clearly derived from the respective *benoni* stems of these two *binyanim* in a linear fashion:[22]

(11)

Verb	Gloss	benoni
histagel	adapted	mistagel
histakel	observed	mistakel
hištamet	shirked	mištamet

Liter. N	Coll. N	Gloss
staglan	mistaglan	opportunist
staklan	mistaklan	observer
štamtan	mištamtan	shirker

(12)

Verb	Gloss	benoni	Rel. w/an	Gloss
hicxik	made laugh	macxik	macxikan	funny one
hirgiz	made angry	margiz	margizan	annoying person

In the cases before us, however, it would be difficult to argue for linear derivation of *CaCC+an* realizations from related *pa'al* or *pi'el* bases: in *pa'al*-related *CaCC+an* cases, it would necessitate derivation from the *past* stem; in *pi'el*-related verbs the (present/imperfect) stem would be the correct one, but without the prefix *me+* which is required to distinguish the present/present participle from the future/imperfect stem. In other words, since *CaCC+an* forms cannot be shown to be derived by linear affixation of *+an* to a *benoni* stem, they can only be generated discontinuously, from root plus consonant-vowel pattern.

When trying to determine the relative productivity of word-formation strategies involving the suffix *+an*, one also finds that there are numerous cases whose historical origin is probably linear, but which end up as *CaCCan*—e.g. *gaavtan* "boastful" (see *gaava* "pride"), *parvan* "furrier" (see *parva* "fur"), *yaaran* "forester" (see *yáar* "forest"), etc. Speakers consequently cannot tell from the surface form whether they are dealing with a linear derivation or with discontinuous realization of *CaCC+an*, since synchronically, both interpretations are possible.[23] There are also cases in which *both* strategies can be shown to have appplied, and to be equally acceptable even at the literary register: both *taxbulan* and *taxbelan* "resourceful person" are attested (see *taxbula* "ruse, strategem"), as are *taxsisan* and *taxsesan* "strategist" (see *taxsis* "strategy"). In most instances of multiple realization, however, the colloquial *CaCC+an* variant is *clearly* the preferred one: *yazman* "initiator" is commoner than *yozman* (see *yozma* "initiative," or *yozem* "initiate, *benoni* form"), *zalelan* "glutton" is more frequent than *zolelan* (see *zolel* "devour food, *benoni* form.") Productivity tests usually also indicate preference for the discontinuous *CaCC+an* (supposedly substandard): literary *katalogan* "cataloguer" is reinterpreted as *katlegan*, *pulmusan* "polemist, disputant" as *palmesan*, *sixletan* "rationalist" as *sxaltan*. It appears, then, that discontinuous *CaCC+an* is reinforced by linear derivation which on the surface looks like *CaCC+an*, and that whenever both strategies are attested, or when speakers are given a productivity-measuring task, the *CaCC+an* variant tends to be preferred.

In MH, then, discontinuous derivation continues to exist productively, and is in no danger of losing its productivity owing to Slavic (or Yiddish) general[24] preference for linear derivation. Whatever claims are made with regard to the rest of the grammar, it would be very inappropriate to regard MH word-formation as non-Semitic.

Since discontinuous word-formation is a hallmark of Semitic languages, and as such constitutes perhaps the *first* condition for characterizing a language as Semitic,[25] one can state with considerable certainty that at least *typologically*, MH *is* Semitic. The crucial question is whether labeling a language as Semitic can be determined solely on the basis of genetic development, or must also take typological considerations into account. In the latter case, the productivity of non-linear word-formation processes would in itself suffice to characterize MH as Semitic, and the considerable MSH component in syntax would reinforce the classification—irrespective of how many of the same structures can also be found in Yiddish (or in Slavic).

One may claim that even in the syntactic domain, today's MH is closer to BH and MSH than it was, say, forty years ago: there are significantly more cases today of *smixut* dependency constructions, etc.[26] The argument can be made that had Hebrew continued to develop uninterrupted for these 1,800 years, it could have become less "Semitic" than it is today[27]—which is what happened, for instance, to Neo-Syriac (in which "ergative"-type structure has pushed aside the earlier "active" structure under the influence of Persian and Turkish, ultimately resulting in loss of the original inflected forms of the verb[28]), and certainly to African Semitic pidgins, which are no longer Semitic. Even if MH resulted from a kind of "creolization" process,[29] its increasing Semitization, primarily in morphology, is gradually "decreolizing" it. Typologically, then, even if MH was not distinctly Semitic to start with, it certainly is today.

Wexler's main argument, regarding the diachronic *genetic* development of MH, is, as stated above, beyond the expertise of this reviewer. However, evidence appears to be stronger for Yiddish origin of MH than for Slavic origin of Yiddish. The development of MH on a Yiddish base is a reasonable hypothesis, and many unexplained phenomena fall into place with the notion of an underlying Yiddish syntax, modified by Hebrew structures already in operation in Yiddish and by elements of MSH syntax brought about through extensive use of Mishnaic clauses and phrases in the initial revival stage (primarily in the literary register, but to an extent in the colloquial as well.)[30]

The weakness of this monograph is not in the theory; on the contrary—it is an exciting hypothesis, which appeals to the intuition of this reviewer (in its Yiddish-to-MH argument). Rather, it is lacking in the amount of syntactic evidence that it invokes. There *must* be much more support there for Yiddish syntactic structure than offered in the book, particularly from more complex levels of subordinate clauses of different types and at different levels of subordination. Apparently, the author felt that "the message *had* to go out" before he was able to fully explore the potential of Yiddish-syntax-in-MH evidence. Further research into this specific issue may significantly strengthen his argument.

A monograph like *The Schizoid Nature of Modern Hebrew* is an important and welcome contribution to the study of MH and its origins, to research on language revival, and in particular to the issue of determining language affiliation. The author should be congratulated on having the courage to boldly state a hypothesis which others in the field have long considered a taboo. Although the evidence is incomplete, the proposed theory can shed new light on many questions, linguistic as well as extra-linguistic, and will probably initiate a healthy, productive debate among Hebraists and other scholars. Even if that were the *only* merit of the Wexler hypothesis (which it certainly is not), it would still make the publication of this book a very worthwhile enterprise.

Notes

1. e.g. see G. Goldenberg, "*Ruaḥ ha-safa u-mdiniyut lešonit le-'or hitpatḥuyot be-safot šemiyot ḥadašot,*" *Zixronot ha-'akademya la-Lašon ha-'ivrit* 21 (1981), pp. 36–39.

2. Some of the typically-Semitic phonemes of BH were either weakened or merged in ways similar to what is found in MH. There is evidence for the weakening of the pharyngeal *'ayin* to glottal *'alef* or its complete loss already in the Dead Sea Scrolls. Except for the so-called "oriental" traditions, i.e. those observed by Jews from Arabic-speaking countries, the distinction between *t* and the emphatic (or pharyngealized) *ṭ* has not been preserved. Furthermore, there is ample support from losses and neutralizations of phonemes that have taken place in other Semitic languages and dialects, which look very much like what we find what we find in MH when we compare it with BH: merger of the pharyngeal *ḥ* with the velar *x* in favor of the latter, absence of distinction between emphatic *ṣ* and non-emphatic *s*, disappearance of *q* or its merger with other phonemes, etc.

3. Unless marked otherwise, stress is word-final throughout.

4. But one also finds *xavéyrim* "friends, ms.," *xalóymes* "dreams," where deletion is blocked. Why?

5. The question of why Yiddish blocks spirantization in *some* Hebrew words which do spirantize in MH, as in *lepóxes* "at least," is harder to answer, and may depend on time of borrowing, substratal influences, etc.

6. *Ze taluy miménu* "it depends from him" instead of *ze taluy bo* "it depends 'in' him," *histakel al* "look on" instead of *histakel be* "look at" and *ecel* in the sense of Fr. *chez* are probably Yiddish in origin; the use of *nora* "awfully" as a superlative in *hu nora nexmad* "he is awfully nice" etc. probably goes back to Yiddish *šréklix, mitxašek li* "it 'self-desires' to me = I feel like" to *es glist zix mir, ose xaim* "'makes life' = has a good time" to *maxt a lebn, lo holex* "doesn't go" to *'s geyt ništ, asa li xor baroš* "made to me a hole in the head" to *er hot mir gemaxt a lox in kop, hu menadned li al an(e)šama* "he 'shakes to me on the soul' = he bores me; he does not let go" to *er farnúdet mir di nešúme, hu ose li et amávet* "he 'makes to me death' = he torments me (mentally)" to *er maxt mir dem toyt, ani maxzik miménu* "I 'hold from him' = I believe in him" to *ix halt fun im, ze yikax arbe zman* "it will take much time" to *dos vet némen a lánge cayt,* etc.

7. See E. Y. Kutcher, *A History of the Hebrew Language* (Jerusalem-Leiden: Magnes-Brill, 1982), p. 219.

8. Although in normative MH the first three items carry final stress, the normal accent is as above. Colloquially one also hears

Yiddishized *bekícer, aíker, leáxis*. The non-final stress certainly betrays Yiddish intermediacy.

9. *op. cit.* p. 222.

10. e.g. see H. B. Rosén, *Contemporary Hebrew* (The Hague: Mouton, 1977).

11. See M. H. Segal, *A Grammar of Mishnaic Hebrew* (Oxford: Clarendon Press, 1927), p. 204.

12. As pointed out to me by Benjamin Hary, July 1992.

13. As pointed out to me by Yael Ziv, July 1992.

14. See Kutcher, *op. cit.*, p. 214.

15. *ibid.*, pp. 213–214.

16. H. Blanc, "Some Yiddish Influences in Israeli Hebrew," in U. Weinreich (ed.), *The Field of Yiddish II* (The Hague, 1965), pp. 185–201.

17. *op. .cit.*, p. 216.

18. See S. Bolozky, "Word formation strategies in the Hebrew verb system: denominative verbs," *Afro-Asiatic Linguistics* (*Monograph Journals of the Near East*) 5:3 (1978), pp. 111–136; S. Bolozky, "Strategies of Modern Hebrew verb formation," *Hebrew Annual Review* 6 (1982), pp. 69–79; S. Bolozky, "Semantic productivity and word frequency in Modern Hebrew verb formation," *Hebrew Studies* 27:1 (1986), pp. 38–46.

19. See S. Bolozky, "Continuous and Discontinuous Word-Formation in Modern Hebrew," paper presented at the North American Conference of Afro-Asiatic Linguistics, March 6–8, 1991, Berkeley.

20. BH forms like *na'ămán* "pleasant, lovely," *barqán* "briar, thorn," *'avdán* "ruin, destruction" can only marginally be claimed to constitute realizations of *CaCC+an*, and those that look like BH N+*an* are probably realizations of discontinuous *CoCC+an* (*qorbán* "sacrifice," *'ovdán* "ruin, destruction") and *CiCC+an* (*'inyán* "matter," *qinyán* "property, possession," *binyán* "building," *kivšán* "oven, furnace, kiln," *miškán* "dwelling; temple").

21. The reviewer has not been able as yet to distinguish the *different sources* for cases whose origin is medieval.

22. Below, the colloquial variants contain #*mV*+, which marks the *benoni* in all verb patterns except for *pa'al* and *nif'al*.

23. Included are also forms in which a base vowel is elided, as in *safkan* "skeptic" (see *safek* "doubt"*)*, *psantran* "pianist" (see *psanter* "piano"); or *e* is maintained or added for phonetic *reasons, as in pardesan* "citrus grower" (see *pardes* "citrus grove"), *marpekan* "aggressive, pusher" (see *marpek* "elbow"); or *a* is inserted in the environment of a historical glottal, as in *mahapxan* "revolutionary" (see /*mahpexa*/ "revolution"). Also relevant are derivations from segolate bases, as in *raftan* "dairy farmer" (see /*raft*/ > *réfet* "cowshed"), *yarkan* "greengrocer" (see /*yark*/ > *yérek* "greens"). Occasionally,

colloquial reduction obliterates the distinction between strategies, as in literary *kalkalan* "economist" (see *kalkala* "economy") becoming *kalkelan* and *mada(')an* "scientist" (see *mada* "science") turning into *mad(')an*.

24. Though not total. Slavic languages do display *some* discontinuous morphology, particularly in shifts from one aspect to another, in a manner that is similar to what English does in its set of strong verbs, as in sing-sang-sung, ring-rang-rung; take-took-taken, shake-shook-shaken; blow-blew-blown, grow-grew-grown; etc. As pointed out in A. Spencer, *Morphological Theory*, (Oxford: Blackwell, 1991), and in S. Bolozky, "Awareness of linguistic phenomena in the native language and its implications for learning Hebrew," *Bulletin of Hebrew Higher Education* 1:2 (1986), pp. 14–17, such patterns should be handed by root+pattern discontinuous mechanisms not unlike those used in the description of Semitic languages.

25. As noted in Kutcher *op. cit.*, p. 222, a language such as Amharic is still Semitic typologically owing to its morphological structure. Had it been defined on the basis of its syntax alone, it would have been considered an African non-Semitic language.

26. As this reviewer has been reminded by Shlomo Izre'el, personal communication, July 1992.

27. See Kutcher, *op. cit.*, p. 200.

28. See Goldenberg, *op. cit.* p. 38, quoting E. Y. Kutcher, "Two 'Passive' Constructions in Aramaic in the Light of Persian," *Proceedings of the International Conference on Semitic Studies* (Jerusalem, 1969), pp. 132–151.

29. As argued in S. Izre'el, "*He-hayta thiyat ha-'ivrit nes? 'al tahalixim šel pijinizácya vekreolizácya bi-ycirat ha-'ivrit ha-ḥadaša*," *Proceedings of the World Congress of Jewish Studies* 9 Section 4:1 (1986), pp. 77–84.

30. As suggested to me by Ora Schwarzwald, personal communication, July 1992.

Part II

Culture and Society: Gender, Ethnicity, Community

Does Gender Matter?

Madeleine Tress

Lesley Hazleton, *Israeli Women. The Reality Behind the Myths*, New York: Simon and Schuster, 1977.

Natalie Rein, *Daughters of Rachel. Women in Israel*, Harmondsworth, Middlesex: Penguin, 1979.

Geraldine Stern, *Israeli Women Speak Out*, Philadelphia and New York: J. B. Lippincott, 1979.

Deborah Bernstein, *The Struggle for Equality. Urban Women Workers in Prestate Israeli Society*, New York: Praeger, 1987.

Beata Lipman, *Israel: The Embattled Land. Jewish and Palestinian Women Talk About Their Lives*, London: Pandora, 1988.

Lisa Gilad, *Ginger and Salt. Yemini Jewish Women in an Israeli Town*, Boulder: Westview, 1989.

In a society as complex as Israel's, with its uneasy coexistence between modern and traditional social classes, how do we set criteria for measuring the empowerment of women? Is women's liberation determined solely by public sphere activity? Should mandatory education for girls be taken for granted? Are universal suffrage and compulsory military service for women determinants? Where does labor force participation fit into the grand scheme of things? Are Sephardi and mizrachi women immigrants from North Africa and the Middle East liberated because they no longer live in mother-in-law-dominated households? What about their daughters undergoing a period of unmarried adulthood?

Do all prominent women in public life "count"? Do we determine feminist achievement by the number of women who either hold political office or are on the central committees of the various political parties? If so, then how do we assess women, who in their positions of power, have never articulated women's issues per se such as Golda Meir when prime minister or Tehiya's Geula Cohen? Do we compare them to Meretz's Shulamit Aloni, whose political career has focused on gender-related issues?

These are not easy questions to answer in a society where, despite more than one hundred years of Zionist-related settlement and forty-six years of statehood, the national question remains primary, superseding questions of class and gender. For example, the six volumes under review represent most of the book-length manuscripts in any language on the role of women in the Zionist enterprise. In and of itself, this number reveals both how seriously women's issues are considered and the state of the women's movement in Israel. Moreover, five of the six volumes were written by non-Israelis.[1] Ironically, the process of self-examination and study by Israeli women themselves is less advanced than it is in the works of authors from other parts of the Middle East (e.g. Egypt's Nawal El Saadawi) or North Africa (e.g. Morocco's Fatima Mernissi).[2] For many Israeli men and women, gender remains a non-issue.

The feminist critique that does exist of Israeli society tends to focus on two issues: (1) the role of Jewish law (*halakha*) in Israeli society and how that oppresses women; and (2) the hegemony of militarism and its concomitant dependence on women as symbols of the nation who assume the burden of reproducing it, so that the construction of gender is intimately tied up in the Zionist project itself.

The critique, however, fails to take into account the interactive relationship between Judaism and Zionism, considering the role of religious law and tradition to be much more coercive than hegemonic. It is this reviewer's contention that halakha and militarism are not mutually exclusive, but interdependent.

Moreover, the books written by Lesley Hazleton, Natalie Rein, and Geraldine Stern all presume that in order to be Israeli, one has to be modern and Western. Their subtexts are unabashedly Orientalist, so that Western ideas and values are always touted as better, no matter what their relationship to the East. The West is rational, developed, superior, and human. The East is aberrant, underdeveloped, and inferior. In the particular case of the Zionist project, anyone who was not directly involved in it, such as the Sephardim and mizrachim, the ultra-Orthodox (*haredim*), and the Palestinians, became at best invisible, and at worst the proverbial Other.[3] As we shall see in the course of this chapter, Orientalism also permeated the Israeli women's movement. It was never able to expand beyond an urban intellectual and professional base, comprised mainly of Ashkenazi women from English-speaking countries.

It is on these two issues that this review will focus. More specifically, it will concentrate on how the interaction between classical Judaism and Zionism influenced gender relations in the Israeli economy, polity, and society, and how an Orientalism inherent in the Zionist project has held back the development of a gender-specific movement.

I shall begin by examining the role of women in Jewish law (halakha) and tradition (*aggadah*) as the guide for this exploration. This normative role will be juxtaposed against the actual role of Jewish women, both in the Diaspora before the advent of the Zionist enterprise and in Palestine/Israel. By focusing on the role of classical Judaism in Zionism we can see how the "new Jewish woman" operated in a sphere in which religion was hegemonic. This, in turn, interacts with Israeli militarism to create a climate in which women's traditional roles are idealized.

Classical Judaism–Zionism–Women

Zionism, like other forms of nineteenth-century European nationalism, used older, mythical images as a means of legitimacy. By borrowing two key concepts from classical Judaism, the Chosen People and the Promised Land, the Zionist project would unite in time (the present) and space (the biblical Land of Israel) a Jewish Diaspora that had little in common besides religious practice (or the collective memory of it) and a history of persecution, as members of this religion, throughout the ages.

Much of the imagery of the Zionist movement was borrowed from the discourse and symbols of classical Judaism. In addition, pre-state society (the Yishuv) continued to use the Ottoman millet system, in which each religious community was remanded to its own authorities in personal affairs. The British Mandate retained the system both to encourage Jewish settlement and to protect the settlers from the Arab majority, under the guise of respecting minority rights. For the Jewish community, halakha became the adjudicator of all personal matters, making even the most self-proclaimed atheist and socialist pioneer partly subject to religious authority.

It is not my intention here to restate how halakha oppresses women. All of the books under review discuss the relationship between Judaism and women. However, they all ignore the innate structural and ideological relationship between classical Judaism and Zionism. Instead, three (Hazleton, Stern, and Lipman) focus on halakhic injunctions against women. There are entire chapters in both Hazleton and Stern that focus on how halakha constrains Israeli women. Both point their fingers at the 1953 Rabbinical Courts Jurisdiction Law (Marriage and Divorce), as the reason why women remain "second-rate citizens" (Aloni in Stern, p. 25), who compose the "third Israel" (Hazleton's term). Yet, with the exception of Lisa Gilad's ethnographic portrayal of Yemini women in *Ginger and Salt*, there is little discussion of the halakhic role of women aside from the family laws in any of these volumes.

Halakha traditionally excluded women from religious study. Jewish women were required only to keep the dietary laws (*kashrut*) and the Sabbath, but were not required to pray, except for their own satisfaction. This meant that women were either illiterate, or did not know Hebrew. In all instances, their linguistic abilities would affect their participation in social and cultural life after they had immigrated to Palestine.

Religion became the privilege and responsibility of men, facilitated by the women who confined their activities to the private realm of home and family. Women would receive great esteem by fulfilling their supportive role of bearing and raising children as well as providing harmonious homes so that men could study. As we shall see later, religion and militarism would conflate in Israel to reinforce this role.

The rabbinic literature credits women with more compassion and concern for the unfortunate than men,[4] as a consequence of their "natural" function. Simultaneously, their place was circumscribed in the area of power and politics.

This came to a head in the Yishuv with the 1920 elections for the founding Assembly of the Elected, the body that would become the Israeli parliament. A struggle over universal suffrage ensued between secular and religious Zionists, an incident ignored in all of the books under review, and downplayed by most students of Zionism.[5] Simply stated, elections for the Assembly were postponed for nearly two years for fear of alienating religious-Zionists from the state-building enterprise. Special voting booths were built for Orthodox men in Jerusalem, and the male head of household was given the right to vote on behalf of all the eligible female voters in his household. Although these concessions were made for this election only, they were to set the stage for later political deals that would help determine the Jewish character of Israel, and concomitantly subdue any programs that empowered women in the political or social realms.

In other spheres, women had greater power. They were allowed to participate in charitable behavior and good deeds (*tzedakah*). By the sixteenth century, a distinctive print-literature emerged in Europe that emphasized gender-related charitable obligations. Women's roles as helpers were also reflected when they first entered the European labor market en masse in the nineteenth century. Like their gentile cohorts, Jewish women went into the "feminine occupations" such as teaching or nursing, as well as office work and consumer goods production. Woman's work in the private sphere became socialized. In the economic realm, she was engaged in many of the same things she had done in the household, albeit in a new locale and under new conditions.

Women in the Economy

The women involved in early Zionist settlement were also involved in socialized private-sphere work. One of the great Israeli gender-related myths, unfortunately propagated in Geraldine Stern's *Israeli Women Speak Out*, is that Yishuv "women did almost every job the men did, building, running tractors, managerial jobs" (p. 100).

The historical record, however, reveals another experience. Both in rural and urban areas, Zionism needed a rapid increase in the Yishuv population if it was going to create a socio-economic base for expansion. Women were admitted to kibbutzim only in numbers large enough to maintain necessary services. They were rarely engaged in agricultural work, and instead found themselves in traditional roles, concentrating on cooking, sewing, laundering, or child care exclusively. Even when women tried to dress, behave, talk, and work like men, hoping those tactics would bring them equality, they were not considered full kibbutz members. For example, at Degania, men worked for the Palestine Office of the Zionist movement and the women worked for the men.

As Deborah Bernstein's excellent study on urban working women in the Yishuv demonstrates, women were quickly relegated to service work, which constituted 46.5 percent of the female labor force by 1930. Most of this was as domestics. Industrial employment in general was usually temporary, and paid low wages. Women's major contribution to the labor force in the Yishuv was indirect as maintainers and reproducers of it, rather than as producers themselves.

The sexual division of labor has continued into statehood. Child rearing is the most valued of all female activities, followed by housekeeping. Indeed, only 2.5 percent of Israeli women do not marry by the age of forty. Woman's ascriptive role has been continually underscored. If the goal of the Zionist movement was to create the new Jewish man, the new Jewish woman was still a traditional one, albeit with a communal purpose.

In the first years of the state, sex role differences were exacerbated. The first- and second-generation Yemini women immigrants in Gilad's study had different expectations of the labor force than the pioneers (*halutzot*) described by Hazleton, Rein, Stern, and Bernstein. The immigrant generation from Yemen believed that women should only manage households. Once in Israel, mothers found that they had to work outside of the home in order to provide their children with a good education and to supplement their husbands' low incomes. Ironically, work outside the home enabled women to gain more authority in it, more independence from the family unit, and even allowed them to engage in politics (Gilad, p. 2).

Regardless of country of origin, Israeli women are concentrated in low and middle echelons of the labor market. They composed 38.6 percent of the labor force in 1982, but only 13.8 percent of all administrators and managers (Bernstein, p. 165). In 1988, 38 percent of Israeli women worked outside the home. Less than 10 percent of Israeli academicians are women, although they comprise the vast majority of primary and secondary school teachers. While they seem to have made some inroads as physicians in the state-run medical system (Kupat Holim), much of this is due to the fixed hours they have working in a clinic, thereby making it easier to carry out their duties as wives and mothers in nuclear families.

Israelis consider anyone with a career to be selfish and exploitative,[6] and the primacy of motherhood has translated into a widespread ambivalence about woman engaging in high-commitment careers at a possible cost to family life.[7] Moreover, as Dafna N. Izraeli points out, the combination of Soviet immigration with stagnant economic growth in the past decade means that any equal opportunity for women will be suspended for the foreseeable future. Women will not advance much simply because the state is not confronted with a skills shortage.[8]

Women in the Polity

Success in Israeli politics is often dependent on a strong military background, and despite universal conscription, women are not found in the upper echelons of the military. There is only one woman general in the Israeli Defense Forces (IDF), and within the IDF, there is sex segregation: Women are not assigned to combat and are frequently involved in "helping" roles—as office and kitchen workers. The IDF as the great class equalizer of Israeli youth still socializes young women to accept traditional roles.

Women had been involved in the various anti-British militias of the Yishuv, the most glaring example being Geula Cohen in Etzel. However, there were limits to military exercises. The Hagana, like the IDF it would become, trained women to use guns but never allowed them to participate in guard duty. During the 1948 Arab-Israeli war, women were embodiments of the national front. "Women soldiers were essential for convoy duties, since they could conceal guns and grenades under their clothes and evade detection by the British troops manning the roadblocks, who did not search women" (Hazleton, p. 20). They were not, however, engaged in combat.

Even with the advent of the IDF Women's Corp, known as Chen, restrictions still exist.[9] Military women generally replace men in jobs considered within women's capacity, so that men can be released for frontline service. Even General Amira Dotan, the founder of Chen, has no qualms about this. When Lipman interviewed her, Dotan said, "I don't think women should drop bombs or become pilots, though. That goes back to the traditions of Judaism and also, because we are stationed here in Israel, it is allied to the Muslim tradition" (p. 42). Female conscripts do, however, spend their time receiving "countless hours of cosmetics advice and demonstrations, given by cosmetics companies who volunteer their time 'for the army' " (Hazleton, p. 133), although they receive very little sex education, which is consistent with Israel's pro-natalist policy.

Women also spend two years in the military as opposed to a three-year requirement for men. Moreover, after their three years are over, men serve in the reserves for about one month per year until they are fifty-five years old. Women spend their "reserve" duty reproducing (male) soldiers for the State. Marriage, then, is related to national security. Israeli militarism, rather than expand opportunities for women, sharpens the division of labor, giving women an even clearer domestic base.

Although Israel has produced its share of prominent women, they are poorly represented in public life. Women can become members of parliament and judges in the High Court, but the 9.2 percent of parliament members in 1993 who are women comprise the largest proportion since the State was founded in 1948. Much of women's lack of visibility in the parliament is related to their role in the military. Outside of parliament, there is not a single woman mayor in Israel, and halakha, which adjudicates all personal matters for Israeli Jews, forbids women from either sitting on a bench in a family court or being a witness in one, since it does not acknowledge her right to sign a document.[10]

Because of the particular history of the Zionist project, the State itself has been the agent of social change. It plays a contradictory role vis-à-vis women. It has challenged and weakened part of the system of patriarchal gender relations with its secular equality laws, but has reinforced it through militarism and its use of halakha to adjudicate personal matters.

Sexual equality is mentioned in the Declaration of Statehood in 1948; the basic laws passed in 1949 declare that women are equal in the entire legal system. It should be pointed out, however, that neither statement has any legal binding (Hazleton, p. 23). The Equality of Sexes Act was passed in 1951 and there has been equal pay for equal work since the mid-1950s. The Equal Opportunity in Employment Bill was passed in 1982.

In contrast, the 1953 Rabbinical Courts Jurisdiction Law severely circumscribed the rights of women in the private sphere. The National Insurance Act, also passed in that year, allowed women to retire at the age of sixty, so that they would no longer have a "double-day." Since 1987, there has been parity in retirement age. Fully paid, three-month compulsory maternity leave has been in effect since 1956. A 1988 Equal Opportunity Law grants the right to "parental leave" to care for a newborn or sick child. However, there have been very few cases of men taking advantage of this legislation.

Women in Society

The rabbinic tradition always approved of women's public-sphere participation as long as it was confined to tzedakah. Voluntary and philanthropic organizations, including many of those associated with the Zionist project, fell into this purview, with women either creating alternative institutions or providing services for women in need.

As Bernstein demonstrates, organizations with a specific social and economic agenda were another matter. The most prominent of them, the Women Workers' Movement, basically surrendered its advocacy for women to the Orientalist mentality of the fledgling Jewish State. The movement viewed mizrachi immigrants as primitive women who needed to be taught how to behave in "modern" Israel. This strategy not only diverted the movement from issues concerning working women, but also alienated Sephardi and mizrachi women from gender-specific issues in much the same way that pioneering Zionism (*halutziut*) estranged the mizrachim in general. Israel was "exceptional" inasmuch as a genuine class-based politics as a force of opposition never developed. This was a consequence of the particular history of Israeli social democracy, which did not develop out of the class experience, despite proclamations by the halutzim that they composed the working class.[11] Similarly, the development of the women's movement in the 1970s was exceptional for it was not rooted in 1960s new left politics, as it had been in Western Europe and North America.

The Israeli Women's Movement was founded by Marcia Freedman and Marilyn Safer, two émigrées from the United States.[12] At first the movement held seminars on women's issues at the University of Haifa. All of Israel's early feminists, like Freedman and Safer, were urban, professional, and from English-speaking countries. Indeed, many early consciousness-raising groups were conducted in English. Natalie Rein, who was a movement activist, writes that consciousness-raising led to an analysis of Israeli children's books so feminists could study role structure and identification. They also brought up questions about abortion, pregnancy, and birth control. By the mid-1970s, the women's movement had branches in Haifa, Beer-Sheba, Tel Aviv, and Jerusalem, and about one thousand women as followers.

Marcia Freedman, who began her political career as a member of Ratz, the Citizens' Rights Movement, started her own Union of Women for Equal Rights in Israel, which ran unsuccessfully for parliament in conjunction with the Women's International Zionist Organization (WIZO). The party platform addressed the problems of housewives, employed women, and soldiers, of prostitution, rape, and wife beating, of children's rights, and of the image of women in the media.

Israeli feminism contested none of the basic premises of the Zionist enterprise, particularly its militarism and its retention of the national question as primary. Indeed, feminists such as Freedman thought it was important to win the demographic race against the Palestinians, albeit with a new twist: To give birth to an out-of-wedlock child would be considered politically progressive, serving as "another form of protest against the age-old mandate of men over women" (in Stern, p. 63). Freedman also called for the establishment of community centers "in which much of the work in running a home would be communalized" (in Stern, p. 55), but failed to say who would work in these centers. Presumably, it would be Sephardi, mizrachi, and Palestinian women who were largely invisible in the movement.

The women's movement in Israel was not at odds with the ethos of Zionism but the way in which it functioned. During the 1970s, its point of contention with the State was "not over its policy of territorial expansion with military aggression, but over how best to carry out this policy with women's aid."[13] Chen would symbolize part of this. Women in Black—a group that gained prominence after the Palestinian intifada began in 1987 and which calls for an end to the occupation of the West Bank and Gaza—was still light years away.

Feminist Orientalism

The elitism that tainted the women's movement in the 1970s also permeated much of the early writing on women as well. Stern's book, for example, consists entirely of interviews with Ashkenazi women, with two exceptions—Geula Cohen and Violet Khoury, who at the time *Israeli Women Speak Out* was published was the mayor of Kfar Yassif. Cohen, despite her mizrachi background, fits into the pioneering profile that has excluded Sephardi and mizrachi women. Khoury, in contrast, is the "good Arab." She is a Christian who sees social laws, such as compulsory education for women, that pertain to women as progressive. It should be noted that nowhere in this interview does either Stern or Khoury contest the official Israeli view of the post-1948 Palestinian exodus, nor does either mention that Palestinian citizens of Israel lived under military rule until 1966.

Rein's Orientalism, in contrast, is much less subtle. She refers to the Judaism practiced by the Sephardim and mizrachim as "a religion primitive in its application and unaffected by the natural development of time" (p. 57). Mizrachi women "became mere breeding machines and the butt of planners and politicians" (p. 57). Hazleton, like Stern, while mentioning Israel's mizrachi majority, is concerned primarily with the pioneering experience.

Perhaps on these grounds alone one should be thankful that the early books are all out-of-print. They are more than compensated for by the other three, which all make important contributions to the study of gender relations in Israel.

Gilad's study concerns the transition in the lives of women who emigrated from Yemen to Israel. This is an ethnographic study and by no means a feminist tract. It is not a book for generalists on the status of Israeli women. Gilad presupposes a cerebral audience conversant in the vocabulary of post-modern anthropology. Her work is significant for it is the only work on Israel women to give voices to subaltern women, thereby enabling them to speak to a largely Western audience that might have otherwise stereotyped their existence. Gilad shows how Yemini women were able to use their "menial" positions outside the home as a means of empowerment. No matter how lowly their occupation, they felt "liberated" because they were no longer secluded in the domestic realm. Gilad also eloquently focuses on the consequences of gender in the immigrant experience. More importantly, however, she sees Israel as a Middle Eastern country and continuously refutes the subtext of Western cultural superiority found in the earlier works.

Bernstein's study, in contrast, focuses mostly on gender relations in Yishuv urban areas. She examines the roles of both Ashkenazi and Yemini working women as part of the urban labor force. Tradition, and political and economic conditions all worked against Yishuv women. Building the country—settlement, immigration, defense—was primary, and social issues never came to the fore. An epilogue reflecting fifty years later on the Yishuv urban experience provides a more compelling analysis of Israeli women today than either Hazleton or Rein.

Lipman's set of interviews is the least scholarly of the three books, but the most accessible to a general audience. She does, in addition, have a keen sociological eye, as evidenced by whom she interviewed for the book. Women from nearly every walk of life in Israel and the occupied territories are represented—Israeli and Palestinian, hawk and dove, secular and religious, Ashkenazi and Sephardi/mizrachi, Zionist and non- or anti-Zionist, and every possible permutation and combination therein. Like Gilad and Bernstein, Lipman does focus a critical lens on the Zionist project.

What Is To Be Done?

The failure of the women's movement to gain any momentum in Israel parallels the failure of pioneering Zionism to accommodate those individuals who were peripheral to the state-building project: the indigenous Palestinian population, the haredim, and the Sephardim and mizrachim. Instead of a burgeoning women's movement, identity politics came to the fore, which was reinforced by the occupation of the West Bank and Gaza. The State used religious discourse to legitimate its quest for a Greater Israel. Judaists such as Gush Emunim were able to surround the state and civil society with their ability to combine militarism and halakha in such a way that even Israeli secularists gave their tacit consent to this project.

These various identity politics also gave renewed primacy to the national question, particularly what to do about the Palestinians. Feminists such as Shulamit Aloni, while still articulating women's concerns, have become outspoken critics of the occupation. Israeli and Palestinian women have come together for the first time, to discuss various solutions to the Israeli-Palestinian conflict within the context of their roles as women. Women began gathering in silent vigil outside of government offices on Friday afternoons (the Women in Black), recognizing that a dialectic exists between gender inequality and the national question, for Israel's militarism reinforces both. These women are fighting not only against vestiges of patriarchy but also against a society in which the creed of militarism, which is exclusively male despite universal conscription, has invaded private life. The only movements that can truly create an autonomous capacity for action are those which contest this kind of domination.[14]

Opposite them is a particularly gender-related identity politics, best articulated by Geula Cohen, whose concern is the transmittal of culture and tradition in which nurturing capabilities are important: Israeli women should not only be biological mothers in Israel, but also care for "the family of all Israel at the same time" (Cohen in Stern p. 183). In this worldview, woman's domestic role becomes a ritualized public one for she is the mistress of the home, and those institutions most closely associated with the home such as education. By keeping kashrut and the Sabbath she is the carrier of the morality that makes public communal life possible. She is lauded as a wife and mother; any other role she may have—for example, as a worker, student, or citizen—is ignored.

In 1985, Na'amat, the current incarnation of the Women Workers' Movement, instituted the slogan "Be a Man, Give Her a Hand," during its "status of women month." Nowhere in its literature did it advocate a redefinition of roles inside the household, however.

Alice Shalvi, a religiously observant feminist and critic of the occupation, when interviewed for Lipman's book, commented that the Israeli press does not take women seriously. "Women's issues go on the women's page, that's all, with the recipes and fashions, and beauty, and not the political aspects of women's lives" (Shalvi in Lipman, p. 105).

Obviously, the primacy of the national question and its concomitant militarism is one reason why the press does not take women seriously. More importantly, Israeli women have not taken themselves seriously, confusing the notion of prominent women with concern for women's issues. A new wave of Israeli scholarship is beginning to contest basic premises of the Zionist conception of women in both civil society and the State. It is the hope of this reviewer that the literature on Israeli women will continue to grow and be of the caliber of Lisa Gilad, Deborah Bernstein, and Dafna N. Izraeli. Perhaps in some future volume of this series the list of books to be reviewed will not only be longer, but will also be in-print.

Notes

1. Indeed, none of the six writers were born in Israel. Deborah Bernstein, the only Israeli in the list, was born in the United States, but immigrated to Israel as a child.

2. El Saadawi and Mernissi are inarguably quite privileged compared to the masses of Middle Eastern women. Both are urban intellectuals with Western-style or Western educations. Nevertheless, even within these parameters, they still have no real Israeli counterparts.

3. My use of the term Orientalist, while ultimately derived from Edward Said's *Orientalism* (New York, Vintage, 1979), comes closer to the usage found in Ella Shohat's *Israeli Cinema: East/West and the Politics of Representation* (Austin: University of Texas, 1989). My concern here is less with the depiction of the "Orient," i.e. the Middle East, in the post-Enlightenment period (Said's concern) and more with the relationship between the Zionist pioneers and the others they confronted in Palestine. It is for this reason that I include the *haredim* among Orientalism's subjects, for although Western in origin, they rejected the Enlightenment and the modernism that went with it.

4. Judith Baskin, "The Separation of Women in Rabbinic Judaism," Yvonne Yazbeck Haddad and Ellison Banks Findly eds., *Women, Religion, and Social Change* (Albany, N.Y.: SUNY Press, 1985), p. 6.

5. The exceptions are Shabtai Teveth, *Ben-Gurion. The Burning Ground. 1886–1948* (Boston: Houghton Mifflin, 1987) and S. Zalman Abramov, *Perpetual Dilemma: Jewish Religion in the Jewish State* (Rutherford, N.J.: Fairleigh Dickinson University, 1976).

6. Dafna N. Izraeli (in "Culture, Policy, and Women in Dual Earner Families in Israel" in Suzan Lewis, Dafna N. Izraeli, and Helen Hootsman, eds., *The Dual Earner Family in Comparative Perspective*, [Newbury Park, Calif.: Sage, 1991]) writes that the word "careerist" in Hebrew (fem. "careeristit") has always been a pejorative term.

7. Dafna N. Izraeli and Ephraim Tabory, "The Political Context of Feminist Attitudes in Israel," *Gender and Society* 2 (1988):463–481.

8. Izraeli, "Culture, Policy, and Women."

9. Chen is an acronym for Chet Nune, Woman's Corps, but also means "grace" in Hebrew.

10. The contamination of halakha into civil life came to a head in 1987 over the case of Leah Shakdiel. Shakdiel, an orthodox Jew and feminist, was elected to the religious council, a civil body, in Yerucham, a development town in the Negev. The local rabbinate objected to her appointment. Shakdiel brought the case to the High Court, which ruled in her favor.

11. Shlomo Swirsky, "Their heart is not in the East." *News from Within*, 14 November 1988.

12. Freedman has since returned to the United States. Safer remains in Israel, and is a faculty member at the University of Haifa.

13. Dina Hecht and Nira Yuval-Davis, "Ideology Without Revolution: Jewish Women in Israel." *Khamsin* 6 (1978): 4.

14. Alain Touraine, "Triumph or Downfall of Civil Society," David Reiff general ed. *Humanities in Review*, Vol. 1 (New York: Cambridge University, 1982).

Studies on Ethnicity

Walter F. Weiker

Eliezer Ben-Rafael and Stephen Sharot, *Ethnicity, Religion, and Class in Israeli Society*, Cambridge: Cambridge University Press, 1991.

Guy H. Haskell, "Components of Identity: The Jews of Bulgaria in Israel," *Shofar*, 8, no. 1, (Fall 1989), pp. 47–60.

Vered Kraus and Robert W. Hodge, *Promises in the Promised Land: Mobility and Inequality in Israel*, Westport, Conn.: Greenwood Press, 1990.

Sammy Smooha, *Social Research on Jewish Ethnicity in Israel 1948–1986*, Haifa: University of Haifa Press (available in New York from the American Jewish Committee), 1987.

Shlomo Swirski, *Israel, The Oriental Majority*, London and New Jersey: Zed Books Ltd., 1989.

Walter F. Weiker, *The Unseen Israelis: Jews from Turkey in Israel*, Jerusalem Center for Public Affairs and University Press of America, 1988.

Alex Weingrod, *The Saint of Beersheba*, Albany: State University of New York Press, 1990.

Books on Israeli ethnicity (defined in reference to Israeli Jews in terms of one's country or region of origin) continue to appear, and its role in shaping Israeli society continues to be a subject of debate. Interest has continued in part because ethnicity's possible connection to important social and political issues has come to public attention in visible ways such as the allegation that voting (at least since the 1977 election which brought down the Labor governments which had dominated Israel since independence), has had as one of its most significant dimensions the basic cleavage called variously Ashkenazi/Sephardi, Oriental/Occidental, and Asian-African/European-American. There is also considerable speculation about the role the large Russian *aliyah* may have, and there have been numerous comments in the press and elsewhere that one of its consequences will be to modify, if not reverse, the balance between those two major groupings in the population of Israel.

Many questions which are important for both Israeli society and for the development of general and cross-national theories of ethnicity are raised in these studies. Those arising in Israel but which also have potential broader significance include: What are the interrelations between ethnicity and social class? What are trends associated with generational change? Are there parallels to what Herbert Gans in studies of the United States has labeled "symbolic ethnicity"? Is it possible that both ethnic and class cleavages could be superseded by a religious cleavage as the most salient one for many Israelis? In what ways may ethnicity be more or less disruptive of social harmony in Israel than it is in other countries in which there are also populations with multiple cultural heritages? How do the developments in Israel fit into various definitions of social "integration"?

Three Approaches

The debate is equally vigorous among scholars as it is in the media and the general public. A useful perspective in which to consider the studies reviewed in this chapter is Smooha's codification of three "approaches," which he calls cultural, class, and pluralist, and which are summed up succinctly in the opening essay of his bibliography.

1. He characterizes the "cultural approach" as perceiving "ethnicity as conflicting with modernity and which holds that under the pressures of industrialization and national integration cultural differences will be blurred, assimilation intensified, and ethnicity enfeebled around the world" (p. 19). This hypothesis is examined in Ben-Rafael and Sharot's study of four ethnic groups (Moroccans, Iraqis, Romanians, and Poles) in Beersheva. (The research, done in 1982/83, has also been the basis of several important journal articles, which unfortunately are not included in their bibliography, and of Ben-Rafael's earlier book *The Emergence of Ethnicity: Cultural Groups and Social Conflict in Israel*, 1982.) They examine the interrelations between ethnicity, class, and religion by classifying each of their 826 respondents on each of these three scales.

Religion is the least complex. The two Oriental groups are on the whole sharply in contrast to the two European ones. "Among the Moroccans, at the present rate of intergenerational erosion, it would take another three generations before they drop to the current Polish level of observance of the dietary laws, and another six generations before they reach the current Polish level of observance of kiddush" (p. 99). From another angle, differences in religiosity are found not to be very disturbing to most Israelis when they are expressed by others in personal terms, and it is only the haredim (ultra-Orthodox) who threaten to make religion a volatile social and political issue.

Ethnicity and class are less simple phenomena. For the Romanians and Poles the situation is relatively easy: as "veteran" communities and ones at the top of the social and political structure they have little reason to be intent about the need to preserve their ethnic culture. Whether there is development of a more conscious Ashkenazi grouping, whose nascence Alex Weingrod saw more than a decade ago ("Recent Trends in Israeli Ethnicity," *Ethnic and Racial Studies* 2, 1979) is still in some doubt, with about as many of Ben-Rafael and Sharot's Polish and Romanian respondents rejecting such an identification even as their third choice (after Israeli and/or Jewish) as accepting it (Ben-Rafael and Sharot, table 8.4.)

Among Moroccans and Iraqis, on the other hand, specific ethnic identification (as differentiated from the broad ethnic category of Oriental Jews) is favored by a significantly larger proportion than is the case with the two European groups. This is partly the result of perceived discrimination, and here the class factor comes into play when it is found that the lower socio-economic strata find political ethnicity more salient than do those individuals who have had greater upward mobility. This is particularly the case among Moroccans, who have generally been seen by many Israelis as the group most different from Israel's dominant culture and at the lowest end of the social and economic scale. (It should be noted, though, that for the most part all ethnic groups have been resistant to political parties based specifically on ethnicity.)

In this regard one of Ben-Rafael and Sharot's important foci is on "mobiles" and on class consciousness: "politicized class consciousness is weak in Israel, but the data on other dimensions, such as class images and dissatisfactions, are similar to those found in other industrial societies" (p. 154). That this is true despite the perceptions of very considerable social and economic gaps is accounted for in part by the intensity with which immigrants to Israel have pursued their identification as being both Jewish and Israeli, a phenomenon often described as the ideology of *mizug ha'galuyot*, the fusion of the exiles, and which also has, in Ben-Rafael and Sharot's view, lessened the overall intensity of ethnic politics, as mentioned above.

The intersection of ethnicity and class has varying effects on different segments of the population. Instructive here are their findings on friendship networks:

> Blue-collar Moroccans and Iraqis are the only categories whose broad ethnic networks are more homogeneous than their class networks. Among white-collar Moroccans the odds of class heterogeneous networks are about equal to

the odds of their ethnically heterogeneous networks, but among the Iraqi, Polish and Rumanian white-collar categories, the difference in odds is especially great, and they tend to combine ethnic openness with class closure. (p. 109).

Similarly, their respondents believed that discrimination was considerable on the basis of ethnicity, but "when we turn to the frequency and the effects of discrimination that were reported by those discriminated against, it is the class factor that emerges as the important one" (p. 200).

A specific point which the authors make is that these findings mean that the description of recent Israeli voting since 1977 as largely an Ashkenazi/Oriental contest is a much too simple analysis.

2. The "class approach" is represented dramatically by the sociologist Shlomo Swirsky. Known earlier in English only by articles in *Dissent* and the *British Journal of Sociology*, the welcome translation and updating of his 1981 book in Hebrew paints a stark picture of Israeli stratification. Seeing none of the mitigating factors that Ben-Rafael and Sharot identify, Swirski contends that Israeli society is sharply polarized on the basis of ethnicity because ethnicity in turn coincides with class. He maintains further that Ashkenazi Israelis are intent on preserving their political, economic, and cultural dominance, and that toward that end it is necessary to keep the Oriental groups subordinate. His book contends that these goals were the ones which gave rise to policies like sending Oriental immigrants to Development Towns, assigning their children almost automatically to less challenging school classes, etc. Swirski's text is followed by a section called "Oriental Activists Speak."

In support of his thesis he has some interpretations of specific phenomena which are novel. Regarding the rising proportion of ethnic intermarriage, for example, he writes:

> Hardly anyone has ever stopped to consider the racist implications of such a "hope" or solution. For looking strictly at the class position of the groom and bride, intermarriage does not necessarily result in a "fusion" of

classes, but can simply mean moving up, or down, the class scale for one of the parties, bringing about no change whatsoever in the class structure of society. What lies behind the celebration of intermarriage is, rather, a belief that it can lead to the "uplifting" of the Oriental partner, either through the transfer of the genes of the Ashkenazi partner to the couple's children, or through the influence of the "cultural environment" that the Ashkenazi partner imposes in the home (p. 23)

This is not the place to assess Swirski's arguments, except to note that, while other Israeli scholars would probably take exception to them, his viewpoint undoubtedly represents the opinions of some members of the *Edot ha-Mizrach*, and it is a thesis of which all observers of Israel should be cognizant.

At least part of his argument, however, is supported by the research of Vered Kraus and the late Robert Hodge. Through elaborate statistical analysis they conclude that the most important factor in mobility and inequality in Israel is education, not ethnicity, father's occupation, or culture. In this regard Israel is very much of a meritocratic society, they assert, and individual members of any ethnic group can and do display social mobility with educational attainment. They also note other significant facts such as that "ethnic group membership was found to be of lesser consequence in explaining the ethnic gap in education among immigrants than among second-generation Israeli Jews" (p. 174); and that "as primary and then some secondary education became nearly universal, the threshold of social exclusion moved up to secondary school completion, only now it was from this level that the ethnic and national differentials continued to rise" (p. 174).

Since the distribution of quality education is politically controllable, it becomes possible that there has been at least a tacit process of maintaining patterns of European domination. Though Kraus and Hodge stop before maintaining that this was a deliberate aim of the dominant groups in Israel, they note that the process of allocating educational resources in a number of countries has been such as to at least implicitly resist supplying equal opportunity to potential competitors, whether they be from ethnic groups or from other sources, and they can find no other explanations for the continued class gaps among ethnic groups in Israel.

3. The third approach, which Smooha calls the pluralist one, is the one which he himself favors. It holds, among other things, that large generalization about "universalistic, uniform trends with respect to ethnicity in industrial societies" should be avoided, that each society must be analyzed in terms of its specific dimensions of 'cultural diversity' and 'social separation,' that "inequality in the distribution of resources is the central axis around which group relations revolve in a pluralistic society," and that "of all the factors at work in pluralistic societies, the political factor is the most important" (pp. 43–47).

Applying this approach to Israel, Smooha asserts that the most divisive cleavage in Israel is between Arabs and Jews, that second in gravity is the division between religious and non-religious Jews, and that in this context . . .

> ethnic pluralism is less severe and institutionalized. It is prevented from gaining legitimacy and consequently is bound to be eroded through various measures taken against it in the name of the official policy of consensus-building, including efforts to moderate ethnic differences, upgrade ethnic integration, and grant rewards according to merit. When all is said and done, no ideological dispute exists between Orientals and Ashkenazim regarding the character of the State and the final goal of the relations between them—namely, equality and assimilation. These features destabilize Israeli ethnic pluralism, but do not detract from its significance. (p. 48)

He notes, to be sure, that the process has worked only very imperfectly, and that "the Orientals' economic consolidation and social mobility notwithstanding, an ethno-class structure is taking shape in Israel" because "virtually the entire disadvantaged Jewish population is Oriental, as is most of the Jewish working class" (p. 53; for a detailed exposition see his study *Israel: Pluralism and Conflict*, 1978).

The three approaches are very usefully summarized on twenty-one criteria in diagram form, at the end of his essay, and Smooha concludes by warning that at this stage in the development of Israel and of Israeli sociology, "since it is clear that no simple immediate way exists to decide which interpretation is best, there is no practical possibility of selecting among the three perspectives" (p. 74).

Another important matter is the scope of studies in Israeli ethnicity. Sammy Smooha has done a useful service in pointing to some important lacunae by documenting how heavily studies to date have been concentrated on the Edot ha-Mizrach (Jews from Asia and Africa), and even here the coverage is very uneven. His bibliography has thirty-five entries for Moroccans, eighteen for Yemenites, twelve for Iraqis, seven for Tunisians, four each for Libyans, Iranians, Kurdish Jews and Bene Israel (Indian Jews), and three each for Ethiopians and Georgians (where to count the latter is ambiguous in geographic terms but apparently clear for most Israelis). By contrast, he found four studies which deal with Rumanian Jews, two each with Russians, Americans and Caucasians (from the Caucasus), and one each with Austrians, Germans and Poles. The listing of topics is also instructive about the pattern of researcher interests. There are seventy-nine entries under inequality (stratification, class structure); fifty-nine under prejudice (stereotyping, social distance); fifty under cultural differences; thirty-seven under separation; thirty-one under attitudes and perceptions, ethnic; twenty-nine under culturally disadvantaged pupils; twenty-six under social mobility; twenty-two under psychological differences (cognitive skills, personality); and twenty-one under religion (differences in religious attitudes, observances, rituals and styles).

As mentioned earlier, one of the gaps in research on Israeli ethnicity is the absence of studies of non-Oriental communities. Some were included in the early work on immigrant absorption by Shmuel Eisenstadt, Judith Shuval and others, but they have seldom been examined since then or treated in full-scale terms. A small start has been made in remedying this by the recent appearance of work on two "middle groups," i.e. non-Oriental Sephardim. Both groups are considered to be among the most successfully integrated of those which arrived after the founding of the state. In both cases, the reasons for their successful integration included their pre-immigration history, the circumstances of their immigration, and their position in Israel's social structure.

The Jews in Turkey consisted of two groups, the middle and upper-middle classes, and the poor. The former in particular were relatively well-integrated into Turkish society in that they were not discriminated against even if they were in some senses second-class citizens in an Islamic country. One of the reasons for this was that they kept in their place and did not assert themselves very publicly in either politics or economics. Few were Zionists, but all had strong Jewish consciousness, and they came to Israel with some skills from an already modernizing society. Almost all the poor (who had nothing to lose by leaving Turkey and who were strongly motivated to become upwardly mobile), and many of the educated Jews who were strongly idealist, came almost as soon as the Israeli state was established, and others have been coming ever since.

In Israel they maintained the same characteristics. They were determined to fit into their new society and not to make waves. Thus they stayed primarily in private-sector occupations like commerce, factory work, and the professions; they made no efforts to get into politics or into the limelight as a group; and they made no particular moves to perpetuate a specific Turkish-Jewish culture.

Several circumstances in Israel made it appropriate and possible to follow such a path. One was that most came and had their initial Israeli experiences during a period when cultural assimilation was the dominant ideology, rather than the emphasis on maintaining subcultures which became at least tacit government policy later. Another was that they could avoid being involved in the Ashkenazi/Sephardi or the European-American/Asian-African division because they were not really in either camp: they were Sephardim but not

Oriental, i.e. from Arab countries. (See Walter F. Weiker, "Stratification in Israeli Society: Is There a Middle Category?" in *Israel Social Science Research*, 1, no. 2 [1983]; 30–56.) In fact, it was never clear to many Israelis just who the Jews from Turkey were, and they are a community which was almost unique in Israel in not having any particular public "image." It is only in the last few years, in the context of Israel's emphasis on cultural pluralism, and with an opportunity at hand with the five-hundredth anniversary of the expulsion of Jews from Spain and Portugal and their welcome in the Ottoman Empire (an event marked with major events in Turkey, Israel, the United States and elsewhere in 1992) that they have begun to try to put themselves on Israel's cultural ethnicity map.

The Jews from Bulgaria present a different case. In the interwar period they were perhaps the most determinedly Zionist diaspora community in the world, and in Bulgaria they were able to display it publicly and to organize numerous institutions to prepare themselves for eventual immigration to a Jewish homeland. They came en masse within two years after the founding of the Israeli state. Although many established themselves initially in a concentration in Jaffa, their Zionism soon impelled them to integrate rapidly, and their skills were useful in enabling most of them to become part of the middle class. In addition to bringing with them much European culture they were also Sephardim, however, and like the Turks they could avoid being drawn into that volatile dispute, though in recent years some Bulgarian Jews have expressed impatience with what they see as the tendency of some Israeli Sephardic organizations to ignore them. I hope that Prof. Haskell will extend his research about this group.

Another form of cultural expression in Israel is one which can be given several labels including ethnic, cultural, religious, traditional, group solidarity, identity-seeking. As is well known, a phenomenon of public celebration of holidays and other observances by particular groups has been going on in Israel for some years. The best-known are the Moroccan *mimouna*, held each year on the day after Passover, and the *seherrana* of the Kurds. The former, in addition to its cultural aspect, has had distinct political overtones as well.

Alex Weingrod's *The Saint of Beersheba* describes and analyzes another form of such expression, a *hillula*, a memorial celebration commemorating the death anniversary of Rabbi Chayim Chouri. Chouri immigrated to Israel in 1955 after a seventy-year career in Jerba, an island off the coast of Tunisia, and in Gabes, the home of Tunisia's largest Jewish community. When he died in Beersheba in 1957 his tomb became the destination of an annual pilgrimage. Weingrod describes its events in great detail. In regard to matters of interest for the study of ethnicity, he found that most pilgrims are Tunisians (with smaller but still significant numbers from elsewhere in North Africa), that they include persons from all social classes and of many ages (though there was a predominance of those in the lower strata and of older persons who often had had association with Chouri in Tunisia), and people from many levels of religiosity. While many come because of "traditional" reasons such as beliefs in Chouri as a *zaddik* or saint, who even now "possesses great magical or mystical powers and that taking part in the pilgrimage and prayer at his grave is both rewarding in itself and may also have certain beneficial consequences" (p. 40), for others it is largely a social event.

In a particularly useful final chapter Weingrod puts the *hillula* into the context of similar expressions not only in Israel but in such other places such as England and America. Like other researchers, he also asserts its importance for Israel by pointing to the interrelations between ethnicity and other factors:

> The *hillula* is by no means an isolated event. On the contrary, it is part of the overall experience of all who participate in it. While at one level it may appear to be naive and spontaneous, at other levels this *hillula* is a resounding statement of major social trends. What this means is that the pilgrimage is closely connected with a variety of social and cultural processes taking place within

contemporary Israeli society. It has not only an internal dynamic and message, this celebration (and others like it) is also a formidable occasion whose tones are loudly heard throughout the Israeli social system. Social stratification and inequality, immigration and ethnicity, the links between politics and culture—these are among the significant themes expressed during the pilgrimage to Rabbi Chouri's grave. (pp. 69–70)

Conclusion

As was the case when Walter Zenner discussed ethnicity in an earlier volume in this series, there remain some lacunae in research on Israeli ethnicity. The studies reviewed here make some advances with Smooha's codification of the three approaches, with Ben-Rafael and Sharot's work at looking at ethnicity, class and religion in combination, with Weingrod's look at a pilgrimage ceremony in comparative perspective, and with two studies of non-Oriental groups. It is also notable that a team of four Israeli scholars has recently published what to my knowledge is the most thorough study to date of an ethnic group: Tova Bensky, Yehuda Don, Ernest Krausz, and Tikva Lecker-Darvish, *Iraqi Jews in Israel: Social and Economic Integration* (Bar-Ilan University Press, 1991, Hebrew). They are reportedly making plans for similar studies of other ethnic communities. (There is also interesting work on Syrian Jews by Walter Zenner, for example, "The Cross-National Web of Relations of Syrian Jews," in G. Gmelch and Walter Zenner, eds., *Urban Life* (1988) and "Middleman Minorities in the Syrian Mosaic: Trade, Conflict and Image-Management," *Sociological Perspectives* 30 (1987).

Building on many earlier studies of numerous topics concerning the role which ethnicity may play in the ability of Israel to fashion a harmonious society, with these volumes Israeli sociology has taken some important additional steps which can lay the groundwork not only for more comparative Israeli studies, but also for enabling knowledge about Israeli ethnicity to increase its contributions to the development of a larger cross-national ethnicity theory.

It may be increasingly possible, for example, to advance in the examination of just how important "situational" factors are. Certainly such ones as the speed with which Israeli society has grown, the large size of the cultural gaps among the groups which are being asked to assimilate, the importance of Jewishness as a characteristic knitting the society together (not only vis-à-vis the Arabs who make the "outer context" of Israel another possibly unique factor, but also as a response to the entire history of the Jewish Diaspora and anti-Semitism), and others may indeed make Israel a somewhat unique case. It might be compared to at least some other countries of immigration and of a considerable multiplicity of ethnic groups, however—the United States, Canada, and Australia come to mind. Another avenue of exploration might take advantage of such facts as that there are Russian Jews in Israel from a number of *aliyot* from the days of the Yishuv to the current arrivals, who could well be the subjects of a longitudinal study which could be replicated in other countries to test hypotheses about generational ethnicity, "symbolic ethnicity," and others. The opportunities are rich and many.

The Search for Israeliness: Toward an Anthropology of the Contemporary Mainstream

James Armstrong

Virginia Dominguez, *People as Subject, People as Object: Selfhood and Peoplehood in Contemporary Israel*, Madison: University of Wisconsin Press, 1989.

Tamar Katriel, *Communal Webs: Communication and Culture in Contemporary Israel*, Albany: State University of New York Press, 1991.

I

These two books are the most recent entries in what is becoming a genre in the anthropology of Israel, the search for what it means to be Israeli and how that meaning is reflected in everyday life. Other earlier works which share this focus on mainstream culture and symbolism include Katriel's *Talking Straight* and Shokeid's *Children of Circumstances*.[1] This relatively new trend in Israeli ethnography is indicative of the upheaval in both anthropology and mainstream Israeli culture. Cultural anthropologists are increasingly challenging the objectivist-empirical orientation or what Van Maanen terms "realist" ethnography.[2] In the process of doing so new forms of ethnography are being generated and new questions are being formulated, especially ones about the role of the anthropologists in the representation of "their" people and in the making of ethnography.[3]

On the Israeli anthropological scene, the shift in emphasis toward questions about mainstream collective identity and how it is created in everyday life seem to mark the uncertainty that Israelis are experiencing about the direction of the state and contents of their peoplehood. The Americanization of Israeli culture, political, ethnic and religious divisiveness, government scandal and ineptitude, and the Intifada, among other things, are increasingly driving secular Israelis to a sort of collective reappraisal. Understandably, anthropologists and others, both inside and outside Israel, are participating in the reappraisal, as both these volumes clearly indicate.

Like much recent ethnography, the works by Katriel and Dominguez share in the reflexive nature which allows readers to experience both the research and analysis with the author. Although Dominguez much more consciously and consistently advocates and participates in this mode of ethnography, Katriel's voice can be detected throughout her work. Clearly, both authors have been influenced by postmodern concerns with subject-object relations and cultural critique. And, both focus on the analysis of discourse and ritual to arrive at their conceptions of what Israeliness is, how it is reflected, and who determines its contents. Neither claims to offer a complete characterization, rather both are attempting to interpret slices of the historically and culturally complex phenomenon that I will refer to as Israeliness.

Still, there is much to differentiate these two works and the two authors. Dominguez, bringing the traditional distance from the object of her research with her, is a non-Jewish ethnographer. Katriel, in contrast, is a native, who has the problem of creating some distance between herself and her subject.[4] Katriel focuses more on the everyday and the mundane, while Dominguez tends toward the interpretation of more exceptional events and rituals in Israeli life. Finally, Katriel's methodology, a sort of structuralist ethnography of communication, is more formal and clearly articulated than Dominguez's looser semiotic approach.

II

I must admit I was attracted to *People as Subject, People as Object* by the mere fact that both Dominguez and I are non-Jews who have extensive experience living and doing research in Israel about Israelis. I was grabbed by the confessional tone in the introduction which promised that her dilemmas in coming to grips with Israel and her apparent eventual disillusionment with Israeliness would shed light on similar experiences in my own fieldwork. Dominguez writes,

> During that period [May 1981 to August 1985] I spent thirty-four months in Israel, learned to speak, read, write, and lecture in Hebrew, fell in love, almost converted to Judaism, experienced the fear and agony of war in Lebanon, and went through stages of loving and hating Israel. At some point in the midst of all this I began to "react to Israeli society," and with each negative or emotional reaction I pondered ever more about my construction of the "object." (p. 15)

Although she went to Israel originally with the intent of studying the problem of ethnicity in Israeli society, as she increasingly identified with Israelis, Dominguez "discovered" that there can't be a problem of ethnicity without a sense of collective self. That is, ethnic divisions within Israeli society are only problematic insofar as there is some idealized, subject-constructed sense of peoplehood which is incompatible with those divisions. The potential alienation of foreign participant-observers in Israel may stem from our desire to share in this collectivity. By attempting to submerge ourselves in the object of study, we realize that we are always bound to be strangers, different, outside the boundaries of the Israeli collective self.

For both Dominguez and myself the realization of our "outsiderness," while being disconcerting, was also productive since it generated questions and prevented us both from taking much about Israel for granted. For Israeli anthropologists and sociologists submersion and entanglement in their object of study is a fact of life. Dominguez argues that the longstanding concern in Israeli academia with ethnicity stems from the incorporation of Zionist assumptions about the ideal of collectivity into their analyses of society. Their participation in and involvement with what they study thus predisposes them to particular forms of analysis emanating from their position near the "center," while preventing them from having access to "outsider" perspectives.

Ultimately, Dominguez seeks to address the question of peoplehood by using Israeli collective identities as the object of interpretation. "In what ways is it a representation, an objectification? How is it shaped, molded, altered and perpetuated? And how can it help us learn about the very processes of objectification in which we *all* participate?" (p. 19). She hopes to approach answers to these questions through the analysis of public discourse. To a certain extent, then, this book is not about Israel, but rather it uses Israeli examples to explore the process of objectification both by the author and by Israelis themselves. Nonetheless, those of us who may be somewhat less concerned with the problems of objectification can still learn something about Israeliness from this volume.

Dominguez draws her data from a wide variety of sources, most of them less than typical for anthropological research. Much of her data is taken from Israeli newspapers and magazines. She relies heavily, but not exclusively, on the *Jerusalem Post* and includes a significant section on the use of the term *tarbut* (culture) in *Koteret Rashit*, a now defunct news magazine aimed at an intellectual audience. In addition, she explores the issues raised in public meetings and public performances, especially those which focus on ethnicity, such as a presentation by S. N. Eisenstadt at the 1982 Israeli Sociological Association's annual meeting and a presentation and panel discussion centered on storytelling and folklore at the First International Conference and Festival of Jewish Theatre.

Each of the six chapters, which comprise the body of the book, seeks to disclose the ways public discourse, on then current issues, articulated, created, or negotiated Israeli collective identity or contentions about that identity. Although ethnicity, including the increasingly vocal assertion of the Edot ha-Mizrach (Eastern ethnic groups) to full-fledged participation in the mainstream, is a repeated theme, Dominguez also considers Yom haAtzma'ut (Independence Day) as a ritual, newspaper representations of the Lebanese during the war in Lebanon, and the controversy around "Who is a Jew?".

Generally, her analyses are insightful and interesting, occasionally counter-intuitive, but certainly worth considering. I was especially impressed with her careful demonstration of the dilemma of an admittedly pluralistic society, or one that is increasingly willing in some contexts and in certain ways to acknowledge pluralism, having to create and recreate its peoplehood. Dominguez asks,

> Can a people really exist without a *culture* by which they can be identified and distinguished from others? Can a *people* really be culturally pluralistic? And, if part of the Zionist project is the cultural and social reunification of the Jewish people (after centuries of dispersion), what form will (or should) that Jewish culture take, who will decide what to promote, on what do they base their arguments, and what do the arguments reveal about the assumptions of peoplehood? (pp. 101–102, italics in original)

Her answers to these questions are complex and they help to shed light on the debate about ethnicity in Israel and on the terms for increasing legitimation of ethnicity in Israeli Jewish society. She clearly sees the negotiations between Ashkenazim and Sephardim/Orientals to be controlled by the Ashkenazim. I also liked her hint in a later section of the book that Israeli mainstream accommodation to pluralism might, in part, be the result of the realization that Lebanon fell apart because it could never successfully create a sense of collective identity.

The heavy focus on ethnicity is understandable. Dominguez went to Israel to investigate ethnicity and it certainly was a central issue in Israel in the early 1980s. She even refers to it at one point as "the Israeli obsession with ethnicity" (p. 180). Her analyses indicate that it was played out in a variety of contexts important for defining versions of Israeliness.

It seems to me, however, that she fails to appropriately contextualize the "obsession." Although she was in Israel for the 1981 elections, she doesn't mention the degree to which ethnicity was used by both major parties as an issue in their campaigns. Begin, for example, repeatedly appealed to potential Likud supporters' feelings of ethnic discrimination which fueled their opposition to the Peres-led Labor Party. Acts and threats of violence toward Labor and other "left-leaning" parties dominated by Ashkenazi voters were carried out by non-Western Jews. Labor supporters belittled the instigators of these actions as antidemocratic and primitive.[5] Furthermore, she largely ignores earlier outbreaks of ethnic unrest, such as the Israeli Black Panther movement of the early 1970s. To fully appreciate the significance of ritual attempts at self-objectification by Edot ha-Mizrach, the use of *tarbut* in public discourse, policies regarding the integration of Ethiopian refugees into Israel culture, or any number of other issues discussed in this book, it is necessary to tie them into the context and the mood of the period. The meaning of these phenomena for Israelis, as well as the ability of readers to understand them, is situated in the ways they touch upon each other. Unfortunately, this is missing in the book.

Another way that Israelis create their collective sense of self is through the sense they have of others, and Dominguez does not ignore this. In perhaps the most easily followed chapter of the book, entitled "On Authorship and Otherness," she considers how the boundaries between self and other are drawn. She makes it clear, at least from her point of view, that the boundaries are not simply a matter of a simple us/them opposition, but include both considerations of Jewishness and degrees thereof and of Israeliness. Thus, Arabs can be Israelis and still others, while Jews, even ones who live in Israel, can lack the necessary attributes to qualify for insider status. She seems surprised that Israelis rarely employ the term *goy*, to refer to non-Jews and accounts for this by arguing that the boundaries of otherness are not clear.

In contrast, I would argue that for secular Israelis, at least, the goy-Jew distinction is irrelevant because the assumption is that everyone is a Jew, except Arabs, who are (or were) all but invisible to Israelis.[6] For Jews in the Diaspora, where their peoplehood is at least partly created through their objectification by the dominant culture in a way similar to the experience of Israeli Arabs, *goy/goyim* is a meaningful term. Dominguez's analysis, here, might have been informed by a consideration of the process of becoming "Jewish" that Israeli *yoredim* experience in the United States.[7] Dominguez, by the way, encountered the experience of Israeli Jews assuming her to be Jewish, but chose to ignore the implications of this mistake.

Furthermore, the ways Israelis construct otherness is strongly influenced by their history. Although Dominguez makes reference to the significance of Zionism in the creation of Israeliness, and by implication otherness, she never explicitly outlines the role that Zionism plays or how it has been redefined in response to the Israeli experience. Clearly, the development and expression of Zionism in both Europe and pre-state Israel against a background of intense secularism that devalued both religion and non-Western cultures played an immense role in how contemporary mainstream Israelis view others. It is difficult to account for how Israelis objectify others, including the "others" who are now contesting the hegemony of Eurocentric culture in Israel, without understanding the roots of their ideological system.

Although not particularly significant, I take exception to several other assertions Dominguez makes. In her analysis of Yom ha-Atzma'ut, she argues that the plastic hammers, used by kids as noisemakers and to bang others on the heads, are ritual substitutes for the military parades which were a feature of the celebration in the 1950s and 60s.[8] I guess I don't think unusual things are necessarily symbolic. Furthermore, the meaning of the hammer, if it is symbolic, might not be "veiled aggression" or "symbolic violence." A Freudian might find something sexual in them. I don't mean to detract from what is, however, an interesting consideration of how Yom ha-Atzma'ut, as the only secular holiday, is problematic for all Israelis.

Dominguez's analysis of the common structure of ethnic "celebratory assemblies" is also questionable. She views the stage presentations as collective storytelling, in which the stories share a "script" that includes

> ... jokes about kibbutznikim, Ashkenazi accents, unyielding clerks of the government bureaucracy, and Ashkenazi self-importance. In nearly all, a second generation male gets involved with a stereotypically Ashkenazi female who is initially met with suspicion especially by the older family members but who is eventually accepted by the young man's family. All, without, exception include a life cycle ritual. . . . All end on a positive note. (pp. 147–48)

I recognize this as the outline of the popular 1965 Israeli film *Sallah* written by Ephraim Kishon and starring Chaim Topol. If these celebratory assemblies borrowed their script from the movie then they don't constitute a collective script, just a convenient, ready-made, effectively entertaining representation of the immigrant experience and the ideal of being full participants in the mainstream. I do agree with Dominguez's claims that these performances signal the value of inclusion and integration, and the desire on the part of actors and spectators to make a claim to the collective identity by adding to the culture rather than commandeering the mainstream. In this sense, they are seeking to control their own objectification.

On a more personal note I am disappointed that in *People as Subject, People as Object* Dominguez fails to reveal more of herself. Under most circumstances this would not bother me, but in her introductory remarks she reveals much about herself in a way that promises that her analyses would include the confrontations, emotions, and conflicts which led to particular insights. Although this element is sometimes present, it seems too protected. This, I'm sure, is partly a personal reaction, stemming from my desire to share more strongly with her experiences as a non-Jew in a position that closely resembles my own research experiences. At the same time, not being privy to her personal dilemmas in research and analysis prevents us from completely understanding the process of objectification in which we (the readers and the author) are participating.

III

Katriel's book represents a continuation of her earlier work on *dugri* speech in that it analyzes public communicative events as a means of elucidating the meaning of Israeli life.[9] The breadth of her new work is greater than that of *Talking Straight*. She covers a range of kinds of communications, including ritualized interaction among children, discourse and rhetoric on children's radio programs, conversations at family picnics at military camps, and the use of fire inscriptions in "civic rituals."

For the most part, Katriel draws her data from everyday events and mundane exchanges. She exhibits a keen awareness of her position vis-à-vis the subject she engages. As a participant in and ethnographer of her own culture, she acknowledges the need to defamiliarize herself with her subject. She calls this process "encirclement," which might be defined as the moment when mundane acts "shed their accustomed air of 'naturalness' and become interpretive sites for the exploration of cultural sense" (p. 2). Her goal in this process is both descriptive and critical, as she seeks to demonstrate how "experiences of solidarity and community" are enacted in the Israeli socio-cultural landscape.

The title, *Communal Webs*, is informative here. It is taken from Clifford Geertz's spider web metaphor for culture. Katriel claims, "This metaphor connotes not only a sense of active production of symbols and meanings, but also a sense of cultural members' enmeshment in their own meaning productions" (pp. 4–5). It is important to realize that her emphasis on the collective aspects of the "individual/communal dialectic" derives, in part, from her work on the self in American cultural contexts. The existence of a theory of culture which gives substance to the ideas and connects the various examples is a real advantage in this book. Even if we disagree about the adequacy of this theory, it serves to contextualize what, in its absence, would seem like isolated examples of Israelis communicating. Furthermore, the web metaphor suggests that Katriel doesn't intend to give a complete nor a fixed representation of how Israelis communicate their Israeliness.

The main strand tying together Katriel's various explorations of Israeli cultural communication is *gibush* or crystallization. This term encapsulates the significance of the Israeli emphasis on the integrated collective. It is a key symbol necessary for understanding the organization of Israelis' assumptions about themselves and their social contexts. Katriel's initial realization of the significant place *gibush* occupies in Israeli collective identity came through educational research. In this research, teachers often complained about the problem of achieving *gibush* in the classroom. In social contexts *gibush* is always desirable, but the *gibush* metaphor is not limited to social groupings and situations. It extends to the psychological referents, such as personality. Katriel writes,

> ... speaking of the 'crystallized' group or the 'crystallized' person suggests the attainment of some idealized standard of form and order in the social and personal domain, respectively. While used for such diverse 'products,' the *gibush* metaphor implies a cultural conception of sociological and psychological processes as involving a movement of solidification, of in-gathering from a scattered state of 'atomized' particles to a state of well-integrated stability. (p. 29)

This strand of Israeli culture is critical to understanding Israeliness, at least as it is revealed by mainstream secular Israelis. In reading this analysis I was struck with flashes of recognition which helped make sense of a range of personal experiences I encountered in Israel. The emphasis in Israeli social life on group activities and on the solidarity of the group intrigue me. I have always interpreted them as expressions of the Israeli collective orientation. Still, it was difficult for me to understand why dissension surrounding group-oriented activities always caused so much fretting and anxiety, while dissension regarding almost anything else (e.g., politics) was expected. I also wondered why the Israelis I was close to felt so open about discussing group discord with me, but avoided the topic with members of their *chevra* (friendship group). Katriel's analysis of *gibush* allows me to make sense of these issues, as well as a number of other "oddities" in Israeli social interaction. I also believe that this concept is important for informing Dominguez's assertions about the problems that legitimated ethnic pluralism entail for a society that values *gibush*. The need or belief in the need for crystallization with which young Israelis are socialized, and with which adults make sense of that process, explains the dilemmas around and contentions over ethnicity and peoplehood so central to Dominguez's analyses.

Unlike many structural and symbolic forms of analyses, Katriel's methodology incorporates some focus on process as well as structure. Thus, the cultural forms with which she is dealing are alive, prone to change and reinterpretation. For example, in her analysis of picnics, she concerns herself not only with the symbolic content of family outings with their soldier children at military camps, but also with how these outings represent the process of reducing the distance between family and soldier. This reduction of separation serves to create an atmosphere of direct familial support and involvement which contrasts with the *gibush*-creating segregation from family experienced by previous generations of army recruits. Thus, the government, responding to divisions in Israeli polity over occupation, can subtly appropriate parental support for uncomfortable policies by engaging them more directly in the military experiences of their children. This example also illustrates the complex way that Jewish values centering on the family get entangled with the Zionist value on *gibush*.

Much of *Communal Webs* focuses on ritualized social exchanges among Israeli children in peer-oriented contexts. Katriel's main examples are *brogez* (ritualized conflict), *bihibudim* (ritualized sharing), *hahlafot* (ritualized swapping), and *sodot* (secret sharing). In each case the relationship to *gibush* is effectively interwoven and the connections among these childhood communicative acts are clearly specified. Some attempt is made to relate the implications of these rituals to the ethos of Israeli mainstream adulthood. More emphasis on adulthood would have made for a more compelling introduction to the "roots of the Israeli experience." I don't want to leave the impression that I think Katriel should have written a different book. I am very pleased with this one. While most Israelis will identify immediately with the childhood experiences revealed in Katriel's insights, most other readers need more details.

In concluding this section, I want to deal with one last issue which strikes me about Katriel's point of view. Katriel has significant ethnographic experience in the United States which, in her words,

> ... has helped [her] retain a much needed freshness of outlook, a second-best to the celebrated culture shock which ethnographers have traditionally thrived on. In particular, [her] exposure to American versions of the celebration of the 'self' has helped [her] recognize the profound communal focus that still permeates Israeli culture despite the much discussed 'Americanization of Israel' (p. 4)

From this one might expect that some effort would be invested by the author in discussing how collectively centered values, as expressed in the rituals she analyzes, contend with, incorporate, or avoid Americanization. These comparisons would help American readers anchor the Israeli experience in their own, while simultaneously incorporating more process into the analysis of the production of Israeli culture.

If Americanization is irrelevant for *gibush* or for the social contexts in which Israeli children perform their rituals, then that should be pointed out. My sense is that Katriel believes that the impact of Americanization is somewhat exaggerated. I would counter that the traces left by Americanization, especially the emphasis on the self, will not look so American when they become incorporated into Israeli cultural and social life. The results of this process will be found as redefined and competing strands in the web of Israeli mainstream culture.

IV

Although neither of these books present as complete a representation of contemporary mainstream Israeli culture as their titles promise, they go a long way toward providing an understanding of Israeli collective identity, at least as it existed in the early and mid-1980s. Dominguez focuses on the forces contending for a role in determining collective identity without ignoring either the divisiveness or the integrative elements involved in the construction of a mainstream culture. Katriel is more concerned with how Israeli identity is integrated and symbolized in everyday communicative acts, but she acknowledges the tensions that are present in Israeli society. Katriel's focus on how Israelis create different but connected representations of their collectivity in their communicative rituals does more to inform Dominguez's work than the converse. Still, the difference between the two books is not in the quality of insights but in the focus of analyses. It is quite possible that these differences are the product of outsider as opposed to insider perspectives, but they also derive from theoretical concerns: Katriel's experience with Americans' celebration of self and Dominguez's original interest in ethnicity. For both authors the process of distancing, disengaging, and defamiliarizing was analogous, but their starting points were sufficiently dissimilar to result in revealingly different, yet complementary, recognitions of Israeliness.

Notes

1. Shokeid, M., *Children of Circumstances: Israeli Emigrants in New York* (Ithaca: Cornell University Press, 1988); Katriel, T., *Talking Straight: Dugri Speech in Israeli Sabra Culture* (Cambridge: Cambridge University Press, 1986). Most other examples of this genre are in the form of articles by both Israeli and American authors, including a number of non-anthropologists.

2. Van Maanen, J., *Tales of the Field: On Writing Ethnography* (Chicago: University of Chicago Press, 1988).

3. Cf. Marcus, G. and M. Fischer, *Anthropology as Cultural Critique: An Experimental Moment in the Human Sciences* (Chicago: University of Chicago Press, 1986); Rosaldo, R. *Culture as Truth: The Remaking of Social Analysis* (Boston: Beacon Press, 1989).

4. Actually Katriel is not a Sabra. She came to Israel as a child. For my purposes and in comparison to Dominguez she "qualifies" as a native.

5. There are a number of articles, including several by anthropologists, which document the significance of ethnicity and how it was used by both major parties in the 1981 elections. See, for example: Aronoff, M., "Political Polarization: Contradictory Interpretations of Israeli Reality," in M. Aronoff, ed., *Cross Currents in Israeli Culture and Politics* (New Brunswick, N.J.: Transaction Books, 1984); Louis, A., "Ethnic Politics and the Foreign Policy Debate in Israel," in Aronoff, *Cross Currents in Israeli Culture and Politics*; and Cohen, E. "Ethnicity and Legitimation in Contemporary Israel," *Jerusalem Quarterly*, no. 28 (1983):111–24. Interestingly, Dominguez cites none of these articles even though she cites each of the authors extensively and had an article of her own included in the Aronoff volume.

6. Yoram Dinur argues that Israeli Jews are oblivious to the presence of Arabs in their company. Arabs, at least prior to the Intifada, were for all intents and purposes invisible (*My Enemy, My Self* [New York: Doubleday, 1989]). My own experiences in Israel through the 1970s and early 80s support Dinur's contentions. Israelis rarely talked about either Israeli Arabs or those living in the occupied territories. Their presence was acknowledged only when it could not be avoided.

7. Shokeid, op. cit.

8. My memory, confirmed independently by two Israeli consultants, indicates that the plastic hammer first appeared as part of the celebration of Purim.

9. *Dugri* or straight talk is a speech style that embodies the ethos of the Israeli sabra, especially the values promulgated by early socialist-Zionists and redefined in the development of Israeli society (Katriel, op. cit.).

Part III

Social Analysis

From Apparatus to Populus: The Political Sociology of Yonathan Shapiro

Uri Ram

Yonathan Shapiro, *The Formative Years of the Israeli Labor Party: The Organization of Power 1918–1930*. London: Sage, 1976. (In Hebrew, *Ahdut HaAvoda HaHistorit*, Tel Aviv: Am Oved, 1975.)

Yonathan Shapiro, *Democracy in Israel* (In Hebrew, *HaDemocratya Be-Israel*). Ramat Gan: Massada, 1977.

Yonathan Shapiro, *An Elite Without Successors: Generations of Political Leadership in Israel* (In Hebrew, *Elit Llo Mamshichim*). Tel Aviv: Sifriyat Poalim, 1984.

Yonathan Shapiro, *The Road to Power: Herut Party in Israel*. Albany, N.Y.: State University of New York Press, 1991 (In Hebrew: *LaShilton Bechartanu*. Tel Aviv: Hakibbutz Hameuchad, 1989.)

Yonathan Shapiro occupies a special place in Israeli sociology. Until his emergence in the field in the early 1970s the sociological discourse in Israel was totally dominated by one school, the functionalist, or modernization school, which was based at the Department of Sociology of the Hebrew University. This department was directed for almost two full decades by S. N. Eisenstadt, and under his influence Israeli society was interpreted as a highly coordinated and adaptive social system based on a value consensus guided by the nation-building elite of the Labor Movement.[1] Shapiro was the first academic sociologist to pose a comprehensive challenge to this dominant "paradigm" and to offer an overall alternative to it. His own point of departure was the sociology of conflict. Shapiro's life work is dedicated to an historical-sociological analysis of the construction and transformation of the Israeli political elite. This project has so far yielded a series of studies which covers the history of the Israeli political elite from its very beginning to the present time. Four major stages in the formation and transformation of the elite can be discerned in his work:

1. The formation of Ahdut HaAvoda and the articulation of its winning strategy, its rise to domination in the Jewish community, and the molding of the basic parameters of this community's polity (Shapiro 1976).
2. The consolidation of the dominant party under changing conditions of social expansion and the eventual gain of sovereignty (Shapiro 1977).
3. The withdrawal of the generation of founders from the party's leadership and the entailed inheritance crisis with the take-over by the second generation (Shapiro 1984).
4. The rise of the right-wing Likud party and its leader Menachem Begin, and their eventual assumption of governmental power in 1977 (Shapiro 1989).

This chapter reconstructs and interprets the work of Shapiro in the five following respects: (1) it explains the circumstances of the emergence of the conflict perspective, exemplified by Shapiro, in Israeli sociology; (2) it highlights the theoretical assumptions of Shapiro's work; (3) it reconstructs his major theses; (4) it explicates the ideological underpinnings of his work; and (5) finally it offers an overall evaluation of it.

I. The Context of Emergence

Shapiro gained his sociological education at the London School of Economics, and afterwards at Columbia University, New York. The influence upon him of scholars like Ralph Dahrendorf and C. W. Mills, of these schools, proved to be pivotal. Shapiro founded the Social Sciences Faculty at Tel Aviv University and has taught sociology there since 1964. Since the early 1970s he has pursued a laborious historical-sociological project which explores the Israeli elite from the perspective of conflict sociology.

The emergence of conflict-sociology in Israel should be understood against the background of developments in two spheres—the political and the intellectual. Shapiro's first major critical work on the formation of the Israeli elite was published in 1975. This was shortly after this elite suffered the "earthquake" shock of the 1973 October War. The postwar period saw the eruption of a wide public denunciation of the state's leadership. This remonstration expedited the "upheaval" (*mahapach*), the victory of the *Likud* party in the 1977 elections. Yonathan Shapiro was an important figure in one wing of the protest movement, which opposed the abuse of power by the Labor's oligarchy.

The growing political protest and increasing disillusionment of the mid-1970s exposed the Israeli Labor elite for the first time to a comprehensive sociological critique. Prior to this—as Shapiro explains—Israeli sociologists were "not yet capable of demystifying [the Zionist] revolution" and tended to be "very apologetic." They have clung to functionalism because they preferred:

> [A] theory that treats society as a unified social system . . . [and is concerned with] continuity and not change; [functionalism] deals with social integration and views negatively social processes and social organizations and institutions that do not contribute to such stability and integration.[2]

Criticizing the functionalist school, Shapiro is dismayed by the fact that "most of the political sociologists in Israel, when studying their own society, ignore the rich tradition of political sociology which deals with informal political structures, with the covert activities of elites, and with the oligarchies that control ostensibly democratic political parties." He contends that:

> They pay little attention to the political activity that goes on in informal meetings and in secret consultations, the covert operations of pressure groups, or the system of interpersonal relations of politicians and its influence on their policies. The scholars prefer to discuss the formal structure of politics: official agreements between parties, party platforms and public statements of leaders, and public opinion surveys. This is not a lack of sophistication on their part, but an unwillingness to deal with the shadowy side of politics.[3]

At another level the emergence of conflict-sociology in general and the critical approach towards the elite in particular, should be understood against the background of the emergence of similar concern in Western academia in the late 1960s and early 1970s.

II. The Theoretical Orientation

Conflict-sociology is of course as old as sociology itself. Yet in its contemporary shape it was crystallized as a response to the claims of the functionalist school. In the late 1950s and in the 1960s conflict-sociology was being expounded, especially in Britain, from what can be generally described as a neo-Weberian or left-Weberian perspective. While Parsonian functionalism[4] draws heavily on Durkheim's notion of collective moral conscience as the bond of social order,[5] and on Weber's notion of the ethical-cultural foundations of the social order,[6] conflict-sociology endorses Marx's and Engels's ([1948] 1968) view of the inherence of conflict in society.[7] It eschews, however, their insistence on the exclusivity of the economic sources of such conflict, and adopts instead the major insights of Weber's sociology of domination. Robert Michels's study of the workings of the "iron law of oligarchy" in the German social-democratic party[8] served as a prototype for conflict-sociology's analysis of the concentration of power in modern bureaucratic mass organizations.

A most influential early enunciation of this renewed conflict-sociology was Ralph Dahrendorf's study of class conflict in industrial society.[9] In its contention that modern society is conflict-prone but that this conflict pivots around institutionalized authority (and thus is waged between superordinates and subordinates, rather than between property-owners and property-less), this study became an exemplar of the neo-Weberian trend. The core ideas of conflict-sociology may be summarized as follows: first, the central feature of social organization is hierarchy, which entails inequality and domination. Second, the structure of society is determined by the outcome of intergroup struggles. Third, this outcome is conditioned by the distribution of resources among the contending parties. And finally, fourth, social change is driven mostly by conflict.[10]

More specifically Shapiro's work is informed by the sociological tradition of elite studies, which began at the turn of the century with Mosca[11] and Pareto[12] and was revived by C. W. Mills's seminal study of the American power elite,[13] which applies to the study of political structures the basic Marxian-Weberian insights of conflict-sociology sketched above. Mills's foremost contention was that in the United States power—enormous power on a national scale—is concentrated in the hands of a small ruling elite which consists of the incumbents of the top echelons or the "command posts" of the three pervasive bureaucratic institutions of modern society—state administration, the big corporations, and the military. This perspective runs against the grain of liberal and Marxist sociological orthodoxies alike. On the one hand, by emphasizing the concentration of power it repudiates the consensual notion of American society espoused by both functionalists and pluralists; yet, on the other hand, by emphasizing the organizational, rather than economic, basis of power, it also repudiates the ruling-class notions of Marxist analysis. With the required adjustments, Shapiro pursues a similar line with regard to Israel.

III. The Political Elites:
From Bureaucratic to Status Politics

At the core of Shapiro's analysis of the Labor elite is the political-organizational network woven by it, which facilitated its expanding control over vast, nationally accumulated, economic resources and the construction of an autonomous economic infrastructure. These provided the means necessary for the dissemination of the ideas of the elite, which in turn had served to mobilize mass support for it. This mass support, finally, provided the elite with a democratic legitimacy. Thus in explaining the formation of the Israeli polity Shapiro suggests a causal flow—depicted in chart 1—which is distinctly antithetical to the functionalist one.

Chart 1.*
The Causal Flow in the Formation of the Israeli Polity, in Y. Shapiro's Interpretation

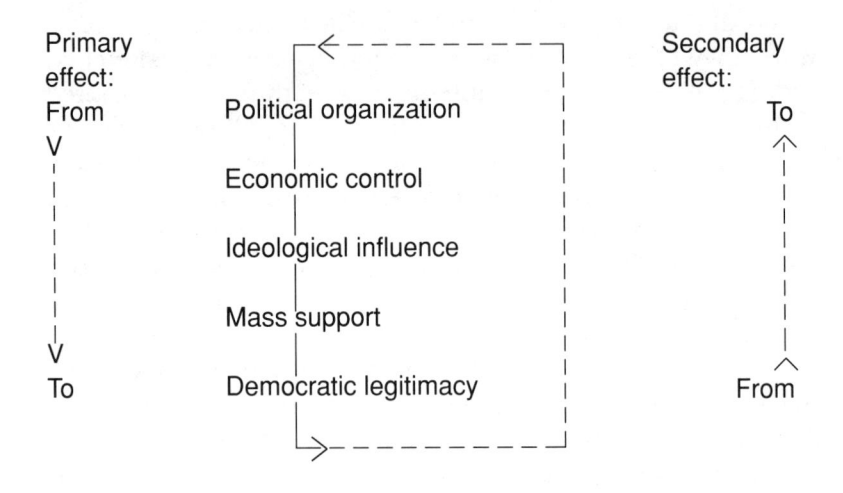

Primary effect:
From
V
↓
To

Political organization
↓
Economic control
↓
Ideological influence
↓
Mass support
↓
Democratic legitimacy

Secondary effect:
To
↑
From

---

*All charts in this chapter were designed by Uri Ram.

The linchpin of this view is that "in the beginning there was the organization," or, put another way, that "in the modern world the organization rules. He who organizes society dominates it" (Shapiro 1977:59, 128). Yet, there is one striking dissimilarity between the elite examined by Mills and the one examined by Shapiro. In the latter's case the major institutional site of the elite is a political party, in a way which takes after the structure of the Soviet elite, while in the United States parties are largely fragmented, diffused and belong to the second, intermediary, ring of power rather than to the primary one.

The distinction between Shapiro's interpretation and that of the nation-building perspective is made transparent by their diverse comparative frameworks. The functionalists consider Israel under the Labor regime in the frame of reference of Western democratic societies whereas Shapiro considers it more akin to a Soviet-type society. The major similarity between the Russian and the Zionist revolutions stems, in Shapiro's view, from the subordination of the economy to political control and the accumulation of power by the means of a disciplined centralized organization. From this angle the Israeli analogue of the Soviet Communist Party is Ahdut HaAvoda which was established in 1919, which was transformed to Mapai in 1930, and became the Israeli Labor Party in 1968.

Shapiro's interpretation of the formation of the Israeli elite diverges sharply from that of the functionalist perspective in its view of particular group interests, rather than universal social ideals, as the principal drive behind it. In his interpretation the founders and leaders of the party brought with them from East Europe the socialist political culture which is focused upon "organization and discipline rather than a world-view" (Shapiro 1975:29). Following his assumptions Shapiro considers political moves as consequences of strategic interests, rather than of normative commitments (a case in point is the dispute between *Gdud HaAvoda* (Work Brigade) and the Histadrut [Shapiro 1975:85;

also see ibid.:153–54, 156, 177]). He narrates the history of the Labor movement as a fray of organizational bickering, handled in meeting rooms among committees composed of a small number of leaders and conducted behind the backs of the rank-and-file, in which giant organizations were constantly engaging each other in quarrels over national resources, while at the same time constantly splitting from within into suborganizations, which did the same with regard to the portion of resources accruing to their umbrella institutions. Thus it was the Histadrut against the Zionist Organization, Gdud HaAvoda against the Histadrut, the party apparatus against the Histadrut apparatus, the Workers' Councils against the central leadership, the economic branches against the political forums, and so on and so forth—almost a struggle of all against all for resources, especially economic ones (as, for instance, the struggle over Mapai, [Shapiro 1975:81–82]; or over the public works office of the Histadrut, [Shapiro 1975:119–20]).

While for Eisenstadt and his associates a normative purport in the form of the "pioneering ideology" is considered as the cornerstone of the Labor movement's practice, Shapiro's regard for "ideology" in the sense of "worldview" or "social ideals" is very low, to say the least. The whole rationale for the establishment of the would-be leading Labor party Ahdut HaAvoda was—in his view—the competition over financial and human resources among contenders in the Jewish community in Palestine. The founders' main concern was the following:

> If they do not succeed in convincing the Zionist organization to allocate to them its funds and to deposit in their hands responsibility for the absorption of immigrants, it was feared that the workers would not join their organization and submit to their authority. On the other hand, if they do not mobilize the majority of workers in their organization and under their leadership, it was feared that the Committee of Representatives (of the Jewish Agency—U.R) and the Zionist organization would refuse to allocate the funds to them and would prefer to conduct the economic activity in the country the way they would find fit. (Shapiro 1975:30)

The simultaneous plunge along these two intersecting routes—the recruitment of members by the use of public Zionist finance, and the acquisition of public Zionist finance due to the authority over immigrant manpower—was the crux of that elite's politics. The would-be elite consolidated its standing in a series of bureaucratic skirmishes it waged against both outside competitors and internal contenders, in each case using its accumulated advantages to further improve its instruments of power.

First, the party had to consolidate its own control over the *Histadrut* (Shapiro 1975:37–76). This was accomplished in general by the organizational design of the institution, in which power was deposited at the top, and by the formation of a network of auxiliary organizations which augmented the same concentration of control from the top over various activities of the Histadrut. In the case of the establishment of the Histadrut, as well as in many other analogous cases, the elite's strategy was to present a united left front vis-à-vis the (then non-socialist) Zionist movement, and at the same time to aggregate its own power vis-à-vis the smaller leftist components inside the front.

To put it graphically, even if somewhat crudely, the leadership of Ahdut HaAvoda succeeded in locating itself in a narrow bottleneck linking the "outside" and the "inside" of the Jewish Yishuv. A great portion of the resources flowing from the outside (the Zionist movement) had to be piped through this bottleneck, and in turn distributed through it. (For instance, between 1919 and 1923, 2.5 million English pounds, out of 16 million transferred to Palestine, were channeled through the Histadrut. This represents the largest single channel of its kind [Shapiro 1975:23].) This strategic location is depicted in chart 2. In Shapiro's interpretation the political-organizational ingenuity of an elite which turned itself into an indispensable link between Jewish diaspora finance and Israeli manpower has been the primary cause of the success of the Labor movement (for a succinct discussion see Shapiro 1977: 86–89).

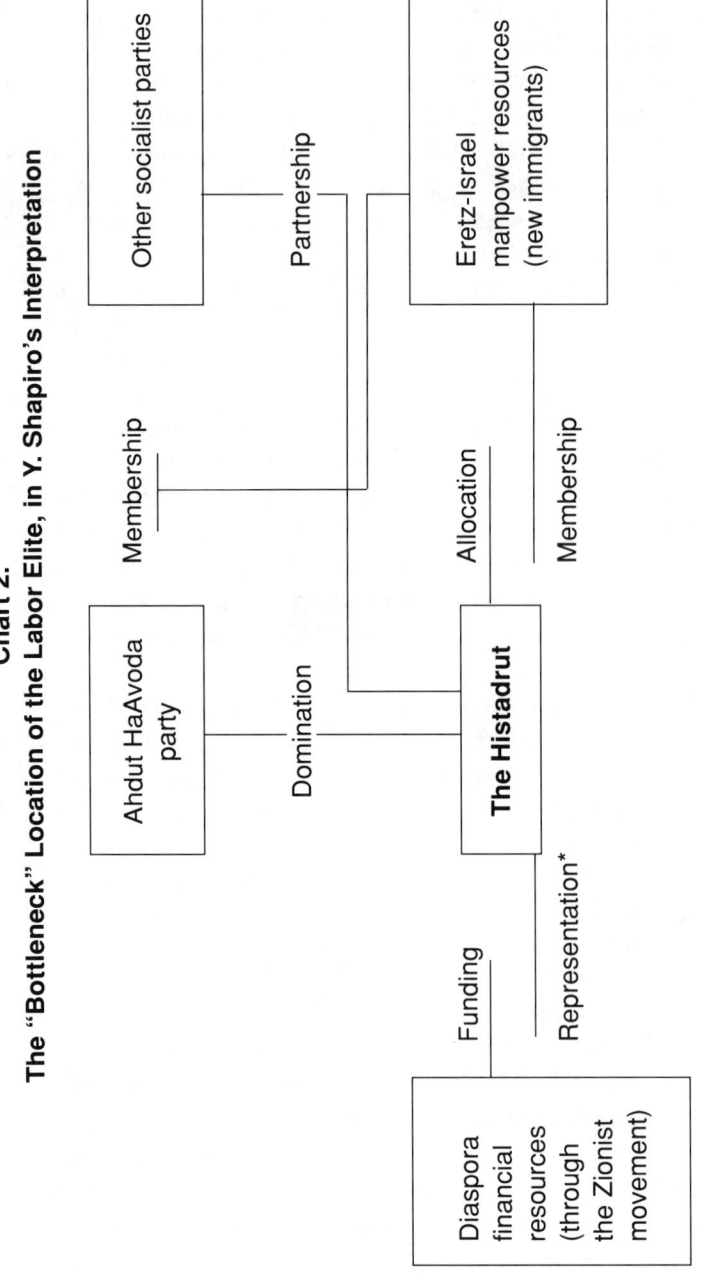

Chart 2.
The "Bottleneck" Location of the Labor Elite, in Y. Shapiro's Interpretation

```
┌─────────────────┐                          ┌─────────────────┐
│ Ahdut HaAvoda   │      Membership          │ Other socialist │
│ party           │──────────────────────────│ parties         │
└─────────────────┘                          └─────────────────┘
         │                                            │
         │                    Partnership             │
         │                                            │
         │ Domination                                 │
         │                                            │
         │                                   ┌─────────────────┐
         │                                   │ Eretz-Israel    │
         │                      Allocation   │ manpower        │
         │                 ┌─────────────────│ resources       │
         │                 │                 │ (new immigrants)│
         │                 │                 └─────────────────┘
         │                 │                          │
         │                 │                          │
         │                 │                          │ Membership
         │                 │                          │
         ▼                 ▼                          │
    ┌──────────────────────┐                          │
    │   The Histadrut      │──────────────────────────┘
    └──────────────────────┘
         ▲           │
         │ Funding   │ Representation*
         │           │
    ┌─────────────────┐
    │ Diaspora        │
    │ financial       │
    │ resources       │
    │ (through        │
    │ the Zionist     │
    │ movement)       │
    └─────────────────┘
```

*Formal representation in the Zionist movement was by political parties, not by the Histadrut as such.

While Shapiro does not deny that the political system established by the Labor movement is democratic he considers it a restrictive and formal democracy, subject to oligarchic duress. Actual authority was firmly concentrated at the summit of the apparatus. This prevailed first and foremost in the internal power structure of the party itself, and from there spilled to the pre-state polity and was later bequeathed to the state. The authority of the oligarchy was achieved by several mechanisms. At numerous places in his writings one finds allusions to the intricacies of The Apparatus, i.e., the bureaucratic methods of political control utilized by the ruling elite (for a discussion of the mechanisms of oligarchic rule see in addition to references below Shapiro 1977:62–68). Among the control mechanisms, Shapiro notes at various places the following: *Indirect representation*, which guaranteed that executive institutions are always elected by a small group of professional politicians, not directly by the public. *Nomination Committees*, which guaranteed that individuals owed their place to party functionaries rather than to the open constituencies. *Implementation and cooptation of leaders* in key positions in exterior organizations, as well as by the cooptation of leaders of such organizations (cf. Shapiro 1975:30–33). *Party discipline*, which guaranteed party control over elected representatives in various institutions by the formation of an abiding party position on all matters on the agenda before the formal process began (cf. Shapiro 1976:158). *Vertical links* among party units, which guaranteed their direct connection to the party headquarters, rather than to each other (thus preventing the formation of competing power centers such as trade unions or regional offices) (cf. Shapiro 1975:171). *Top leadership coordination*, which guaranteed that holders of key positions in a variety of organizations associated with the Labor movement, such as party, Histadrut and government work in informal understanding (Shapiro 1975:178). *Informal power structure*, the conduct of many of the activities specified above in a covert manner, which left democratic assemblies devoid of substantive power while retaining mostly ceremonial functions (Shapiro 1977:101–102).

Thus, by and large, authority flowed in the oligarchic course, that is from top to bottom, rather than in the democratic pattern, that is from the bottom upwards. Hence while the supreme executive committee of the party was supposed to be the carrier of the members' will, as a matter of fact the broader the institution was the less authority it exercised.

Comparable oligarchic methods of representation obtained in the larger polity. The two parliamentary institutions that governed the Yishuv, the Zionist Congress and the Assembly of Delegates, and in turn their respective executive bodies, as well as the Histadrut's institutions, were all arranged on similar principles. And the same has remained valid for the Israeli parliament, the Knesset, today. Hence, as Mills and other elite sociologists argue in other cases, despite the semblance of formal democracy, power is concentrated in the hands of a small ruling elite.

The oligarchic concentration of power removed the political decision-making process from the public domain to the domain of administrative coordination, from members of the polity to functionaries of it; the content of politics assumed the form of bureaucratic activity. The activists of Ahdut HaAvoda became managers in the institutions of the Histadrut and this bureaucratic activity became the content of their role as political activists. They became bureaucratic-politicians (Shapiro 1975:59). Adopting a typology of Brzezinski and Huntington,[14] Shapiro distinguishes two models of politicians: electoral-politicians and bureaucratic-politicians. In Ahdut HaAvoda, which exemplifies the latter:

> Internal organizational struggles determined the organizations' policy and the political future of the bureaucratic-politicians, with almost no intervention on the side of their voters, who in most cases were not aware of these internal affairs. The ideological and personal struggles were conducted according to the rules of the game of bureaucratic organizations—strategy of meeting rooms'—under the spread wings of the apparatus which

functioned more as a barrier than as link between the leadership and the rank and file. (Shapiro 1975:206; also see ibid., 73–74 and 82–85)

With the passage of time Ahdut HaAvoda's successor, Mapai, grew to have three major types of activists, among whom different kinds of social power were divided. Members of the agricultural settlements, though devoid of actual power and representing a minority in the party, were the depositaries of its pioneering image and thus retained a "status group" prestige. The incumbents of the apparatus were not highly esteemed but compensated themselves with a higher standard of living and social security, thus retaining an economic class power. The top leadership, sharing in the prestige of the settlers and leaning on the economic power of the bureaucrats, held the reigns of political power. The combination of three faces of power—symbolic, economic, and political—made Mapai not simply a ruling party, but a *dominant* one. Needless to say, Shapiro's tripartite analysis draws on Weber's famous class-status-and-power conceptualization.[15]

At the end of 1977, the Labor movement's five decades of hegemony came to a close and the Likud became the governing party. For Shapiro, who until now tended to portray the elite as omnipotent, this swift transformation of power posed a very delicate problem. How is it, he now came to ask, that the elite that ruled Israel from the 1930s did not succeed in reproducing itself beyond the biological lifetime of its founders and failed to create a generation of successors? (Shapiro 1984:9). From investigating the solid foundations of the house the Labor movement built, since 1977 Shapiro turned to investigating the cracks in the building. Shapiro interprets the decline of the elite in generational terms.

It is Shapiro's contention that the crisis of the Labor elite is rooted in the socialization of its post-revolutionary generation, the Israeli natives—Tsabar in local jargon. This generation, to make the argument tangible, includes the most prominent Labor leaders since the 1970s—Moshe Dayan, Yigal Alon, Yitzhak Rabin, and Shimon Peres among them. The replacement of Prime Minister Golda Meir, a Third Aliyah leader, with Rabin, an Israeli native, in 1974 symbolizes the changing of the guard in Israeli politics from the veterans of the Labor movement to its "youngsters." The "youngsters," however, were already in their sixties, and in no time lost the reins of power to the Likud right-wing party.

The generation of successors was born around the 1920s. Its common experiences which Shapiro deems decisive include, first, schooling in the educational system of the Yishuv under Mapai's domination, and, second, participation in the first large-scale hostilities between Jews and Arabs in Palestine in the years 1936 to 1939 and later in the War of Independence in 1948. While their schooling indoctrinated in them heavy doses of Israeli nationalistic ideology (wrapped up in rigid and barren socialist phraseology), their defense roles ingrained in them military mentality. None of it prepared them to be successful politicians.

Unlike their forerunners who were immersed in both Jewish and European culture, and whose ideological choice had been an act of revolt, the successors knew only the Hebrew language, and consumed unthoughtfully and superficially the convictions bequeathed to them by their parents. They internalized socialist-Zionism narrowly and rigidly, lacking the flexibility of mind and creativity which characterized the founders of that same movement. Yet some of them were incorporated into the ruling elite and would become the top leaders of the 1970s. Their route to the top passed through the youth movements, the communal settlements, and—above all—a prolonged military service.

The only functional niche open to the successors was that of the military profession. A large part of the youngsters of the Yishuv—40 percent of the 14 to 18 age cohort in 1945—were affiliated with the Hagana, which became an almost indispensable stage in their socialization and preparation for public roles (Shapiro 1984:109). The cult of the "pioneer" incorporated a new dimension, that of the "fighter." The two fused almost completely with a new organizational form adopted by the Hagana, especially by its elite unit, the Palmach. Palmach units were located in kibbutzim and divided their time between military training and agricultural work. So much so that, in Shapiro's words, "the *Kibbutz* has become a military combat unit" and for the generation of successors "military defense has become the essence of Zionism" (Shapiro 1984:114 and 117 respectively). In terms of the intergenerational relations within the elite, the prevailing pattern of the seniority of the "founders" was reproduced:

> The ruling elite succeeded in integrating the youngsters in military frameworks which were kept under its effective control. The youngsters turned into obedient underground fighters, but the revolutionary generation continued to set goals and directions. (Shapiro 1984:118)

This analysis leads Shapiro to the verdict that the successors were prepared only for executive roles, not for political leadership roles. They lacked both the vision and the know-how for political life, and did not succeed in elaborating a worldview of their own suitable for the circumstances of post-independence, industrial and democratic society, in which—when they finally assumed leadership—the ideology of the lingering elite was rapidly declining in coherence and influence. Mostly, they joined the ranks of the growing bureaucratic class, especially in the military, government, and public economy. They became Israel's army generals, senior government officials, and economic executives. Mapai itself became, even more than it used to be, a party of the bureaucratic class.

The old elite, however, grew older and lost its grip on the social (Oriental immigration) and political (occupied territories) changing circumstances, yet kept on blocking its young guard from top political positions. When the old elite finally vanished—a process that began already in the 1950s but did not culminate until the 1970s—and the turn of the successors finally arrived, the minority of them who did opt for political roles faltered as soon as they received power. They lacked the internal cohesiveness and ideological persuasiveness needed for a coordination of a dominant elite. Their military background did not train them to deal with complex problems of a different—political—nature. Since the source of their prestige was their defense expertise, and since they could think only in military terms, they designed the failed policies that Israel adopted with regard to the occupied territories of 1967 and the Palestinian issue (Shapiro 1989:166–69).

༺༻

The Labor movement reached its lowest ebb in the elections of 1977, after which it never recovered its role as the pillar of the Israeli polity. Broadly speaking, Shapiro's analysis of the political "upheaval" of 1977 is based on Weber's influential classification between traditional, legal-rational, and charismatic types of political domination and legitimation (Shapiro does not recognize this conceptual lineage, and at a certain point by interpreting Weber's concept of charisma quite narrowly even denies it. See Shapiro 1989:111.)[16] Shapiro's analysis of the "upheaval" can be conceived in terms of a transition from a legal-rational, or bureaucratic, polity, to a charismatic polity. This is manifested in the major transformations he discerns in the Israeli political culture. Up to 1977 political parties were operated by strong apparatuses, political divisions clustered around class issues (social distribution), and the political process was carried out by bureaucratic committees. This, as I demonstrated, forms the gist of Shapiro's image of the Israeli polity under Mapai's domination. Since 1977 parties tend to be operated by the personalities of celebrated leaders, political divisions tend to cluster around status concerns (social prestige), and the political process is practiced by masses in city piazzas. This captures the nature of the Likud party and the impact it exerted on Israeli politics at large, as is summarized in chart 3.

In this interpretation of the Likud party Shapiro takes his cue from two cases he considers comparable: the case of the European radical right, especially Fascist movements in

Chart 3.
Major Characteristics of the Israeli Political Culture Before and After 1977, in Y. Shapiro's Interpretation

	Before 1977	After 1977
The Party system	Multi-party system and a dominant party: Mapai (Ma'arach; Avoda)	Multi-party and two major parties competition
Emulated models	European social-democratic parties and the Soviet Communist Party	European radical-right movements (fascism) and Latin American (Argentinean) populism
Party organization	Apparatus party	Leader party
Party concerns	Class interest (group rewards)	Status concerns (group prestige)
Rewards for support	Material rewards (offices, budgets, etc.)	Symbolic rewards (nationalistic myth, etc.)
Political culture	Pragmatic, moderate, compromising, programmatic, rational	Radical, extreme, inciting, mythical, emotional, totalistic
Style of politics	Politics of meeting-rooms (organizational politics)	Politics of the piazza (rhetorical politics)
Leading values	Collectivism	Romantic nationalism

the pre–World War II era, and the case of Latin American populism, especially Argentinean Peronism (see Shapiro's Introduction in his 1991:7–14). What is common to both references is a "politics of resentment" of unestablished or disestablished groups against the established order; these groups find an outlet through rallying behind demagogic leaders who exploit group-myths to create excitement and skirt the democratic process. (The main difference between Fascism and populism being the social stratum to which each appeals—the former to declining middle classes, the latter to uprooted proletarized peasantry. See especially Shapiro's reference to G. Germani 1978, in Shapiro 1991:11.)

Two generational units took part in the "upheaval" of 1977: the Likud's historical leadership and the Oriental masses. They were united by a resentment towards a political regime which derided them and frustrated their aspirations.

The members of the veteran leadership were born in the decade 1910 to 1920 and experienced the formative stage of their political socialization in Poland in the 1930s. Its immediate model of emulation was Pilsudski's antidemocratic Polish militaristic nationalism. More broadly it drew inspiration from the antiliberal and antisocialist chauvinistic wave that swept large parts of Europe during their adolescence. In Poland they formed a youth movement named Betar. Betar became the radical wing—and military flank—of the major right-wing opposition to the growing power of the Labor movement, the Revisionist party, which was formed by Zeev Jabotinsky in 1925. It is Shapiro's contention that Herut acquired its basic characteristics in Pilsudski's Poland: the authoritative leader principle, the hierarchic and disciplinary structure, the protomilitary attitude, the nationalistic fervor, and the animosity toward socialism. Betar was literally a "brown shirt" movement (cf. Shapiro 1989:35–50).

Betar's successor in the state era was Begin's Herut party. It refrained from an explicit ideological program containing policy objectives and plans (especially on social and economic issues) and preferred instead to engage in "symbolic discourse" centered around myths of national glory and heroism. The role of "ideology" in Shapiro's discussion of Mapai is replaced by "myth" with regard to Herut, though the basic instrumental function remains the same. Deprived of governmental levers and economic infrastructure of its own, Herut could not satisfy its adherents in the instrumental sense, and so instead it provided them with great aspirations and nourished their deprived sense of status. The party also refrained from the construction of an organizational structure—either democratic or bureaucratic—and operated on the basis of a "leader principle." The exalted leader was not only the source of authority in the party but the symbol of its ends. Though occasional elections for the leader did take place, they had a ceremonial character.

To retain his leadership stature in face of successive electoral defeats (up to the 1960s the party remained around the 13 percent mark), Begin caused the departure of activists of the militant right-wing flank who were critical of his parliamentarian commitments, and later neutralized the only flank in the party which had a rudimentary bureaucratic organization, the trade union. Subsequently he remained an absolute leader, considered as the "commander" of the party, operating it with personal aides ("colonels") and appealing directly to supporters without intermediary institutions (one method to neutralize such institutions was to inflate the number of their members so as to turn them into an audience rather than a decision-making forum). His major instrument was rhetoric in which he appealed to emotions rather than to the logic of his listeners.

Without care for consistency Herut joined with the Liberals to enhance its legitimacy, and at the same time started to cater to the Oriental proletariat. It was the Six Day War, however, which pushed Begin to the foreground of Israeli politics. The Eretz Israel myth for which he himself served as a symbol, to which he was committed from youth, and which later condemned him to political desolation, suddenly and unexpectedly came true (or at least could be thus presented). The political discourse reshuffled from rational to symbolic idiom.

What forged the alliance between the Herut Polish leadership and the Oriental proletariat was what Shapiro calls "status politics." Both groups suffered from status deprivation. Both were blocked (though for different reasons) from

Israel's primary channel of mobility—public administration. Both, in other words, were barred from the bureaucratic dominant class—the class of Mapai. The drive for mobility which is usually an individual issue—according to Shapiro— became a group concern, and the vote for Herut transferred it to the political level. The Orientals did not vote for a greater Israel, neither for a better welfare system, wages, or housing (though all these were also promised by Herut), but for pride, and in the deliverance of pride no one was as expert as Menachem Begin (Shapiro 1989:178–80).

IV. Ideology: Neither Left nor Right

It is difficult to tell where Shapiro's sociology ends and his ideology begins. As a sociologist his major project is a critique of the deformities of democracy in Israel. These are also the concerns of him as a political figure. In 1973 Shapiro joined active political life (for a short while). He became a founding member of one of the protest movements in the wake of the 1973 war, the Shinui ("change") party. Shinui was, in Shapiro's own testimony, a party which wished to install in Israeli public life "the fine qualities of a productive and ethical middle class, qualities so much missing from the country's public life."[17] Shapiro chaired the platform committee of the party, and the basic program produced by it reflects the democratic concerns outlined above. In a spirit of "moderate critique of the *Histadrut* culture and values of the Labor movement,"[18] it emphasizes the need for public accountability of representatives, for reduction of governmental intervention in the economy, for the installation of merit criteria in the civil service, etc.[19] Though Shapiro later retreated from party activity this episode certainly locates him right in the center of the Israeli political map. Shinui offers upper-middle-class voters of a free-market orientation a third way (even if only an illusionary one) between the étatist "left" and the nationalist right.

Shapiro maintains that Israeli democracy practices only the *formal* or procedural principle of representative institutions, free elections and majority rule, while failing to fulfil the *liberal* principle of respect for the rights of individuals and of the minority. This is true—in different ways—for both the political culture of the Labor movement and of the Likud. The former was in his view collectivist and bureaucratic, the latter nationalist and chauvinistic. None is committed to the rights and liberties of the individual. While in the Labor era democracy suffered from the encroachment of party apparatus over the governmental civil service, elected institutions, and economic management, in the Likud era civil society and polity fall prey to irrational and erratic "piazza politics" and to demagogic leadership.

Shapiro's own political agenda consists of the cultivation of liberal political culture in Israel. Shapiro, then, distrusts bureaucratic socialism and detests populistic nationalism. Rejecting both the left and the right he almost by default opts for the center. He is a true advocate of middle-class liberalism.

V. Critical Evaluation

To sum up, Shapiro's conflict-sociology interpretation of Israel repudiates the idealistic image of the Israeli elite portrayed by functionalist sociology, and the understanding of the nation-building process in terms of institutionalization (and eventually routinization) of fundamental values. It also rejects the image of the Israeli polity as a pluralist (or consociational) Western democracy. Relying on analyses of bureaucratic oligarchies and power elites, and in turn, on analyses of populist and fascist movements, Shapiro portrays the Israeli leadership in colors reminiscent of the Soviet red and, in the recent period, of the Fascist brown.

Shapiro's analysis has some limitations. Its concept of politics tends to reflect the concept of politics of its object of study—the dominant party elites—and becomes instrumental and cynical. Its notion of Israeli politics is consequently extremely instrumentalist and elitist: the goal of political activity is the "accumulation of power and domination" for their own sake (Shapiro 1975:81). Politics is mainly an affair of leaders ("Public opinion usually does not awaken unless members of the leadership take steps to awaken it" [Shapiro 1977:125; also see Shapiro 1975:13]), and democratic politics is not a public affair, but rather an exchange between a dominant group and other organized interest groups or parties (Shapiro 1977:143-44). By the laws of oligarchization the goals of political activity tend to recede to the background, the instruments of politics to seize the foreground. Politicians look for power for power's sake or for status for status's sake.

This concept of politics not only limits the meaning of democracy—which Shapiro strives to broaden—but also hinders a fully contextualized analysis of politics. Neither social programs nor political economy can be conceived in this approach, except as instruments of power. On the one hand no room remains for non-elite politics, for social movements, or indeed for any articulation of genuinely democratic—let alone socialist—collective interests and identities. Paradoxically, by Shapiro's account it almost emerges that if democracy is to thrive politics should be avoided as much as possible. On the other hand class interests remain opaque and the political economy behind politics is reduced to a mean in a power struggle without an insight into its inherent workings. Thus, for instance, though public finance is of crucial importance to the analysis, it appears only as an external resource, a cash injection into the system from the outside. While this may well be a valid observation in itself, it does not explain the relative success with which this resource was utilized productively to form a viable economic infrastructure for the Jewish community. By the same token the social economy of the Oriental proletariat is reduced to the status and symbolic levels, without a comprehension of the proletarionization involved and the justified social claims made.

The same narrow concept of politics—power for power's sake—also explains another major deficiency of Shapiro's analysis: a lack of due consideration for the geopolitical context in which the elite operates. The story he narrates is of internal power and status struggles. Wars appear twice as crucial to the fate of the elite (1936–1948 and 1967–1973). Yet, they are not conceptualized in Shapiro's analysis, but rather are left as a *deus ex machina*. The imperatives of the national conflict are not well integrated into the scheme. All these defaults became the points of entry for other critical perspectives which emerged in Israeli sociology in the 1970s.[19]

Despite these notable weaknesses Shapiro is the single most significant sociologist to have turned the tables of Israeli sociology in the early to mid-1970s, just before the appearance on the scene of other sociological trends. By redirecting attention from order and consensus to conflict and domination he was able to offset the Eisenstadtian romanticization of the labor elite in its youth and the trivialization of the changes it underwent in its older days. In Shapiro's interpretation the "pioneering" group became an "oligarchy" and collective equality was exposed as a disguise for hierarchical distribution of power and reward. No less defiant is his bold exposure of Likud politics for what it really is, again a first account of this kind from the pen of an established Israeli sociologist, and evidence for the development of the discipline away from political conformism and complacency and toward an open critical stance. The exposition of the "shadowy side" of Israeli politics and the deciphering of its instrumental mechanisms (in the case of Labor) and symbolic mechanisms (in the case of the Likud), and the portrayal of collective portraits of different "generational units" of the Israeli political elite is undoubtedly a most original and significant contribution to the Israeli sociological agenda.

Notes

1. Eisenstadt, S.N., *Israeli Society*, (London: Weidenfeld and Nicolson, 1967).

2. Shapiro, Yonathan, "Political Sociology in Israel: A Critical Review," in *Politics and Society in Israel: Studies in Israeli Society*, Vol. 3, edited by Ernest Krausz, (New Brunswick: Transaction Books, 1985), pp. 7–8.

3. Ibid, p. 9.

4. Parsons, Talcott, *The Social System*, (New York: Free Press, 1951).

5. Durkheim, Emile, *The Elementary Forms of the Religious Life*, (London: Allen Unwin, [1912] 1954).

6. Weber, Max. *Economy and Society*, Vols. 1 and 2, edited by Gunther Roth and Claus Wittich. (Berkeley: University of California Press, [1922] 1978).

7. Marx, K. and F. Engels, *Manifesto of the Communist Party*, in *Selected Works*, (London: Lawrence and Wishart, [1848] 1968).

8. Michels, Roberto, *Political Parties: A Sociological Study of the Oligarchical Tendencies of Modern Democracy*, (New York: Free Press, [1911] 1962).

9. Dahrendorf, Ralph, *Class and Class Conflict in Industrial Society*, (London: Routledge and Kegan Paul, 1959).

10. Collins, Randall, "Conflict Theory and the Advance of Macro-Historical Sociology," in *Frontiers of Social Theory: The New Syntheses*, edited by G. Ritzer, (New York: Columbia University Press, 1990), pp. 68–87. 1990.

11. Mosca, G, *The Ruling Class*, (New York: McGraw Hill, [1896] 1939).

12. Pareto, Vilfredo, *The Mind and Society*, 4 vols., (New York: Harcourt, Brace, [1916] 1935).

13. Mills, C. Wright, *The Power Elite*. (Oxford: Oxford University Press, 1956).

14. Brzezinski, Z. and S. P. Huntington, *Political Power, USA/USSR*, (New York: Viking, 1964) pp. 144–150.

15. Weber, Max, *From Max Weber*, edited by H. H. Gerth and C. W. Mills, (New York: Oxford University Press, 1946) pp. 180–195.

16. For Weber's typology, see: Weber, Max. *Economy and Society*, Vols. 1 and 2, edited by Gunther Roth and Claus Wittich. (Berkeley: University of California Press, [1922] 1978), pp. 212–299.

17. Shapiro, Yonathan, "Epilogue," in *Shinui Movement: From Protest to Political Party*, edited by Shira (Shapira) Ben Zion, (Tel Aviv: Shira Public Relations, No Date), p. 100.

18. Ibid., p. 13.

19. Ibid.

20. Ram, Uri, "Civic Discourse in Israeli Sociological Thought," *International Journal of Politics, Culture and Society*, 3: 1989, pp. 255–272; and *The Changing Agenda of Israeli Sociology: Theory, Ideology and Identity* (Albany, SUNY Press, forthcoming).

Governing in a Turbulent National Policy Environment

Giora Goldberg and Efraim Ben-Zadok

Yehezkel Dror, *A Grand Strategy for Israel*, Jerusalem: Academon, 1989. (Hebrew.)

Yehezkel Dror, *Memorandum for the Israeli Prime Minister: II. To Build a State*, Jerusalem: Academon, 1989. (Hebrew.)

I

Yehezkel Dror, one of Israel's leading social scientists, is internationally known for his pioneering studies in public policy analysis. Dror has recently completed a monumental work of five volumes in Hebrew where he provides a long-range analysis of Israel's fundamental policy and security issues followed by recommendations for breakthroughs in national policy making. The first volume, *A Grand Strategy for Israel*, is reviewed here. This introductory volume presents a general overview and guidelines to the other four volumes. It includes a brief and practical discussion of the most urgent policy and security issues faced by the State. Each of the other four volumes is written as a memorandum for the Israeli prime minister. The second memorandum, *To Build a State*, which is reviewed here, analyzes the functioning of the Israeli political-administrative system and its current problems of governance. It also offers recommendations for improving the system.

The other three memoranda for the Israeli prime minister were not yet published at the time of writing. The first one, *The State of the Nation*, assesses Israel and its policy environment in the context of historical processes. Another memorandum, *The Logic of Zionism*, examines the principles of Zionist ideology in light of present and future political conditions. It also develops an updated systematic approach for Zionism to effectively guide Israeli policy making. The final memorandum, *A Grand Policy for Israel*, offers recommendations for breakthroughs in policy making.

Our review of the two 1989 volumes, *A Grand Strategy for Israel* and *To Build a State*, begins with a brief discussion about the three legitimacy principles on which Israel's political culture is based. The conflicts among these principles provide one common explanation for the turbulence of the Israeli policy environment. We will use the principles and their conflicts as a theoretical framework throughout the review. To a certain extent, Dror acknowledges the difficulties created by the conflicts among these principles. He does not explain, however, the turbulence in the policy environment through the three principles and the constraints that their conflicts impose on the policy environment. According to Dror, the problem is not such objective constraints of the policy environment, but basic deficiencies in Israel's leadership, politics, government, and administration.

With respect to the first legitimacy principle, Israel is a Jewish nation-state. This principle mixes the two elements of a particularistic Jewish ethnic-national identity and Jewish religion to the extent that it is very difficult to distinguish between the two. The second legitimacy principle maintains that Israel is a secular liberal democracy. This principle promotes the universal political and social values which are prevalent in other western democracies. The third legitimacy principle presents Israel as a "security state." Its survival is constantly threatened and endangered and, therefore, national security and defense affect every aspect of life in the country.

These three legitimacy principles of the political culture are in constant tension with each other. For example, the tension between Israel as a Jewish nation-state and as a liberal democracy is manifested in the policies towards the Arabs, i.e., Israeli Arabs and Palestinians. Although Arabs do not share Jewish ethnic-national or religious identities, they should have full equal rights as the members of a democratic state. However, Israeli Arabs are deprived of certain formal rights, not to mention informal ones. The Palestinians in the West Bank and Gaza Strip are not even Israeli citizens. This unequal treatment is further reinforced because Arabs are viewed by the Jewish majority as a "hostile minority" and a threat to national security. It illustrates the tension between Israel as a liberal democracy and a "security state." An example of the tension between Israel as a Jewish nation-state and a "security state" is the use of Jewish moral-religious code to exempt orthodox *yeshiva* students and women from compulsory military service.

The deep tensions among the three legitimacy principles are frequently interpreted as creating a highly turbulent national policy environment. There are few other examples of national policy environments that must constantly "check and balance" among such deep tensions in the political culture.

Extreme political groups in Israel demand to solve the complexity of these deep tensions by eliminating one or two of the legitimacy principles or, at least, by significantly reducing their importance. For example, in order to maintain the Jewish character of the State, the ultra-Orthodox are ready to sacrifice democratic and security values. In contrast, the Arab minority rejects the centrality of Jewish nationality and religion in the State. Extreme right-wing groups are prepared for a full (Kach) or a partial (Gush Emunim) elimination of the State's democratic foundations in order to preserve its Jewish character. Extreme left-wing protest groups (Peace Now) are ready to trade off security values in order to sustain Israel's democratic character.

Indeed, when only one principle of this complex triangle of legitimacy principles is significantly involved, ideological and political consensus is relatively high and the national policy environment is less turbulent. For example, reaffirming the principle of a Jewish nation-state through the Law of Return, Israeli Jews accepted the absorption of immigrants from the Soviet Union as their basic commitment despite the heavy economic burden of absorbing such a massive wave of immigration. In contrast, the hesitant policies against the Intifada since December 1987 reflect the tension between Jewish moral values, or universal democratic values, and the security needs of the State.

There is no hierarchy of importance among the three principles. The relative weight given to each one of them varies according to the changing circumstances and the government in power at the time. Between 1948 and 1963, with Labor's Ben-Gurion as prime minister, much attention was given to the security needs. Among other policies, it was also expressed through the enforcement of military administration over Israeli Arabs. Indeed, this policy was abolished three years after Ben-Gurion's final resignation from the government. The military administration was a policy which expressed both the principles of a Jewish state and a "security state." The civil rights of the Arab population, however, were violated through a series of undemocratic restrictions. Between 1977 and 1983, with Likud's Begin as prime minister and the religious parties as the crucial component in the coalition government, much emphasis was given to policies that emphasized the Jewish character of the State. Gush Emunim settlement in the West Bank at that time was one such policy which also has served security needs. By definition, the policy deemphasized the demands of the Palestinians. The relative ineffectiveness of the Israeli government since the early 1970s perhaps could be explained by the growing emphasis on conflicting Jewish and democratic values while the burden of security and defense has not decreased.

According to Dror, however, the source of this ineffectiveness is not the three legitimacy principles, their conflicts, and the constraints that they thus impose on the policy environment. Rather, it is the political-administrative system itself which must be reformed. This argument is the underlying thread of *To Build a State*, which is reviewed in the following section. The reform derived from this argument is the structural backbone for *A Grand Strategy for Israel* which is reviewed in the section thereafter.

II

The argument, in Dror's words, is that the basic problem is not objective "ungovernability," but rather, it is the government's "inability to govern." Israeli politicians and policymakers deny their responsibility by disregarding their own shortcomings and instead, they blame what they view as an objectively turbulent policy environment and a highly complex local society. There is no objective ungovernability, Dror maintains. The role of government is to continuously improve itself despite the difficult and changing circumstances. The ungovernability argument, which is frequently adopted by the political system, is distorted and misleading. Instead, it is the inability to govern, i.e., basic deficiencies in leadership, politics, government, and administration.[1]

Again, to a certain extent Dror acknowledges the three principles and their impact on the policy environment. He even devotes a chapter to the question, "Is the Jewish nation capable of maintaining a state?" In this chapter Dror recognizes the constraints that the high standards of Jewish moral and democratic values traditionally imposed on policy making and implementation.[2] However, he clearly adopts the inability to govern as his chief explanation while discounting the ungovernability explanation. Because Dror does not provide empirical evidence for either explanation in *To Build a State*, he could be legitimately criticized by the many politicians, policymakers, and academics who support the ungovernability explanation.

Given the lack of empirical evidence on either the ungovernability or the inability to govern—two explanations that might best be evaluated by history—the ungovernability explanation, or more specifically, the difficulties imposed on the policy environment by the three principles and their conflicting interactions, is still very potent and attractive. Clearly, no major policy in Israel can rely on only one of the three principles. Rare exceptions might be all-out wars. Yet even the 1982 war in Lebanon became a controversial moral issue since its first week. Moreover, there is no one balanced formula, for the relative weight of each of the three principles, to guide policy in Israel permanently. Their relationships constantly change according to the time and circumstances. Thus, ungovernability remains a valid and no less important explanation.

Furthermore, we see Dror providing some justification for the ungovernability explanation in his discussion of three major deficiencies in the Jewish nation's capacity to maintain a state. These are the impracticality of Jewish moral values for politics, and the absence of both statehood and democratic traditions. All three originate in the legitimacy principles of the political culture which were mentioned earlier. All three explain to some extent the instability of the Israeli policy environment and actually lend support to the ungovernability argument which is rejected by the author.

Dror's practical values for politics are derived from his "raison de Zionism," or the ideological logic of Zionism which he aims to revise and update in one of the coming volumes. These values are based primarily on Rome's raison d'etat rather than Jerusalem's Jewish moral code which is often impractical for politics. That is, as the author explains it, a high priority is given to the instrumental survival and growth of a strong state rather than to its moral behavior in politics and international relations. These practical values, the base of the modern state, take precedence over Jewish thought which stresses, for example, the restraining of rulers to protect individuals.[3] The author continues to explain that Jewish moral values might have facilitated the survival of a nation without a state for two millennia, a unique phenomenon in and of itself. However, between these values and *realpolitik* among states there is tension and perhaps even a contradiction. Moreover, Jewish moral values explain the collapse of

Jewish states in the biblical past more than the traditional speculations on unusual historical circumstances or Israel's central geo-strategic location. Dror concludes that the emphasis on Jewish moral values and the simultaneous neglect of modern state values is a major deficiency in the nation's capacity to maintain a state.[4]

Two more deficiencies are the absence of both statehood and democratic traditions in the Diaspora. That is, Israel lacks the gradual state-building process of a Western democracy which involves centuries of development of centralized government, public discipline, and liberal policies. Instead, the young state experienced a fast process which resulted in much illegal activism, an undisciplined public, and unrestrained strikes.[5]

A quick glance at the early period of statehood shows that Ben-Gurion was aware of these three deficiencies. His efforts to organize a strong centralized government and to promote "statism" as a national value encountered these deficiencies. However, he did not shy away from giving priority to Labor's political interests over "statism-based" interests. A case in point was the prominent status granted to the General Federation of Labor (Histadrut). "Statism" as a national value attracted little attention after Ben-Gurion's resignation.

Although the deficiencies above do not support Dror's "inability to govern argument," his overall analysis of this problem—which raises concern over Israel's capacity to survive and its possible decay as a state in light of the growing power of its enemies—should be taken very seriously. His analysis includes eight weaknesses, or "governing pathologies," which significantly limit the healthy functioning of the Israeli government.[6] These weaknesses portray a government which constantly produces incremental policies, or "muddles through" with small conservative and compromising steps, relying heavily on past political positions.[7] The decision-making pattern of this government frequently tends to be confused and paralyzed; problems tend to be solved through ritualistic, symbolic, and even mystic means with little intention to implement.

In discussing these weaknesses, Dror adds an insightful comment on the famous Israeli "improvisation ability" which was very effective under the uncertain and changing conditions of the Yishuv and the early-state periods. Currently, this improvisation ability is significantly reduced due to the maturing of the state. The issues have become too complex to be handled via improvisation. Further, a crisis management system, which could respond effectively to the new complexity, has never been established.[8]

In light of the deficiencies, weaknesses, and inabilities that are detailed in the volume, the author's conclusions are not surprising. These are:

> Both the government and its functioning pattern are less and less appropriate to the policy environment and the goals. . . . The level of the ability to govern is much lower than what is required and, in light of the needs, the functioning of the government is on a sliding curve. . . . In general, the decision-making processes of the Israeli Government and its committees are primitive.[9]

To overcome these shortcomings, Dror proposes a reform strategy for the Israeli government. This strategy, which he calls "Selective Radicalism," focuses on drastic improvements in a small number of critical areas of governance. In these areas the author suggests a variety of "institutional innovations," namely: formation of top management in the context of an overall reform in public administration; establishing a College for National Policy for top elected and appointed officials; institutionalizing participatory democracy in the community, neighborhood, and workplace levels; enlightening (educating) the public, specifically in regard to political and democratic ideas; establishing a National Council to discuss and recommend administrative changes and ethical rules; strengthening the authority and the power of the prime minister; creating a central Policy Planning Unit in the Office of the Prime Minister; appointing a national policy review advisor to the prime minister; developing a computer-based Decision Support System (information system); improving the analytical level of government's discussions and decision-making processes; improving the functioning of high-level staff; developing an effective and regulated crises management system by the government; establishing a National Institute for Policy Research and Development; introducing Mission Budgeting procedures which include allocation by major activities and their expected outputs; organizing quasi-independent management of specific national projects; improving the routine monitoring of implementation; improving agenda-setting and the analytical level of discussions in the Knesset; developing mechanisms to centralize democratic power, to form consensus, and to make crucial national decisions; and strengthening citizen participation in national projects and local governments.[10]

For Dror, this reform strategy is the right direction, rather than drastic constitutional changes which he views as "false solutions." He argues against the adoption of three such changes: a formal constitution; a reform in the national elections based on individual candidates (rather than party lists) and districts; and a presidential (rather than a parliamentary) system. Dror believes that such drastic changes, taken from a completely different policy environment, namely the United States, will further destabilize and reduce the flexibility of the already troubled Israeli political system.[11]

Clearly, Dror's reform strategy is logically derived from his inability to govern argument and he should be commended for "speaking truth to power" and offering these "institutional innovations" in such critical areas of governance. At the same time, proponents of the ungovernability argument would disagree with his relatively preventive rather than drastic measures. They tend to advocate the constitutional changes above as the ultimate structural remedies for an exceptionally problematic policy environment with a government which is under tremendous time and work pressures. They support drastic changes dictated from the top down which will settle the inherent conflicts among the three legitimacy principles of the political culture (e.g., a formal constitution in order to determine state-synagogue relation).

III

Nevertheless, Dror is Israel's leading policy analyst and his work is based on a wealth of research and practical consulting experience to the Israeli government as well as foreign governments. His analysis of the Israeli inability to govern and how to correct it is extremely valuable and should be carefully read by anyone who is interested in policy improvement in Israel. Many of his "institutional innovations" do not contradict the constitutional changes proposed by the proponents of ungovernability and might be adopted by them as well. According to Dror, many of the innovations are required in order to develop and implement *A Grand Strategy for Israel*,[12] the title of the volume to be reviewed in this section.

This volume is the first published document to design an overall Israeli strategy. For this alone, it represents a significant contribution to the literature. A Grand Strategy is "an approach, a thinking framework and a perception, which is expressed in unique ways of thinking."[13] It provides long-range (twenty to thirty years) broad and coherent (interdependent) policy and security principles from which routine decisions can be prescribed. It encourages creativity and encounters neglected areas in policy making. It is absent in Israel.[14]

A Grand Strategy and the "institutional innovations" required to develop and implement it are absent in Israel for many reasons. Yet the root of the problem, according to Dror, is the prevalent Israeli penchant for "motivated irrationality." This includes distortion of reality, as well as of its perception and interpretation, due to ideologies, values, hopes, fears, and emotions. It leads to biased and emotional thinking rather than objective thinking. It served the Zionist movement well at its inception when it had nothing to lose, and "a self-fulfilling prophecy" process could only contribute to achieving what was seen as almost impossible. "Motivated irrationality" is a major obstacle at present, however, because the circumstances are completely different. The author calls for high-ranking public officials, readers, and even himself to repress and restrain this penchant.[15]

Clearly, "motivated irrationality" is an important determinant of the Israeli inability to govern. The former (cause) and the latter (effect) halt the development and implementation of the Grand Strategy and the "institutional innovations." But for Dror, through such strategy and innovations, Israel can significantly improve its ability to control (govern) the policy environment which, admittedly, is dynamic, demanding, risky, and threatening the survival of Israel for, at least, another thirty to fifty years.[16] His main effort in the book is to prescribe this strategy.

Again, Dror acknowledges the difficulties that the three legitimacy principles of the political culture impose on the policy environment. The tensions among the three principles are portrayed throughout the volume in clashes among the values which represent them. These are Jewish ethnic, national, and religious values; secular, liberal, and democratic values; and security and defense values. The author begins with a long-range assessment which includes clashes among the values of the Jewish and Islamic religions, Jewish and Palestinian nationalism, security needs and liberal democracy rights, and Western and Middle Eastern cultures.[17] The twelve dimensions of the Grand Strategy to which over one-half of the book is devoted,[18] include at least five dimensions where tensions among the three principles and clashes among their respected values are central to the discussion. These are the dimensions about the conflict with the Islam; territory, defense, and borders; foreign policy (and morale); the Palestinian issue; and the national identity and loyalty of Israeli Arabs.[19]

The last dimension, Israeli Arabs, can serve as a good example to illustrate the tensions among the three principles and how Dror's Grand Strategy proposes to overcome them. The author maintains that Israel is "a divided and multinational society." He suggests three interdependent policies to prevent the deepening of the cleavage between Arabs and Jews in Israel. First, full equal rights to Israeli Arabs and their social integration into the larger society (the latter includes housing, lifestyle, military service, and marriage). Second, permanent resident status for Israeli Arabs which includes full equal rights, except for political activity; their rights for political activity would be granted through the Palestinian state (more on that later). Third, an explicit recognition that Israeli Arabs are "an autonomous sub-nationality" with their own culture and symbols, in order to increase their identification with the State. Some of Dror's detailed recommendations for increasing the loyalty of Israeli Arabs include the adding of Arab elements to the Israeli flag and national anthem and enforcing compulsory military service on them.[20] At present, the political feasibility of such recommendations and policies is low. They all represent, however, logical solutions to decrease the tensions among the three principles.

Thus, the three principles and their tensions are covered in the book. Yet the main function of the Grand Strategy is to reach a significant level of control over the policy environment. Specifically, the Grand Strategy is a comprehensive framework to guide and improve policy making and implementation in Israel. It is an applied rather than a theoretical framework and thus differs from most of Dror's major contributions in the past. It will be interesting to see if this direct call to the Israeli government will be generalized to theory building in the future.

Dror's underlying approach is that of the "policy intellectual." This technique of policy analysis reconciles between value-laden assumptions and those that instrumentally assist the politicians in power. As mentioned earlier, the author's values are derived from his "raison de Zionism." His practicality stresses an applied contribution, albeit with a clear distinction between professional analysis and political (party) position. The author acknowledges that this approach can be attacked by Israeli intellectuals and politicians. In his view, their alternative leads to rigid and extensive ideological discussions as well as unprofessional and stagnated policy making and implementation.[21]

Undoubtedly the execution of such an approach, which intertwines values with practice while maintaining intellectual independence and professional integrity, is a difficult task. Dror has been successful, however, in outlining the approach. It will be difficult for politicians from the left or the right to confront his professional conclusions. Of course, his approach might be attacked by non-Zionists. But all they can offer is an alternative ideological line which is shared by only a small minority of Israeli Jews. Or, his approach might be attacked from the school of policy analysis which rejects the use of values in professional work. Yet this value-free school itself is being criticized for its impractical and outdated approach to policy analysis.

A good example of Dror's "policy intellectual" approach is the chapter on the Palestinian issue.[22] Guided by the value of securing the existence and continuity of a strong Jewish state in Israel, a central tenet of Zionism, he methodically develops ten Grand Design policy alternatives to solve this most controversial political issue. Through a detailed and practical analysis he rejects all the alternatives but one: a Palestinian state in what today is Jordan, which will also include parts of the West Bank and Gaza Strip. This "flexible compromise" is the most feasible and practical policy alternative in spite of its risks. Although this alternative can be argued against from certain political positions, it is difficult to criticize its intellectual and professional integrity.

IV

In summary, while Dror characterizes the Israeli policy environment as turbulent and dynamic, he nevertheless suggests that deficiencies in Israel's leadership, politics, government, and administration are the primary determinants of the inability to effectively control the policy environment. He views the Israeli government as "muddling through" incrementally, lacking direction, and incapable of planning and implementing policy breakthroughs. In order to improve significantly the government's control of the policy environment, Dror proposes a variety of "institutional innovations" and a comprehensive Grand Strategy. The former serves as the structural backbone to develop and implement the latter.

Dror's arguments might be controversial. His policy analysis, however, demonstrates intellectual independence and professional integrity. His conclusions and recommendations, therefore, should be taken seriously by Israeli politicians, policymakers, and academics. In the final analysis, however, the question must be raised about the feasibility of developing and implementing the "institutional innovations" and the Grand Strategy.

A possible "window of opportunity" for the adoption of Dror's conclusions and recommendations would be created if a major shake-up in the political system were to take place as a result of a tremendous crisis. Such a crisis would signal to the political system that time is running out and it must save itself from a complete breakdown. The system might then initiate a top-down reform along Dror's guidelines.

Under "conventional" circumstances, a movement towards reform is possible if two major forces were to move in that direction. These are the leading political parties (which determine the distribution of power in the Knesset and government) and the huge government bureaucracy. It is impossible to predict if and when the parties and the bureaucracy will move towards Dror's reform, which in fact reduces their power, albeit under conditions that do not threaten their own survival. Nevertheless, an important trend, common to the parties, the bureaucracy, and even to Israeli public opinion, is an increasing recognition of the value of professionalism in government work. This trend toward professionalism can help to facilitate reform. Thus, important parts of Dror's monumental "true speech to power" might be realized in practice.

Notes

1. Yehezkel Dror, *Memorandum for the Israeli Prime Minister: II. To Build a State* (Jerusalem: Academon, 1989), pp. 49–50, Hebrew.

2. Ibid., pp. 35–47.

3. Shared by American political thought as well, this value, according to Dror, explains some of the many weaknesses of the American government. For this and other reasons, he calls on Israeli academics and practitioners to decrease their emphasis on comparative learning from the American political system which operates in a completely different policy environment. He urges them to learn more from small Western European countries. See Dror, *Memorandum: To Build*, pp. 27–29.

4. Dror, *Memorandum: To Build*, pp. 35–39.

5. Ibid., pp. 39–44.

6. Ibid., pp. 56–58.

7. For more on this pattern of decision making, see Charles E. Lindblom, "The Science of 'Muddling Through'," *Public Administration Review* 19 (1959): 79–88.

8. Dror, *Memorandum: To Build*, pp. 58–59.

9. Ibid., pp. 52–53, 180.

10. Ibid., pp. 108–120, 157–209.

11. Ibid., pp. 88–96.

12. Yehezkel Dror, *A Grand Strategy for Israel* (Jerusalem: Academon, 1989), pp. 33–34, Hebrew.

13. Ibid., p. 23.

14. Ibid., pp. 19–28.

15. Ibid., pp. 33–37.

16. Ibid., pp. 67–70.

17. Ibid., pp. 56–67.

18. Ibid., pp. 119–312.

19. While similar tensions are rarely portrayed throughout the seven other dimensions, security and defense values are central to their discussion. These dimensions are: images of deterrence and friendship; nuclear policy; terrorism and guerrillas; wars; civil defense; research and development; and relationships with the superpowers.

20. Dror, *A Grand Strategy for Israel*, pp. 303–312.

21. Ibid., pp. 12–13.

22. Ibid., pp. 255–301.

Part IV

History and Politics

The Significance of Israeli Historical Revisionism

Jerome Slater

In the past decade or so, there has been a remarkable burst of historical scholarship—most, though not all, the work of Israeli academicians and journalists—on the origins and dynamics of the Arab-Israeli conflict. The sources of this new scholarship are recently declassified Israeli, American, British, Palestinian, and United Nations archives, as well as the private diaries and public memoirs of a number of leading Israeli political leaders, especially Moshe Sharett, David Ben-Gurion, Moshe Dayan, and Yitzhak Rabin. Collectively, these works have come to be known as "historical revisionism," because they have compelled a sweeping reassessment of some of the most critical axioms and widely accepted beliefs about the conflict.[1]

The importance of this revisionism is far more than historical. It has direct relevance for the contemporary conflict between the Israelis and the Palestinians. As Steven Heydemann observes, the "increasingly transparent myths" of standard Israeli historical memory have played "a powerful role in shaping perceptions not only about who was responsible for the Palestinian problem in 1948, or for the continuing absence of peace, but also about what must yet be done to resolve these issues, foremost among them the problem of Palestinians under Israeli rule."[2]

Violence and Terrorism in the Israeli-Palestinian Conflict

One of the central Israeli myths that has been decisively refuted by the new historical scholarship is that the Jews were innocent, largely non-violent victims of fanatical Palestinian violence and terrorism. No part of this standard view can survive objective examination: (1) Given the insistence of the Zionists on creating a Jewish state in Palestine, inhabited primarily by Arabs for thirteen hundred consecutive years, Palestinian resistance to Jewish immigration and political objectives was not necessarily "fanatical," or even unreasonable; (2) when the Palestinians turned to violence, it was usually because they had exhausted political means of protecting their rights, particularly to self-determination and majority rule; (3) the Jews were not merely innocent victims, but were often fanatical, violent, and terrorist themselves.

In the pre-state period, the Irgun and Stern Gang frequently employed terrorism against both the British and against Arab civilians. In the late 1930s, the Irgun began the pattern of planting bombs in Arab marketplaces, firing on Arab buses, and other terrorist actions that were later employed by Palestinian terrorists against the Jews. While Jewish terrorism was officially criticized and disavowed by Ben-Gurion and other mainstream Jewish political leaders, there is substantial evidence that they often tacitly acquiesced in or even collaborated with the terrorism, including some of the worst civilian massacres (e.g. at Deir Yassin in 1948). At the least, they did not eschew the fruits of terrorism, particularly the driving out of the Arabs in the aftermath of the 1948 war.[3]

Until the recent historical scholarship, it was widely accepted that during the 1948 War of Independence, the Palestinian refugees fled Israel more or less voluntarily, in part because of Arab urgings that they do so, in part simply to escape the unavoidable consequences of war. However, this view is now simply untenable, for Flapan, Hirst, Morris, and Palumbo have conclusively established, in copious and painful detail, that most of the Palestinians fled Israel as a direct result of Israeli psychological warfare and intimidation, economic pressures, violence, and outright terrorism, all designed to eliminate as many Arabs as possible from Israel.

The expulsion of the Arabs gave rise to the Palestinian guerrilla movement, dedicated to the defeat of the Jews and the return of the Palestinians to their homeland. Acknowledging no responsibility for the plight of the Palestinians, Israel met the guerrilla attacks with a policy of pure force. Moreover, the policy sometimes went beyond that of massive retaliation against the guerrillas themselves—not merely an eye for an eye, but ten eyes for one eye—to include deliberate attacks against civilians in neighboring countries, even non-Palestinian civilians, the clear purpose of which was to terrorize them into ending assistance to the guerrillas.[4]

Similar policies were employed in Egypt during the 1970-73 Canal War, in Lebanon in the massive raids of 1978 and the invasion of 1982, and in the repression of the Intifada in the occupied territories today, where there have been not only shootings, beatings, jailing and other forms of repression, but even the use of assassination teams—Israeli army units disguised as Palestinian civilians, tracking down and killing alleged activists.[5]

Israeli Expansionism

Another important set of myths examined by revisionism is that Israel has been a defensive, status-quo state which seeks only peace and security and has always been prepared for any reasonable compromise—particularly territorial compromise or partition—to achieve it. However, revisionist scholarship has conclusively demonstrated that from the beginnings of the Zionist settlement of Palestine after World War II through the present all mainline Jewish leaders—not just Jabotinsky, Begin and Shamir, but Weizman, Ben-Gurion, Dayan and others—envisaged the eventual expansion of Israel to include all of "ancient" Palestine, which included lands going considerably beyond even those claimed for "Greater Israel" today. Thus, whenever the Zionist leadership appeared to accept various territorial compromises, including the 1947 United Nations partition plan that led to the birth of Israel, in fact they did so only as a temporary tactic, with the borders to be later expanded as the political and military balance of power shifted in Israel's favor.

In 1919, two years after the Balfour Declaration, the World Zionist Organization submitted a map of the intended Jewish homeland to the League of Nations, including the Gaza Strip and parts of the Sinai, southern Lebanon, the Golan Heights and other parts of western Syria, the West Bank of the Jordan River, and much of what later became Transjordan, to the outskirts of Amman.[6] In 1934 to 1936, in talks with Arab leaders, Ben-Gurion demanded that they accept a Jewish state in all of Palestine, including Transjordan, and Jewish settlement in Syria and Iraq.[7]

Several years later Ben-Gurion decided that Israel must accept a partition, but only temporarily. In 1937 he wrote his son:

> A partial Jewish state is not the end, but only the beginning. The establishment of such a Jewish State will serve as a means in our historical efforts to redeem the country in its entirety.... We shall organize a modern defense force... and then I am certain that we will not be prevented from settling in other parts of the country, either by mutual agreement with our Arab neighbors or by some other means.... We will expel the Arabs and take their places... with the force at our disposal.[8]

A year later, Ben-Gurion told those at a Zionist meeting: "I favor partition of the country because when we become a strong power after the establishment of the state, we will abolish partition and spread throughout all of Palestine."[9]

The Israeli defeat of the Palestinians and the invading Arab armies in the 1948 War of Independence led to the shift in the balance of military power between the Jews and the Arabs for which Ben-Gurion had been waiting. As a result,

Israeli expansionism began. On several occasions during the war, Israel manufactured pretexts to break ceasefires and seize land that had not been allocated to it by the UN partition. By the end of the war Israel included 77 percent of Palestine, instead of the original 57 percent envisaged by the 1947 plan.

The standard view of Israeli expansion in the 1947 to 1948 period is that it was justified because it came about as a result of the Arab refusal to accept the UN partition and the subsequent armed attack against Israel. While there is something to this, the recent reassessments of this period make it clear that there are powerful counterarguments. First, the Arab refusal to compromise was rooted in the fact that they were the victims of the Zionist movement and that their case for insisting on the full measure of their rights was considerably stronger than that of the Zionists. Secondly, the Zionist "acceptance" of compromise was not genuine, but merely tactical and temporary. Moreover, even this highly qualified acceptance applied only to the part of the UN plan the Zionists liked—the establishment of a Jewish state—while they ignored the parts they disliked, including the creation of a Palestinian state and the internationalization of Jerusalem. Finally, it is not clear why the core logic of the UN compromise—to divide Palestine between the Jews and the Arabs on the basis of reasonable demographic and geographical criteria—should necessarily be invalidated because of the initial Arab refusal to accept it.

In any case, Israeli aspirations for expansion were not limited to the 1948 acquisitions. In early 1949 Ben-Gurion told his aides,

> Before the founding of the state, on the eve of its creation, our main interest was self-defense.... But now the issue at hand is conquest, not self-defense. As for setting the borders—it's an open-ended matter. In the Bible as well as in history there are all kinds of definitions of the country's borders, so there's no real limit.[10]

In accordance with this philosophy, Ben-Gurion originally planned to take advantage of the 1948 war to seize all of

Jerusalem and its surrounding areas and much of the West Bank. He felt compelled to abandon this course only under the threat of a full-scale war with the Arab Legion of Jordan and a political if not military crisis with Britain and perhaps the United States.[11]

Moreover, Israel came very close to seizing large parts of the Sinai in the aftermath of the war. In December, 1948, Israel used various pretexts to end the ceasefire agreement with Egypt in order to drive Egyptian armies out of the Negev. To be sure, much of the Negev had been allocated to Israel in the 1947 partition, but Israel did not stop there, continuing on to take all of the Negev, the Gaza Strip, and parts of the Sinai peninsula. It was only after British warnings that it would intervene militarily and a U.S. ultimatum that it would withdraw its diplomatic recognition that Israel withdrew from the Sinai.[12]

Israeli aspirations for the Sinai did not end there, for Ben-Gurion regarded this as only a temporary setback; his archives contain "abundant proof that during the first years following the establishment of the State of Israel, he continued to secretly plan the next stage, in which he would achieve his territorial ambitions."[13] These ambitions were not modest: they included Jerusalem and the West Bank, the annexing of southern Lebanon to Israel and the establishment of a pro-Israeli Christian state in the rest of Lebanon, the conquest of Gaza and the Sinai, and the division of Jordan between Israel and Iraq (then under a pro-Western monarchy). In early 1954, for example, Moshe Sharett recorded in his diary that Ben-Gurion and his protégé Moshe Dayan were pressing for expansion into Lebanon, with Dayan proposing that Israel

> find an officer, even just a Major. We should either win his heart or buy him with money, to make him agree to declare himself the savior of the Maronite population. Then the Israeli army will enter Lebanon, will occupy the necessary territory, and will create a Christian regime which will ally itself with Israel. The territory from the Litani southward will be totally annexed to Israel.

Sharett considered this to be "a crazy adventure"—as indeed it proved to be when Israel actually tried to implement this plan in its 1978 and 1982 invasions of Lebanon.[14]

In 1956, Ben-Gurion proposed the division of Jordan: "Jordan has no right to exist and should be partitioned. Eastern Transjordan should be ceded to Iraq [then under a pro-Western monarchy], which would offer to accept and resettle the Arab refugees. The territory to the West of the Jordan should be made an autonomous region of Israel."[15] As for the Gaza and Sinai, Sharett's diaries reveal that Dayan and Ben-Gurion began planning a war of territorial conquest against Egypt in 1953, even before Nasser came to power and turned to the Soviet Union for arms.[16] Sharett bitterly opposed these plans, and was forced out of office for doing so, clearing the way for the 1956 Israeli invasion and capture of the Sinai, in collaboration with the British and French attack on Egypt.[17] Given the history of Israeli designs on the Sinai, there is reason to suspect that this attack was not merely "defensive," forced on Israel by Nasser's radicalism and the Egyptian military buildup in the Sinai in 1955, though no doubt these were important contributing factors. In any case, there is little doubt that Israel would have indefinitely remained in the Sinai and perhaps annexed it, de facto if not de jure, had it not been forced to withdraw by a combination of blunt Soviet threats of military intervention and severe U.S. pressures.

Finally, Dayan and Ben-Gurion sought occasions to seize the Golan Heights from Syria, even before Syrian shelling of Israeli settlements in the 1960s provided the pretext in the context of the 1967 war. As early as January 1954, for example, Dayan outlined plans to Sharett for Israel to create a series of "accomplished facts" by seizing the Golan if Iraq moved into Syria.[18] Thirteen years later, of course, Israel did capture the Golan, along with Gaza and the West Bank.

Lost Opportunities for Peace

Perhaps the most enduring and the most important of the various myths about the Arab-Israeli conflict—a myth that is an article of faith in Israel and has largely been accepted by the outside world as well—has been that the Arabs have never reconciled themselves to the existence of Israel, have refused all compromise, and with the single exception of Egypt since the mid-1970s, have sought the destruction of Israel. Because of this implacable Arab-Palestinian hostility and rejection, there has been no one (save Sadat) for Israel to talk to about a political settlement, and thus all the wars have been unavoidable, forced upon Israel by the fanatic rejectionism of its Arab enemies. In Abba Eban's famous epigram: "The Arabs never missed an opportunity to miss an opportunity."

But, as with so many other myths about the Arab-Israeli conflict, this one too cannot survive serious historical examination. I shall argue that both parts of the myth are mistaken or seriously exaggerated. On the one hand, the Israelis were far less ready for genuine compromise on the central issues of the conflict—the status of the Palestinians and the final borders of the Israeli state—than the myths imply. At the same time, the policies of the Arabs, including the Palestinians, have been considerably more complex and differentiated: at various times most of the Arab actors have been open to the possibility of genuine compromise.

The 1948 War of Independence

The 1948 war was in fact two wars. In the first, the Israelis fought the Palestinian Arabs; in the second, the Israelis fought the invading armies of Egypt, Jordan, Syria, Lebanon, and Iraq. Though the Israelis defeated both the Palestinians and the Arab states in 1948, the wars never ended and the consequences continue to unfold today. Yet, both wars may have been avoidable.

During the 1930s the conflict between the Jews and the Palestinians seemed irreconcilable, for the insistence of the Zionists on the creation of a Jewish-dominated state in all of Palestine led to vicious mutual violence and terrorism. Moreover, the increasingly desperate Palestinians turned toward extremist leadership, some of whom sought Hitler's help in "solving" the Jewish problem in the Middle East.

However, the failure of the Palestinian revolt of the 1930s, the defeat of Germany, and the determination of the British and later the United Nations to reach a compromise in Palestine resulted in greater moderation or at least realism among the Palestinians. To be sure, some remained violently committed to preventing a Jewish state in any part of Palestine, but by the mid-1940s many others had come to the realization that partition of Palestine and the creation of a Jewish state, however undesirable, was unavoidable.[19] As a result, there were many Palestinian proposals and plans for a settlement, though they came to nought because of the Zionist determination "to achieve full sovereignty at whatever cost."[20] Even so, throughout Palestine many Arab local leaders and villages sought to avoid war by concluding neutralization and mutual non-aggression pacts with their Jewish neighbors.

The UN partition plan presented another opportunity for a settlement, for it envisaged the creation of an independent Palestinian Arab state alongside of the Jewish state of Israel. However, the Israeli leadership secretly collaborated with King Abdullah of Transjordan to thwart the creation of a Palestinian state.[21]

It is possible that if the Zionists had been genuinely willing to accept the *full* compromise political settlement envisaged by the international community (i.e. a Palestinian as well as a Jewish state), not only might the Palestinian-Israeli conflict have been peacefully settled but there might have been no larger Arab-Israeli conflict. There was no massive determination of the Arab world to prevent the creation of a Jewish state per se. Rather, there was a half-hearted, ill-coordinated and relatively small intervention (about thirteen thousand troops), partially motivated by sympathy for the Palestinians, partially by inter-Arab monarchical rivalries—especially Egyptian and Syrian fears that Jordanian annexation of the West Bank would provide the springboard for the realization of Abdullah's dream of territorial expansion and the creation of a Hashemite Kingdom extending over Syria, Lebanon, and parts of Egypt.[22] Thus, a Jewish-Palestinian compromise in 1947, including the creation of an independent Palestinian state in the West Bank, would have gone a long way to eliminating both of the causes of the Arab invasion.

Lost Opportunities Since 1948

Contrary to the widely accepted myths in Israel and elsewhere, there have been no uniformly "rejectionist" Arab states (other than Iraq, not a front-line state), and Israel has had a number of opportunities to reach genuine political settlements with all the major actors—Jordan, Egypt, Syria, and the Palestinians themselves.

The first opportunity for peace occurred in the immediate aftermath of the 1948 war. By March, 1949, armistice agreements between Israel and Egypt, Jordan and Syria had been reached, and in the summer of 1949 representatives from all the leading Arab states except Iraq agreed to meet with Israel at Lausanne, to discuss a general settlement with Israel on the basis of the 1947 UN partition plan. Thus, contrary to the current Israeli mythology, most of the Arab states were prepared to meet face-to-face with Israeli delegates and were ready to discuss a compromise peace.[23]

The Arab position was that peace could be reached if Israel returned to the 1947 partition boundaries and accepted the repatriation of the Palestinian refugees, but Israel insisted that there would be no territorial compromise or return to the former boundaries, that it had no responsibility for the flight of the refugees, and that consequently it would accept the return of few if any of the Palestinians.[24] The Israeli disclaimer of responsibility was of course false; the real reasons for the Israeli policy were the ideological commitment to a Jewish state, the potential security problems posed by any substantial return of refugees, and perhaps above all the fact that Jews had already taken over the villages, homes, and lands of the Arabs.

Would Israeli flexibility have been matched by an Arab willingness to compromise at Lausanne? The territorial issues would have been difficult, for the Israelis could justifiably claim that the Arabs had rejected compromise until they lost the war. On the other hand, if the Arab states were *now* willing to formally accept the state of Israel within its 1947 boundaries, that might well have enhanced Israeli security.

Similarly, there was room for compromise on the refugee issue. The United States, acting as a mediator, proposed that Israel take back 250,000 refugees and promised U.S. financial aid in resettling the remainder in the Arab world; there were many private indications that the Arab states would accept such a compromise.[25]

Thus, Israel bears a considerable responsibility for the ultimate deadlock at Lausanne; carried away by its military victories in 1948, it felt no need to make concessions on either territory or the refugees, concessions that might have brought peace.

Peace with Jordan

A number of revisionist historians, including Bar-Joseph, Melman and Raviv, Pappe, and Shlaim have meticulously demonstrated that Israel could have simultaneously reached peace with Jordan and settled the Palestinian problem—or at least made it strictly a Jordanian problem—at any point between 1948 and 1984, by agreeing to Jordanian sovereignty over the Gaza Strip, East Jerusalem, and the West Bank.

As mentioned earlier, the 1947 UN partition plan envisaged the establishment of an independent Palestinian state, but both Israel and King Abdullah of Transjordan opposed it. Abdullah was prepared to collaborate with Israel, explicitly or tacitly, to divide Palestine and to substitute Hashemite rule for Palestinian sovereignty or a Palestinian state. However, Ben-Gurion and the Zionist leadership wanted all of Palestine, including the West Bank. For the moment, Ben-Gurion reluctantly decided, the strong opposition of Britain and the United States as well as the military power of Abdullah's Arab Legion precluded Jewish seizure of the West Bank, and therefore there was no choice but to remain passive when the Legion occupied the area. But such an unacknowledged, temporary, and reversible acquiescence in Hashemite rule over the area was better than formal agreement to Jordanian sovereignty, let alone Palestinian sovereignty.

The unwillingness of Israel to relinquish its claims to the West Bank and Jerusalem made peace between Israel and Jordan impossible, and it led to reluctant Jordanian participation in the 1967 war, which in turn gave Israel the opportunity it had long sought to seize "Judea and Samaria." From the 1967 war through at least 1984 there were a series of regular though secret meetings between King Hussein of Jordan and Israeli political leaders, to see if a basis could be found for a Jordanian-Israeli political settlement. On a number of occasions Hussein proposed a settlement based on territorial compromise: if Israel agreed to Jordanian sovereignty and political control over the West Bank, Jordan would prevent the creation of a Palestinian state, keep its own armed forces out, and perhaps even allow Israel to unofficially retain some military bases of its own in the area.[26] The Jerusalem issue, highly important for symbolic and religious reasons to both Israel and the Muslim world, would be resolved by a compromise based on shared sovereignty, with Israel establishing its capital in West Jerusalem, Jordan in East Jerusalem.[27]

However, Israel rejected these proposals. Even the Labor government of Golda Meir, which did not claim all of the West Bank for ideological reasons, refused to recognize complete Jordanian sovereignty in the area, especially over East Jerusalem, and insisted on the permanent retention of Israeli military bases and para-military settlements in the Jordan River valley and the mountain passes—by right, rather than by the kind of leasing or unofficial agreement suggested by Hussein.[28]

The "Jordanian option" was available to Israel until 1984, when Hussein was forced to relinquish Hashemite claims in favor of the Palestinians. Given Abdullah and Hussein's willingness to agree to formal peace with Israel, the demilitarization of the West Bank, and the probable continuation in some form of Israeli bases, it is clear that Israel's repeated rejections of this path owed little or nothing to genuine security concerns, especially by comparison with the security problems created by rule over an occupied, rebellious people. The real obstacle to such a solution has been the ideologically motivated Israeli insistence on its full control over, and rights of unlimited Jewish settlement in, "Judea and Samaria," including all of Jerusalem.

Peace with Egypt

Flapan and Shlaim argue that Egyptian participation in the 1948 war might have been avoided if Ben-Gurion had been willing to explore Egyptian overtures; even during the war Ben-Gurion continued to ignore Egyptian peace feelers.[29] On the contrary, Israel engaged in various military provocations in order to provide pretexts for its armed forces to seize the Negev, Gaza, and parts if not all of the Sinai, until international pressures and warnings forced Israel to withdraw from the latter areas.[30] Immediately after the war, Israel ignored Egyptian signals that it would negotiate a political settlement if Israel consented to Egyptian control over Gaza and withdrew from the Arab areas of Palestine and parts of the Negev seized by Israel but not assigned to it by the UN plan.[31]

Even after the overthrow of the Egyptian monarchy and its replacement by the revolutionary government of Nasser, opportunities for peace existed. In 1954 Nasser and Sharett secretly began exploring the possibility of a peace settlement; however, the potentially promising contacts ended as a result of a series of provocative actions against Egypt ordered by Ben-Gurion and Dayan, including the Lavon Affair and major Israeli raids in Gaza.[32] Nasser then lost interest in the possibility of a political settlement, turning instead to the Soviet bloc for arms and a military option.

Immediately following the 1967 war Israel offered to return a demilitarized Sinai to Egypt (as well as the Golan to Syria—though not the West Bank to Jordan) in exchange for a peace settlement. Egypt missed its own opportunities by initially insisting on an unconditional Israeli withdrawal, which in turn led Israel to withdraw its offer. However, by 1969 or 1970 at the latest, following the "War of Attrition," Nasser changed his mind, saying publicly that there could be a durable peace between Egypt and Israel if Israel evacuated the occupied territories. In 1971 Nasser publicly accepted UN Resolution 242, the UN Jarring Plan, and the U.S. Rogers Plan, all of which required the end of the state of war, security guarantees to Israel, and free navigation for Israeli ships through Egyptian-held waterways.

Israel refused all these potential settlements and ignored the Egyptian overtures by Nasser and then Sadat. Sadat then concluded that he had no choice but to break the political deadlock by a limited war in 1973, and that war did indeed initiate a chain of events culminating in the 1979 Egyptian-Israeli peace settlement. However, it is probable that essentially the same settlement could have been reached almost a decade earlier, without war.

Peace with Syria

Syria has widely been considered the most fanatically rejectionist Arab front-line state, but once again the reality is considerably more complex. In 1949 and again in 1952 there were important Syrian peace feelers toward Israel, in which Syria proposed a full peace agreement under which it would absorb up to 350,000 of the Palestinian refugees, in return for water and fishing rights in the Sea of Galilee and other, more minor border changes. The Syrian prime minister, Husnei Zaim, proposed direct meetings with Ben-Gurion to negotiate on the basis of these remarkable proposals, but Ben-Gurion refused even to discuss the matter, essentially because he felt that the price—territory for peace—was too high.[33]

The growing conflict with Syria that culminated in the 1967 war was fueled not only by Israel's refusal to discuss peace on the basis of compromise, but also by a number of unilateral and provocative actions, including the diversion of the headwaters of the Jordan River (which supplied water to Syria as well as Israel) and the carrying out of a number of para-military, agricultural, and other development projects in land owned by Syrian farmers, inside disputed or demilitarized zones along the Syrian-Israeli border.[34] Syria responded to these actions by shelling Israeli settlements and increasing its support for Palestinian guerrilla raids against Israel. The escalating series of clashes in the area culminated in the 1967 war and the Israeli seizure of the Golan Heights.

If Israel had taken advantage of the opportunities for reaching a settlement with Syria in the first few years after the 1948 war, had refrained from provocative actions along the border with Syria in the 1964 to 1967 period, and had not seized the Golan Heights in the 1967 war, it might have had peace with Syria. The chances for a Syrian-Israeli peace settlement obviously diminished after Hafez Assad took power in Syria in the late 1960s, but contrary to the common image it is far from clear that Assad has been rigidly opposed to any compromise with Israel. During the 1970s Assad privately told Kissinger and later Carter that he accepted UN 242 and was ready for peace if Israel withdrew from the Golan and "restored the rights of the Palestinians." In return, Assad indicated he would accept the demilitarization of the Golan, and would consider Palestinian rights to be restored by some form of Jordanian control over the West Bank, rather than by the creation of a Palestinian state.[35]

Syria's position has further moderated in the last few years, following the end of Soviet support for militant policies, the collapse of the Soviet Union, and the emergence of the United States as the dominant power in the Middle East since the Gulf War. It is now publicly stated Syrian policy that it will agree to a "land for peace" settlement with Israel, including the demilitarization of a Golan Heights restored to Syrian sovereignty and political control.[36]

Peace with the Palestinians

Israel might have averted a conflict with the Palestinians and therefore with the Arab world generally, by either of two courses. The best way, both in terms of moral justice and, probably, long-term peace and stability, would have been to have accepted an independent Palestinian state in the West Bank and the internationalization of Jerusalem, as was envisaged by the 1947 UN Partition. The second best solution, as discussed above, was the "Jordanian solution."

From the 1950s through the 1970s Israel's refusal to repatriate the Palestinian refugees, to allow the creation of a Palestinian state, or even to agree to Jordanian control of the West Bank and Gaza resulted in the radicalization of Palestinian nationalism and the emergence of the PLO as the dominant Palestinian organization. In its early years the PLO insisted on the complete "liberation" of all of Palestine and resorted to guerrilla warfare and outright terrorism to achieve this goal. However, by the late 1970s this rejectionist position began giving way—albeit ambiguously, inconsistently and tentatively—to a willingness to seek a diplomatic solution based on compromise with Israel.[37] The gradual evolution of the PLO's position continued throughout the 1980s, until its official decision in late 1988 to accept partition and a two-state solution as the definitive settlement of its claims to Palestine. According to explicitly articulated and authoritative PLO statements, a Palestinian state in the West Bank and Gaza would agree to remain largely demilitarized, to have international peace-keeping forces along its borders to ensure demilitarization and peace, to end terrorism and all forms of attack on Israel from its territory, to enter into some kind of confederal arrangement with Jordan while refraining from alliances with Arab rejectionist states, and in all probability to agree to a settlement of the refugee problem on the basis of a token return to Israel, combined with large-scale international economic compensation for resettlement of the great majority of refugees in Arab lands.[38]

Thus, perhaps as early as the late 1970s, and certainly since 1988, Israel could have reached a just settlement of its conflict with the Palestinians by agreeing to an independent but demilitarized Palestinian state, one that could not plausibly threaten Israeli security.[39] The primary obstacle to such a settlement has been neither Palestinian rejectionism nor legitimate Israeli security concerns, but rather Israeli intransigence, rooted in nationalist, religious, and ideological maximalism.

Conclusion

The implications of Israeli historical revisionism are profound: the myths of Israeli innocence and a fanatical and unavoidable Arab/Palestinian determination to destroy Israel are no longer intellectually respectable, however much they still grip Israeli politicians and public opinion. Zionism and Israel inflicted a number of grievous injustices on the Arab inhabitants of Palestine, and set in motion a chain of events that created the ongoing Arab-Israeli conflict. Blinded by Zionist ideology and the genuine history of Jewish victimization, the Israelis have largely been ignorant of the true history of the Arab-Israeli conflict. Most importantly, throughout the long history of this conflict there have been a number of opportunities in which the conflict might have been settled if Israel no less than the Palestinians and the Arab states had been willing to accept reasonable compromises on the four crucial issues of the conflict: a permanent partition of the historical land of Palestine, Palestinian independence and sovereignty in their allotted land, a partial return of Palestinian refugees to their homes and villages in Israel, and the return of most of the lands captured from the Arab states in the various wars in exchange for genuine peace.

The psychological prerequisite for an Arab-Israeli political settlement is an acceptance by Israelis that their past behavior requires (in both a moral and pragmatic sense) that they must genuinely compromise today, especially with the Palestinians. Or, to put it differently, if the Israelis better understood their own history, free of the distortions and myths that have blinded them, they would be less self-righteous and more prone to compromise: facing their past will help Israelis face their future.

Notes

1. The major Israeli works include Uri Bar-Joseph, *The Best of Enemies: Israel and Transjordan in the War of 1948* (London:

Frank Cass and Co., 1987); Michael Bar-Zohar, *Facing a Cruel Mirror* (New York: Charles Scribners Sons, 1990); Simha Flapan, *Zionism and the Palestinians* (New York: Barnes and Nobel, 1979); Flapan, *The Birth of Israel* (New York: Pantheon Press, 1987); Yossi Melman and Dan Raviv, *Beyond the Uprising* (New York: Greenwood Press, 1989); Benny Morris, *The Birth of the Palestinian Refugee Problem* (New York: Cambridge University Press, 1987); Ilan Pappe, *Britain and the Arab-Israeli Conflict, 1948–51* (London: Macmillan Press, 1988); Livia Rokach, *Israel's Sacred Terrorism* (Belmont, Mass.: Association of Arab-American University Graduates, 1980); Tom Segev, *1949: The First Israelis* (New York: Free Press, 1986); Gershon Shafir, *Land, Labor and the Origins of the Israeli Palestinian Conflict* (Cambridge: Cambridge University Press, 1989); Shafir, "Ideological Politics or the Politics of Demography," in Ian S. Lustick and Barry Rubin, eds., *Critical Essays on Israeli Society, Politics and Culture* (Albany: SUNY Press, 1991); and Avi Shlaim, *Collusion Across the Jordan* (New York: Columbia University Press, 1988).

Non-Israeli revisionist works include Deborah J. Gerner, *One Land, Two Peoples* (Boulder: Westview Press, 1991); Steven Heydemann, "Revisionism and Reconstruction of Israeli History," in Lustick and Rubin, *Critical Essays*; David Hirst, *The Gun and the Olive Branch* (London: I. B. Tauris, 1988); Michael Palumbo, *The Palestinian Catastrophe* (London: Faber and Faber, 1987); Cheryl A. Rubenberg, *Israel and the American National Interest* (Champaign: University of Illinois Press, 1986); and Patrick Seale, *Asad of Syria* (London: I. B. Tauris, 1988).

2. Heydemann, pp. 6–7.

3. J. Bowyer Bell, *Terror Out of Zion* (Dublin: Academy Press, 1979); Flapan, *Birth*, p. 95; Hirst, p. 124; Conor Cruise O'Brien, *The Siege: The Saga of Israel and Zionism* (New York: Simon and Schuster, 1986), especially p. 233; Palumbo, passim.

4. For detailed descriptions of this policy, see Michael J. Cohen, *Palestine and the Great Powers* (Princeton University Press, 1983), pp. 307–309; Hirst, pp. 181–83; Rokach, passim; Rubenberg, pps. 56–57; Avner Yaniv, *Dilemmas of Security* (New York: Oxford University Press, 1987), p. 94.

5. These activities have been repeatedly reported in the Israeli press, even in a 1991 television documentary.

6. A map of the proposed state is included in Flapan, *Birth*, p. 16.

7. Flapan, *Zionism*, p. 144; Shlaim, p. 46.

8. Ben-Gurion's correspondence is cited by Bar-Zohar, p. 16, O'Brien, p. 230, and Palumbo, p. 32.

The Significance of Israeli Historical Revisionism

9. Executive Proceedings of the Central Zionist Agency, cited by Morris, p. 24, and Palumbo, p. 32.

10. Quoted by Palumbo, p. 183 and Segev, p. 6.

11. On the original plans in the 1948 war and the reasons for their abandonment, see Bar-Joseph, pp. 115–18, and a private letter of Ben-Gurion to his friend, Dr. S. Gross, published in the Israeli newspaper *Ha'aretz.*, March 23, 1962, cited by Segev, p. 14.

12. On the Israeli invasion and the withdrawal under severe British and American threats, see John and David Kimche, *Both Sides of the Hill* (London: Secker and Warburg, 1960), p. 260; Pappe; Segev, p. 31.

13. Bar-Zohar, p. 18.

14. The entries from Sharett's diary are on pps. 19–29 of Rokach; see also Segev's citations from Ben-Gurion's diaries, p. 10.

15. Quoted by Melman and Raviv, *Beyond the Uprising;* Press, 1989; p. 53, see also Flapan, *Birth*, p. 51.

16. Rokach, p. 6.

17. Described in Flapan, *Birth*, pp. 50–51. Flapan quotes from Sharett's diary: "I have learned that the state of Israel cannot be ruled in our generation without deceit and adventurism."

18. Rokach, quoting from Sharett's diary entry of January 31, 1954, p. 19. Sharett considered this plan to be part of "the long chain of false incidents and hostilities we have invited, and of the many clashes we have provoked" (p. 6).

19. Flapan, *Birth*, pp. 72–73.

20. Flapan, *Zionism*, p. 285. Flapan later wrote that the evidence that the dominant Palestinian desire was to compromise and avoid war "is so overwhelming that the question arises how the myth of a Palestinian jihad against the Jews could survive so long" (*Birth*, pp. 72–73). Heydemann observes that both Morris and Shlaim also "provide graphic evidence of the way in which efforts at accommodation . . . with local Palestinians were consistently rebuffed by Ben-Gurion" (pp. 13–14).

21. Pappe, pps. ix–xii. This will be discussed in greater detail below.

22. See Flapan, Pappe, and Palumbo for discussions of these and other inter-Arab rivalries as a leading cause of the Arab invasion.

23. This paraphrases Shlaim's conclusions; see especially p. 488.

24. At one point, Israel proposed to absorb 100,000 of the 700,000 refugees, but it soon so hedged and qualified even this offer that it became evident that its real position was no return (Segev, p. 33).

25. Palumbo, pp. 187–89.

26. "The Germans have a military base in Spain. If you agree in principle to restore our sovereignty over the West Bank, including Jerusalem, we could discuss your request later. But first you must agree to the principle." From a transcript of a secret meeting between Hussein and Golda Meir in January 1974, printed in the *Jerusalem Post*, 12 October 1991. For other discussions of the secret meetings and Hussein's willingness to compromise on the security issues, see Henry Kissinger's diplomatic memoir, *Years of Upheaval* (Boston: Little, Brown, 1982), p. 847, and Melman and Raviv, pp. 119–25.

27. The long history of secret meetings and the various territory-for-peace proposals are discussed in Bar-Zohar, pp. 44–45; Michael Brecher, *Decisions in Israel's Foreign Policy* (New York: Oxford University Press, 1974), pp. 484–85; and Melman and Raviv, passim.

28. On Israel's policy in this period, see Yael Yishai, *Land or Peace* (Stanford, Calif.: Hoover Institution Press, 1987), pp. 67–71.

29. Flapan writes: "It is beyond doubt that from November 1947 until 11 May 1948, the Egyptian authorities initiated no steps to prepare for war and staked everything on a last-minute diplomatic solution" (*Zionism*, p. 341). For details on the Egyptian peace feelers, see Shlaim, pp. 312–18.

30. Pappe, pp. 61–63; Shlaim, pp. 320–21.

31. Shlaim, p. 347.

32. In the early 1950s Israel created a spy ring in Egypt, which in July 1954 undertook a campaign of terrorist bombings of British installations in Egypt, designed to look like the work of Egyptian fanatics. However, the Egyptians broke the spy ring and brought the group to trial.

The purpose of the Mossad plot was both to disrupt British and American ties with Nasser and to block the secret Sharett-Nasser negotiations—which they did. Sharett recorded in his diary his bitterness over these Israeli "acts of madness," which evidently were authorized by Moshe Dayan and the hard-line Defense Minister Lavon.

For details on the Lavon Affair, see Stephen Green, *Taking Sides* (New York: William Morrow and Co., 1984), which includes the full text of a 1961 secret report on the matter, from CIA Director Allen Dulles to President Kennedy.

33. On the Zaim offer see especially Segev, pp. 16–18, and an article by Benny Morris based on revelations of the Zaim offer reported by General Arye Shalev, an Israeli delegate to the Syrian-Israeli armistice talks of 1949, in the *Jerusalem Post*, International Ed., 9 December 1989. Brief mentions of the 1949 to 1952 Syrian offers can also be found in Bar-Joseph, p. 245 and Palumbo, p. 182.

The Significance of Israeli Historical Revisionism 199

34. On the Israeli actions that served to escalate the conflict with Syria, see Avner Yaniv, "Syria and Israel: The Politics of Escalation," in Moshe Maoz and Avner Yaniv, eds., *Syria Under Assad* (New York: St. Martin's Press, 1986).

35. On Assad's position in the 1970s, see William Quandt, *Camp David* (Washington, D.C.: Brookings Institution, 1986), p. 57 and Seale, pp. 250–55, 296. In their diplomatic memoirs, Henry Kissinger, Zbigniew Brzezinski, Jimmy Carter, and Cyrus Vance all speak surprisingly well of Assad, regarding him as intelligent, flexible, and realistic, ready to come to grips with the necessity of an Arab-Israeli settlement.

36. *Jerusalem Report*, 31 October 1991; Milton Viorst, "Report from Madrid," *New Yorker*, 9 December 1991; *New York Times*, 12 December 1991.

37. For evidence of the changing PLO position in the 1970s, see Herbert C. Kelman, "Talk with Arafat," *Foreign Policy* 49 (Winter 1982–83); Walid Khalidi, "A Sovereign Palestinian State," *Foreign Affairs* 56, no. 4 (July 1978); John Edwin Mroz, *Beyond Security: Private Perceptions Among Arabs and Israelis* (New York: Pergamon Press, 1980); Edwin R. F. Sheehan, "Step-By-Step in the Middle East," *Foreign Policy* 22 (Spring 1976); Yaniv, *Dilemmas of Security*.

38. See the Israeli news magazine, *New Outlook*, March/April 1989, for interviews with leading PLO officials in which this position is articulated, and especially the enormously important article by Salah Khalaf (Abu Iyad), "Lowering the Sword," *Foreign Policy* 78 (Spring, 1990). Until he was assassinated in late 1990 (probably by the Iraqi secret police, for opposing Iraq's invasion of Kuwait), Abu Iyad was regarded as second only to Arafat in the PLO leadership structure.

This position has recently been confirmed by Faisal Hussaini, widely regarded as the leading PLO figure in the West Bank:

> "I can fully understand why the Israelis say they are afraid that if we have a state, it will endanger their security. So let us sit at the table and agree on conditions to ensure that the Palestinian state will not be dangerous. Let us talk frankly, and see. For example: If they are afraid of an army, I don't want an army. Why have an army?"

Interview with Hussaini, *Jerusalem Report*, 12 December 1991, p. 13.

39. For a full discussion of how a Palestinian state could be reconciled with Israeli security, see Jerome Slater, "A Palestinian State and Israeli Security," *Political Science Quarterly* 106, no. 3 (Fall 1991).

The Utopian Crisis of the Israeli State

Yagil Levy and Yoav Peled

Dan Horowitz and Moshe Lissak, *Trouble in Utopia: The Overburdened Polity of Israel*, Albany: State University of New York Press, 1989.

Baruch Kimmerling, ed., *The Israeli State and Society: Boundaries and Frontiers*, Albany: State University of New York Press, 1989.

Peter Y. Medding, *The Founding of Israeli Democracy, 1948–1967*, New York and Oxford: Oxford University Press, 1990.

Since the Lebanon War, political-sociological discourse in Israel has been increasingly focused on the crisis of the Israeli state. Israeli political sociologists, virtually all of whom belong to the left-liberal camp of Israeli politics, have been grappling with the seeming inability of the state to deal effectively with the problem of the occupied territories. The Six Day War itself, previously celebrated as a great achievement, has now come to be seen as inaugurating the country's fall from grace. Two further points marking this decline are thought to be the Yom Kippur War of 1973 and Likud's assumption of power in 1977.

This sense of deep disillusionment generally characterizes the three volumes under review as well. Although Peter Medding does not deal with the consequences of the Six Day War, he considers it the endpoint of the country's founding period and an important turning point in the course of its development. Horowitz and Lissak focus on the period following that war, and consider the Israeli polity to be "overburdened" by the forces unleashed by its consequences. These concerns are shared by most writers in the volume edited by Kimmerling as well.

The fact that two of the three volumes focus on two consecutive periods separated by the Six Day War—1948 to 1967 in Medding's case, and the post-1967 period in Horowitz/Lissak's— provides us with the opportunity to consider critically the way in which the war has figured in sociological and political discussions in Israel. This examination will then serve as a basis for suggesting an alternative way of conceptualizing the place that war has occupied in Israeli history. Our alternative conceptualization will consider the Six Day War as an integral part of the Arab-Israeli conflict, a conflict which, in turn, will be viewed as constitutive of the Israeli social-political order.

Israeli Political Sociology

The three volumes, especially the ones by Medding and by Horowitz/Lissak, are embedded in the dominant, functionalist discourse within Israeli sociology. The functionalist school, as is well known, has a systemic view of society, seeing it as a composite of specialized roles, each contributing its share to the proper functioning of the whole. The most important regulatory mechanism of the social order, in the functionalist view, is a consensual culture which synchronizes individual interests with society's needs. The existing social order is the starting point of functionalist analysis, while this order itself is not usually questioned.

A key element in the functionalist view of society is the universal character of the state. The state (usually referred to as the "polity" or "political system") is viewed as standing above the fray of civil society, entrusted with regulating, through its rational and "neutral" (Medding 1990: 9, 11) bureaucracies, the competition between the various social interests.

The functionalist school has been the keystone of Israeli social science since the early 1950s. It has inspired the prolific work of S. N. Eisenstadt and his Hebrew University colleagues, who have developed a broad analytic perspective for the examination of Israeli society. The centerpiece of this perspective is the socialist-Zionist consensus forged by the Labor movement. Through this consensus Eisenstadt has sought to explain the evolution of Israel's institutional patterns, their successful functioning in the face of enormous challenges, and the debilitating stress they have come under since 1967.[1] Eisenstadt's heavy footprints are clearly visible in the three volumes, especially the ones by Medding and by Horowitz and Lissak.

Medding's analysis of Israel's founding period—1948–1967— is organized around an effort to characterize Israeli democracy, in Arend Lijphart's terms, as either "majoritarian" or "consensual." A majoritarian democracy is one where power is concentrated in few governmental institutions; a consensual one is where power is more dispersed. Israeli democracy, Medding argues, had been moving gradually from the majoritarian to the consensual type between 1948 and 1967 (pp. 5–7).

The central issue in Medding's discussion is *mamlakhtiyut*, a state-building strategy designed to supplant the factionalism of the Yishuv period with universalist values and institutions. Under the banner of *mamlakhtiyut* the state successfully nationalized such key areas of social activity as the armed forces, education, the civil service and employment services. It failed, however, in its efforts to nationalize the health services (provided, to this day, mostly by the Histadrut), and reform the electoral system, which has encouraged factionalism. The structural tension between state interests and those of political parties, including the ruling party, Mapai, is what prevented political power from being completely concentrated in the hands of the state, even under Ben-Gurion. After his demise, this tension has operated to increasingly disperse political power, thus democratizing the state.

In the best tradition of mainstream Israeli sociology, Medding analyzes *Israeli-Jewish* society under the heading of *Israeli* society (cf. Kimmerling 1989: 270).[2] To appreciate this fact, one needs only to compare his efforts at characterizing Israeli democracy with those of another scholar, Sammy Smooha, who is cognizant of the existence of Arab citizens in the Jewish state. From the perspective of its Arab citizens, Israeli democracy can be characterized as anything but consensual. The choices posited by Smooha,[3] therefore, are majoritarian, ethnic, and *herrenvolk* democracy (he opts for ethnic).[4] But if the central organizing ideology of Israeli society is conceived of as socialist-Zionism, then clearly Arabs can only figure in the analysis as an issue to be dealt with, not as a constitutive element of the social system itself.

Trouble in Utopia is a sequel volume to Horowitz and Lissak's highly acclaimed and widely cited *Origins of the Israeli Polity: Palestine Under the Mandate* (1978). The later volume deals with the post-1967 period, a period in which the Israeli polity, the authors claim, has been overburdened by fundamental value disagreements in the society. Not least among these disagreements has been the one over the very boundaries of the collectivity.

Horowitz and Lissak's theoretical assumptions are informed by Edward Shils' distinction between center and periphery (pp. 20–24). They conceive of the center, long dominated by the Labor-Zionist establishment, as responsible for mobilizing both material and motivational resources for the accomplishment of societal goals. Conversely, the center is subjected to various demands by the different social sectors, and its ability to maintain social integration depends on the degree to which it can satisfy those demands. As long as the society was characterized by consensus over the most basic values, the center could use this consensus to mitigate conflicting demands. This ability has been seriously impaired, however, by the opening up of the Pandora box of dissensus as a result of the Six Day War. Thus the war has led to policy paralysis over the most crucial issues facing the society, and eventually to the downfall of Labor.

The connection between the crisis of the state and the blurring of its boundaries is the guiding thread of Kimmerling's volume as well. We will now focus on Kimmerling's own concluding essay, which summarizes the book's discussion (pp. 265–84), and will turn to other entries in the volume later on.

The main organizing concept of Kimmerling's concluding essay is "control system," a territorial unit which includes several subcollectivities held together by civilian and military bureaucracies and other coercive forces. A control system is created when political power is extended beyond the bounds of legitimate authority, that is, in situations of military occupation. It is distinguished from other types of political systems by its inherent inability to forge a value consensus. Thus the control system is characterized by instrumental power orientation towards the subject groups within it (pp. 266–267).

The complexity of the control system stems from the intermixing of boundaries and frontiers in the relationships between its various collectivities. In Kimmerling's definition, boundaries "separate an entity from 'external elements' which are defined by the boundaries themselves and constitute a necessary condition for the maintenance of a given collectivity's 'internally oriented' identity" (p. 267). "Frontier," on the other hand, is a much more flexible, permeable, open-ended notion, which signifies active interaction and mutual determination between two entities, as well as the possibility of the extension of one into the other, one's replacement by the other, or the total merger of the two.

The common denominator shared by our four authors is their paradigmatic attachment to the functionalist approach. They all take as their starting point the existence of the pre-1967 Israeli social order, constituted by a consensual cultural-ideological framework. For Medding, this framework is *mamlakhtiyut* which subsumes within itself the values of *chalutziyut* but extends them to the entire society. For Horowitz and Lissak the core cultural consensus is also the Zionist ideology, while for Kimmerling it is the Zionist definition of the boundaries of the Israeli collectivity. None of the four authors raises any questions about the pre-1967 social order itself or tries to search for the roots of the 1967 war in that social order.

Furthermore, the way all four authors seek to explain the crisis of the Israeli state is through a discrepancy between normative commitments and contradictory social practices. In Medding's case it is the discrepancy between the universalism preached by *mamlakhtiyut* and partisan particularism. For Horowitz/Lissak the tension is between the integrative function of the political center and its resource allocation function, in view of the excessive demands placed on the center by particular interests since 1967. For Kimmerling the basic problem is the transformation of the agreed-upon boundaries of the collectivity into open frontiers.

The common attachment of these authors to the functionalist paradigm can be further illustrated by their conception of the Six Day War in relation to the Arab-Israeli conflict and to the construction of the Israeli social order. We will now turn to an examination of this point.

Functionalist Discourse and the Arab-Israeli Conflict

As we have noted, all three volumes reviewed in this chapter view the Six Day War as the major turning point in the history of Israel. The import of this view of the war can be fully appreciated only in the context of the functionalist conception of the wider Arab-Israeli conflict.

Medding's book ends with the outbreak of the Six Day War. This event marks, in his view, the endpoint of the founding period of Israeli democracy, as well as a turning point in its evolution. The turning point has to do with the inability of the Labor movement, since 1967, to set the national agenda, that is, to continue to function as the country's dominant political party (pp. 226–229). Thus Medding sees the war as a sudden break in the evolutionary process whereby Israeli democracy had been turning from a majoritarian to a consensual one. Needless to say, he does not even raise the possibility of the war itself being in any way connected to the political processes he is describing in the book.

This *deus ex machina* view of the Six Day War characterizes our other authors as well. None of them consider the war as the possible outcome of earlier developments in the Israeli social system. This is true even for Michael Shalev, a non-functionalist writer who analyzes, in an article in the Kimmerling volume, the strategy used by the Histadrut, since the 1920s, to separate Jewish and Arab workers in the labor market. Shalev differs from most other authors in the three volumes in that he conceptualizes the Arab-Israeli conflict as a major constitutive element in the structuring of the Israeli social order. For the exclusionary strategies employed by the Histadrut towards Arab workers have had profound implications for the *Jewish* labor market as well. Moreover, Shalev's analysis points to the continuation, as well as the changes, in these exclusionary practices, thus undermining the conception of the Six Day War as marking a completely new era in the development of Israeli society. Still, even Shalev treats "Israel's conquest of former Jordanian and Egyptian territory in June 1967" (p. 115) as a disconnected event, without raising the possibility that this conquest may have had something to do with the labor market practices he is describing.

The view of the Six Day War as an abrupt break in the normal evolution of Israeli society meshes well with the general functionalist conception of continuity and change in the social system. Kimmerling has pointed out that all societies are characterized by simultaneous processes of continuity and change. Identifying these processes and deciding which ones are important enough to merit scholarly attention involves what Kimmerling has called "framework decisions." These decisions stem, among other things, from the observer's conception of the identity of the collectivity under study. (Kimmerling himself determined, in a 1992 article, that 1967 was a "break" in Israeli history.)[5]

Following Kimmerling's observation, it may be argued that there is a profound difference in the ways in which continuity and change are conceptualized in conservative and critical (or order and conflict) approaches to the study of politics. Conservative approaches are concerned with the elements which lend the social order the systemic balance required for its continued functioning. Thus functionalist scholars tend to look for regulatory mechanisms, like a consensual culture. Moreover, the political-pluralist bias of functionalism, which results in large measure from its behavioral methodological bias, causes functionalist scholars to have an exaggerated view of changes in patterns of ideological legitimation and political participation, as signifying systemic changes in the social order itself.

Critically oriented scholars, on the other hand, recognize the crisis potential inherent in the social order, which they conceptualize as conflict-ridden. They view the conflict-regulating mechanisms employed by the state as strategies of domination by privileged social groups, designed specifically to blunt this crisis potential. Purely political changes are not viewed by critical scholars as signifying social transformations, unless they accompany structural changes in the social order itself. Thus we have a paradoxical situation in which conservative observers are quick to identify turning points and radical change, while more critical observers tend to see continuity even in processes of apparent change.

This paradox is reproduced, albeit one-sidedly, in the Israeli sociological discourse as well. Functionalist-oriented scholars have seen the Six Day War as a turning point, since it inaugurated changes in the legitimational discourse, in patterns of political participation, in the manifestations of social cleavages, and so forth. However, critical scholars (admittedly a very recent phenomenon on the Israeli academic scene) have so far failed to challenge this accepted truth. To do that, they would have to engage in a critical structural analysis of Israeli society, an analysis that would view the war as rooted in the very foundations of the Israeli social-political order. We will make some suggestions towards an outline of such an analysis later on. But before we do that, we still need to examine the role played by the Arab-Israeli conflict in the functionalist view of Israeli society.

What Israelis usually refer to as "the conflict" is viewed by functionalist scholars as essentially *external* to the Israeli social-political order. The conflict is rooted, they believe, in regional international circumstances encountered by the Zionist project, both before and after 1948. Thus they have never undertaken an etiological study of the conflict, which would examine its development *in conjunction with* the evolution of the Israeli social order, and the mutual *conditioning* of the two. Rather, what functionalist research has done is look for the *effects* of the conflict on Israeli society, which is seen as only reacting to it as an external force.[6]

This analytic failure calls for an explanation, especially since most functionalist writers in Israel belong to the left-liberal camp and believe that it is within Israel's powers to end the Arab-Israeli conflict. Several alternative explanations of this failure might be possible.

One explanation would stem from Yonathan Shapiro's critique of Israeli functionalism. In his own writings Shapiro has analyzed the role of socialist-Zionist ideology in legitimating an unequal political division of labor, which resulted in the disempowerment of various groups in the society.[7] Shapiro thus contributed more than anyone before him to the presentation of a real alternative to the functionalist school. Functionalist writers, he has argued, have tended to adopt the self-image of the ruling elite and to internalize it into the academic discourse. A striking example of this process (not mentioned by Shapiro) would be Eisenstadt's famous distinction between "*oleh*" and "immigrant." This distinction reflected the self-image of the Ashkenazi immigrant workers of the Second Aliyah, who had viewed themselves as "idealistic," and the Yemenite immigrants as "natural," workers.[8] More broadly, as pointed out by Shapiro, Israeli sociology has adopted uncritically the ethos of the *chalutz* and the Labor elite's ideological presentation of Israeli democracy.[9] In a similar vein, it might be argued that the prevailing ideological images of Israel's security situation, such as "society under siege," have also found their way into the academic conceptions of the Arab-Israeli conflict.

Another explanation for the failure of Israeli sociologists to tackle critically the Arab-Israeli conflict, is offered by one of Shapiro's students, Uri Ben-Eliezer. He has argued, following Eisenstadt's own self-criticism of the functionalist school, that Israeli functionalists have taken Israel's belligerent existence as given. They have, therefore, analyzed the institutional arrangements constituted by this reality as functionally dependent on the state of war, rather than as potentially contributing to it or reinforcing it in a dialectical manner.[10]

A further development of this argument may be to point out that functionalist analysis in general has had a great deal of difficulty in conceptualizing direct interactions between subunits within the social system and "exogenous forces" such as international conflict. To paraphrase a famous saying, in the functionalist conception, politics stop at the system's edge.[11] The reasons for this analytic limitation are the centrality of cultural analysis in the functionalist paradigm, its behavioral methodological bias, and its conservative point of view. Thus, functionalists can point to the aggravation of international conflicts through the explicit political discourse prevalent in the societies involved. This has been done, for example, by Gad Barzilai in a recent book on Israel.[12] However, functionalists cannot identify the many nonexplicit ways in which war, and conflict in general, can and do take part in the structuring and maintenance of the social order itself.

Recognizing the possibility, that war and international conflict may have a role to play in the constitution and preservation of the social order, would also run in the face of a number of functionalist assumptions about liberal democratic societies. A universalist state as envisaged in functionalist theory could not possibly manipulate violent conflicts to further its own ends vis-à-vis other social units; it could not engage in a force-oriented discourse in order to discourage

The Utopian Crisis of the Israeli State

political participation; and it could not employ the military for internal political ends. When such things are discovered to have happened, they are invariably attributed to the personal failings of politicians, not to the structural requirements of the system itself.[13]

These shortcomings of functionalist analysis are clearly evident in the Israeli sociological discourse. Even Kimmerling, who has pushed the boundaries of functionalist analysis farther than any other Israeli sociologist, is still confined within the traditional view. He has shown the influence of the Arab-Israeli conflict on the structuring of power mechanisms in the society, both before and after 1948, in light of the need to manage the conflict at the lowest possible cost.[14] However, he has never tried to reverse the path of his analysis, and consider the possible influence of these power mechanisms themselves on the manner in which the conflict has been managed. Nor has he questioned the universalism of the political center, or inquired whether different social groups may have benefited differentially from the accumulation of power in the hands of the state.

In sum, the adherence of mainstream Israeli sociology to the functionalist approach has resulted in a failure to explain the continuation of the Arab-Israeli conflict for over a century. Aside from blaming it completely on the Arabs or, since 1977, on the ideological failings of Likud, Israeli sociologists have had precious little to say about the perseverance of the conflict. By the same token, they have been unable to consider the periodic outbreaks of open military hostilities as anything other than unexpected disruptions of the routine of social life (consider the title of one of Kimmerling's books, *The Interrupted System*).[15]

Thus, the conceptualization of the Six Day War as a watershed event, disrupting the "normal" process of state and nation building in Israel, in the studies here under review, has resulted from their functionalist predisposition. For in the functionalist approach, which does not recognize the Arab-Israeli conflict as a constitutive element of the Israeli social-political order, war cannot be seen as a product of this order. This is especially true with regard to the Six Day War, in which the preliminary belligerent moves, during the time period conventionally seen as the "eve" of that war, were initiated by the Arabs. (See Kimmerling, 1992, on periodization as a "framework decision.")[16]

If war is considered to be a break in the normal course of events, it would naturally follow that its outcome will be seen as having profound implications for the preexisting social arrangements. It is not surprising, therefore, that the Six Day War is seen as such an extraordinary event in the history of Israel. An alternative, and to our mind more realistic conception of the war, as rooted in the Israeli social order, and as signifying, like any historical phenomenon, both continuity and change, could emerge only from a non-functionalist, critical theoretical framework. Some constituting elements of such a framework have been floating in the literature on Israel for quite some time. In the final section of this chapter we will try to put these elements together and present a rudimentary outline of an alternative theory.

The Israeli Social Order and the Arab-Israeli Conflict[17]

Our theoretical endeavor begins with the assumption, articulated in American sociological discourse at least a quarter of a century ago,[18] that the systemic and functionalist conceptions of society embody strategies of domination by privileged social groups. This strategy of domination is ideological, in the original Marxist sense, in that it seeks to present the interests of dominant social groups as identical to the interests of society as a whole.

One of the central symbols manipulated for this ideological purpose is national defense (hardly a revelation to the international sociological community, but a proposition never entertained in mainstream Israeli sociology). The modern state, entrusted, as it were, with a monopoly over the legitimate use of force, is thereby given the authority to determine the collectivity's boundaries and its "national" identity as well. Since the state is identified with the ultimate social value—

The Utopian Crisis of the Israeli State 213

physical survival—it has gained priority over all other social spheres. It has also come to be seen as standing *above* all other social spheres, untainted by their particular interests. Under this universalist guise the modern state has been able to develop and penetrate into every corner of society.[19]

According to Tilly,[20] wars have played a major role in the crystallization of the modern state, and have constituted a key element in its strategy of domination. The creation of existential fears, as much as the defense against existential threats, have strengthened the capacity of the state to penetrate into civil society and gain control over its resources. Thus a dialectical relationship has developed between the legitimational and the violent aspects of state practice: each has reinforced the other and has, in turn, been reinforced by it.[21]

Violent conflict, then, has been an immanent aspect of state-building processes, not only in the third world, but in the Western world as well. And Israel is no exception: the crystallization of a Jewish political community in Palestine/Israel has proceeded hand-in-hand with the development of the Arab-Israeli conflict. The major milestones in the development of the conflict—the transition from local, sporadic altercations during the Second Aliyah to intercommunal strife in the late 1920s, and finally to international belligerency in the 1940s—have also been the major milestones in the crystallization of the Israeli social order.

A number of recent contributions to the sociological literature on Israel can be relied on to substantiate these claims, although these studies do not necessarily utilize the same theoretical conceptualization as we do here:

1. The studies by Shalev (in Kimmerling 1989), Shafir,[22] and Grinberg,[23] which deal with the political struggles of the Labor-Zionist movement to exclude Arab workers from the labor market, illuminate the interrelatedness between the accumulation of power in the hands of the Labor establishment and the intensification of the conflict between Arabs and Jews.

2. A number of Kimmerling's studies have considered the ways in which the conflict has been managed in tandem with state-building processes, such as demographic and territorial accumulation.[24] Kimmerling's arguments concerning the cost-cutting advantages of managing the two processes simultaneously, as well as their mutual conditioning, illuminate the role played by the conflict in the structuring of the political order. It is only a small step from there to our suggestion that conflict-management practices were tailored to the power needs of the emerging political structure.[25]
3. Joel Migdal, in an article in the Kimmerling volume, presents the conflict as a contributing factor to the state-building process. However, like Kimmerling, Migdal does not identify the mutual conditioning of these two processes as originating from identical goals of power accumulation.
4. Ben-Eliezer[26] deals with the transformation of the political discourse of the Yishuv into a militaristic discourse which legitimated the use of violent force for the solution of political problems. Ben-Eliezer ties this transformation, which he locates in the 1930s, to the coming of age of the first Israeli-born generation (the Palmach generation). His arguments also lend credence to the view of the pre-state Jewish political community as utilizing military means, and primarily military thought-patterns, for augmenting its control in the face of challenges from the political right.

This set of arguments does not only improve our understanding of the development of the Arab-Israeli conflict up to 1948. By including the conflict as one element in the construction of the political order, these writers enable us to have a sharper view of various political processes which have taken place in the post-1948 period as well.

Our claim here will be that just as the management of the conflict was used by the founders of Israel to reduce the costs of state building, so it continued to function for the same purpose after the establishment of the state as well. It could be argued, for example, that the state needed the conflict as a means for buttressing its own status as against civil society, in those cases where state power was challenged by various social forces seeking to reduce their dependence on the state.

In general, if state *building* is acknowledged to involve a strategy of violent conflict, and the construction of social arrangements which support the management of that conflict, there is no reason to assume that the same could not be true about state *maintenance*. The militaristic strategy involved in the maintenance stage, however, is not limited to actual military operations. It also includes discursive practices which highlight the centrality of violence in the existence of the collectivity and the role played by the state in managing that violence. It is this violence-management role which legitimates the state's expansion into more and more areas of civil society.

To illustrate this argument we will return now to the question of the Six Day War. We accept Medding's argument regarding the democratization processes which took place in the 1960s, under Levy Eshkol's premiership. Unlike Medding, however, we propose to examine this democratization through the prism of state crisis and the gradual withdrawal of the state from many of its positions in civil society. This withdrawal, we argue, was the consequence, primarily, of the Sinai campaign of 1956 and of the industrialization crisis, both of which had impaired the power of the state.

The Sinai campaign was prepared in total secrecy by Ben-Gurion and a small group of his closest advisers. Later on, these advisers, known as the *tzeirim* (young ones), tried to capitalize on the success of the war in order to increase their political power at the expense of the Mapai leadership. This generated a series of political maneuvers which spilled over into "society vs. the state" struggles. At the center of these was the Lavon Affair, a political scandal raised by the question of who had authorized the attempts to blow up British and American targets in Eygpt in 1954. Much broader issues came to be involved, however, such as the state's authority to conduct clandestine violent operations and the proper limits of this authority. In the context of this debate, Ben-Gurion's authoritarian style of leadership was questioned for the first time, and the ground was prepared for his eventual resignation in 1963. This resignation was a major milestone in the democratization process discussed by Medding (see Medding 1990: 125–31, 180–83).

This political challenge to state authority was compounded by the full-employment crisis which resulted from the country's industrialization.[27] The full-employment situation strengthened the power of workers as against the Histadrut, a de facto state institution charged with controlling the labor force (cf. Shalev, in Kimmerling 1989). This was manifested in the appearance of militant worker committees, in the secession of professionals' labor unions from the Histadrut, and even in ethnic upheaval, such as the Wadi Salib uprising by North African immigrants in 1959 (Medding 1990: 69).

The state reacted to these challenges by partially retreating from its positions in civil society. It reduced its involvement in the economy by, among other things, drastically cutting back its expenditures for public housing. This threw the country into the deepest recession in its history.[28] In addition, the military administration, imposed on the Arab citizens in 1948, was abolished in order to help satisfy the demand for labor. The state also re-legitimated the right, by allowing the remains of Jabotinsky to be interned in Israel, and adopted a number of other liberal practices.

The partial retreat of the state had the effect of restricting the ability of social groups to present it with additional burdensome demands. This was manifested especially in the economic sphere, where the state transferred many of its functions to the free market. In the realm of violent activity, the state resigned itself to the challenges presented by various groups but sought to turn those challenges from the level of state legitimacy to the level of civilian control of the military.

The Utopian Crisis of the Israeli State 217

Parallel to the retreat of the state from some of its positions in society it acted to escalate the friction between Israel and its neighbors. In 1964 Israel reacted to a Syrian military operation with a massive aerial bombardment, a first during peacetime. This was done in the context of the "war for the water," a conflict that had been going on since the 1950s over the utilization of the waters of the Jordan River.[29] In 1966 Israel launched its first daytime retaliatory operation, involving air and armored forces, against Jordan, the Samoua Operation. The escalation process reached its peak in April 1967 when the Israeli air force chased Syrian fighter planes all the way to Damascus and shot down six of them.[30] This was accompanied by a statement of the IDF chief of staff, Yitzhak Rabin, that Israel intended to bring down the Syrian regime.[31]

A few weeks after the downing of the Syrian planes the Egyptian army was deployed in the Sinai and closed down the Straits of Tiran. Israel reacted with a partial mobilization of its reserve forces, which turned within a short time, and in an almost automatic manner, into full mobilization. With the economy virtually paralyzed by this full mobilization, and under increasing pressure from the military, the Israel government decided to launch a preemptory attack against the Egyptian forces in Sinai. As a prelude to this decision, Prime Minister Levy Eshkol was replaced as minister of defense by Moshe Dayan, IDF chief of staff during the Sinai Campaign of 1956 and the dominant figure among the "activist" Mapai Young Guard.

The "necessity" of the way in which the Israeli state reacted to the crisis of May 1967 can be examined on two levels. On the more concrete level, people such as David Ben-Gurion, Moshe Hayim Shapira, and Abba Eban had argued that Israel should exhaust all political means for diffusing the crisis before launching practically irreversible military actions such as full mobilization of its forces. On a more general level, we would argue that the escalation of the conflict which had taken place since 1964 was not "necessary" in the sense of not being mandated by the Arab-Israeli conflict itself. Rather, the scope of Israel's reaction to hostile Arab actions in this period signified, as we have argued, a particular course of action adopted parallel to, and in compensation for, the partial retreat of the state from society.

In view of these developments, the Six Day War, and the continued occupation of the territories taken in that war, appear as a reaction by the state, designed to restore the balance between state and society. Medding is thus wrong, in our opinion, to view the democratization processes of the 1960s as signifying the emergence of autonomous social forces pitched against the state, and the evolution of Israeli society into something resembling the pluralist-functionalist model. In actual fact, these processes signified a partial *tactical* retreat of the state, and of social groups associated with it, in the face of challenges mounted by other groups in society. This retreat was soon reversed by the Six Day War and its consequences.

Our argument cannot be corroborated by empirical evidence at this juncture, for two reasons. First, such an effort would involve a redefinition of the period considered to be leading up to the war, a task which would require much more space than is available to us in this chapter. Second, much of the relevant information is still classified, and is likely to remain so for many years to come, at least on the Israeli side. However, our view of the war is supported by the structural analysis we have presented so far, and by the behavior of the state during the time period which ensued, up to the fall of Labor in 1977.

In the period immediately following the war the state moved in with gusto to recapture the positions it had abandoned in civil society. The incorporation of the occupied territories into the Israeli economy created a sizable market under the complete control of the state. By adopting the right fiscal and labor market policies, the state was able to use this market in order to both end the recession and discipline the Jewish work force. The latter task was achieved through the infusion of large numbers of underpaid, unorganized Palestinian workers into the Israeli labor market (Shalev, in Kimmerling 1989). In addition, the rebuilding of the military after the war, which included not only refurnishing it with war materiel, but doubling it in size as well, generated a great deal of state-controlled economic activity. Other aspects of the reassertion of state power were the slowing down of the liberalizing processes which had taken place before the war, and especially the renewal of territorial expansion, this time, of course, into the newly occupied territories.

An examination of settlement activity in the period 1967 to 1977 would yield interesting results regarding the transformational nature of the war and of Likud's victory in 1977. The Labor-led national unity government moved almost immediately after the war to begin settling the occupied territories. This settlement activity included not only East Jerusalem, the Golan Heights, the Jordan Valley, and parts of the Sinai, it also included settlements in heavily populated areas of the West Bank, such as Gush Etzion and Kiryat Arba, the very places where Gush Emunim would be founded after the Yom Kippur War. The motivating force behind this settlement activity was not Gahal's representatives in the government but rather the representatives of the Palmach generation—Dayan, Galili, and Alon—who enjoyed the hesitant support of Eshkol and, later on, the enthusiastic support of Golda Meir.

Moreover, the settlement activity, designed openly to create faits accomplis of Jewish presence in the territories, was done with the same methods and for the same purposes as that which had preceded the establishment of the state. It also corresponded to the territorial ambitions of the two Labor movement factions which had come now to dominate the government, Achdut HaAvodah and Rafi.

Achdut HaAvodah had never resigned itself to the territorial outcome of the 1948 war. In the early 1950s, its platform stated:

> Any partition of *Eretz Yisrael* artificially breaks the country's objective economic-settlement unity, frustrates the development possibilities of all its parts, undermines its economy, widens the gaps between the peoples residing

in the separated parts, narrows the natural area necessary for the territorial concentration of the Jewish people and harms the country's independence.[32]

The party continued to adhere to this line throughout the founding period (in Medding's terms), and after the Six Day War many of its most important leaders were among the founders of the Greater Israel Movement.[33]

As for Rafi, that party had been founded only two years before the Six Day War, with Ben-Gurion's resignation from Mapai over the Lavon Affair. Moshe Dayan, Rafi's senior representative in the cabinet since June 1967, was the architect of government policy vis-à-vis the Arabs, and the virtual single-handed ruler of the occupied territories. Dayan's position, which became Rafi's position and that of the government as well, was one which "did not deny [the idea] of Greater Israel, but did not endorse it officially either".[34]

Thus, the policy designed to keep the occupied territories under Israeli control, without incorporating them officially into the state, has shown surprising persistence under Labor, Likud, and national unity governments. In actual fact, the only discernable policy difference between Likud and Labor on the occupied territories has been Likud's intensification of settlement activity and its introduction of "quality of life" settlements. This difference can be explained by both the natural momentum gained by the settlement process itself, and by Likud's need to provide material benefits to its followers (which, in the absence of an economic structure such as the Histadrut, it had never been able to do before).

Unlike Horowitz/Lissak, who view this "no peace, no war" strategy as resulting from a political stalemate and the weakening of the political center, we would argue that this strategy represents the reassertion of state power, based on unprecedented cooperation among the dominant elites. This cooperation has manifested itself quite dramatically with the ability of the state not only to hold on to the territorial status quo, but also to undertake bold political moves such as the peace treaty with Egypt, the Lebanon war and then the disengagement from that War, and the economic stabilization plan of 1985.[35]

Even the total disinterest with which the state currently regards the economic plight of recent immigrants from the former Soviet Union is an indication not of weakness but of strength. It indicates that the state is not concerned about having to pay a political price for this policy of benign neglect. At the same time, the state continues to benefit the social groups associated with it by undertaking huge construction projects of dubious relevance to the housing needs of the immigrants and by flooding the labor market with cheap labor power.

In sum, the retreat of the state in the 1960s has been replaced, since 1967, with its total domination of the political space. As a result, the only forms of oppositional political expression available to peripheral groups have been fundamentalist versions of state ideology: the fundamentalist Zionism of Gush Emunim and the fundamentalist Judaism of the *haredim*.

Gush Emunim, as has been pointed out repeatedly, has appropriated the ethos (or should we say myth) of the *chalutz*, and cloaked it with a religious legitimational garb. This was in reaction to the historical exclusion of religious Zionism from the officially sanctioned definition of *chalutziyut*, and the ridicule with which the "knit skullcap" generation had been regarded by its non-religious peers. Another aspect of this effort by young (in 1967) religious Zionists to place themselves at the center of Zionist *hagshamah* (fulfillment) was a drastic increase in their readiness to join front-line combat units during their military service.

Gush Emunim, it has also been repeatedly noted, has not attracted Oriental Jews in any significant numbers. This despite the Orientals' proclivity to be hawkish on the Arab-Israeli conflict. The reason for this failure is that Gush Emunim embodies the efforts of a culturally, but not materially, deprived group to integrate itself into the political center. Oriental Jews, who have been socially and economically, as well as culturally, deprived, have sought other avenues of political expression.

Since the option of Oriental political organization had been effectively delegitimated by the state,[36] Orientals had flocked to Herut and, later, the poorest among them tended to support Kahane. In 1988, after Kahane's party had been disqualified, Oriental voters in development towns and poor city neighborhoods voted in large numbers for ultra-orthodox, *haredi* political parties. As a result, these parties more than doubled their electoral strength, from 4.8 percent of the votes cast in 1984 to 10.7 percent in 1988. By this vote the poorest Orientals have registered their *political* protest against both modernity and *chalutziyut*, two ideological constructs used to legitimate their exclusion from the benefits of Israeli society.[37]

The ability of the state to have such a stranglehold on the political arena is closely related, in our view, to the prominence of the military sphere in Israeli life since 1967, and even more so since 1973 and since the outbreak of the Intifada. This, as Kimmerling has argued, is closely tied to the blurring of the boundaries of the collectivity and the reopening of the frontier. Where we differ from Kimmerling, however, is in his assumption that the debate generated by the reopening of the frontier has been a voluntary interchange among autonomous political forces, each peddling its own vision of the appropriate boundaries of the collectivity.

In our view, just as the Six Day War constituted one element in an ongoing strategy of control, so the construction of the Israeli control system and its maintenance have been direct outcomes of that very same strategy. As Gershon Shafir has shown,[38] the colonial nature of early Zionist settlement inevitably resulted in violent conflict between Arabs and Jews. This conflict continued, in a somewhat different form, during the years of Israel's "normalcy"—1948 to 1967. It reverted back to its original form of intercommunal strife after the reopening of the frontier and the establishment of the control system.

Kimmerling has already pointed to the mechanisms reproducing the control system within its "temporary" boundaries. These mechanisms are connected to the control system's contribution to the regulation of the social division of labor within Israel proper. For example, the influx of Palestinian workers into the Israeli labor market has enabled a large group of working-class Orientals to move into the low managerial and petty entrepreneurial strata. (Other Orientals have been pushed down into the underclass, and it is they who had provided Meir Kahane with his electoral basis and who supported the *haredi* parties in 1988.) Better-situated groups, made up mostly of Ashkenazim, have benefited from the captive market provided them by the state in the occupied territories, by the virtually unlimited pool of cheap labor power available there and by the settlement projects (see Kimmerling 1989: 273–74, 277–78). It is surprising, therefore, that Kimmerling has refrained from drawing general conclusions about the structural role played by the state in regulating the social division of labor, and about the dependence of the latter on the existence of the control system.

The preservation of the control system is also related to the inclusion of Diaspora Jewry as part of the Israeli political community. This has not only caused a sharpening of the distinction between Jews and Arabs, but has also provided the control system with material and political resources needed for its maintenance (Kimmerling 1989: pp. 274–76). Thus, to the extent that the Six Day War had tightened relations between Israel and Diaspora Jewry, it provided the political center with additional resources for meeting the demands of various social sectors. This, together with the very substantial contributions of the occupied territories themselves, made the political center stronger, rather than weaker as claimed by Horowitz and Lissak.

Conclusion

There is no question in our minds that the Israeli state is in crisis. The origins of this crisis, however, do not lie in the Six

Day War, but rather in the very foundations of the Israeli social order which has depended, from the outset, on the management of the conflict between Jews and Arabs. It is this symbiotic relationship between the social order and the conflict which gave rise to the Six Day War (as well as all other Arab-Israeli wars) and to the continued occupation of the West Bank, Gaza, and the Golan Heights.

The unease shown by most authors reviewed in this chapter about the ongoing occupation cannot replace the brutally honest examination required for uncovering its real underlying causes and the interests working for its preservation. The ideological affinity of most of these authors, and of the Israeli "peace camp" in general, to the Labor movement, has prevented them from undertaking this task. For what is required is an analysis not only of the role played by the Labor movement in perpetuating the occupation after 1967, but, much more importantly, of its construction of a conflict-dependent social order as well. Paradoxically, the exaggerated stature granted the Six Day War in the Israeli academic discourse has prevented an understanding of both its origins and its continuing effects on Israeli society. To conclude, the Six Day War still awaits its revisionist historians. Without them, Israeli sociology will remain stunted in its ability to gain a critical understanding of our society.

Notes

1. Eisenstadt, Shmuel N. *Israeli Society*, (London: Weidenfeld and Nicolson, 1968); and *The Transformation of Israeli Society*, (London: Weidenfeld and Nicolson, 1985).

2. See also Deutsch, Karl W., "Introduction," in *Studies of Israeli Society*, vol. 3, *Politics and Society in Israel*, edited by Ernest Krausz, (New Brunswick, N. J.: Transaction Books, 1985), p. 4.

3. Smooha, Sammy, "Minority Status in an Ethnic Democracy: The Status of the Arab Minority in Israel," *Ethnic and Racial Studies*, 1990, 13: 389–413.

4. Peled, Yoav, "Ethnic Democracy and the Legal Construction of Citizenship: Arab Citizens of the Jewish State," *American Political Science Review*, 1992, 86:2 (June) 432–443.

5. Kimmerling, Baruch, "Sociology, Ideology and Nation-Building: The Israeli Case," *American Sociological Review*, 1992, 57: (August) 446–460.

6. Deutsch, op. cit.; Ehrlich, Avishai, "Israel: Conflict, War and Social Change," in *The Sociology of War and Peace*, edited by Colin Creighton and Martin Shaw, (London: Macmillan, 1987).

7. Shapiro, Yonathan, *The Formative Years of the Israeli Labour Party: The Organization of Power, 1919–1930*, (London: Sage, 1976); *Democracy in Israel*, (Ramat Gan: Massada, 1977) in Hebrew; *An Elite Without Successors: Generations of Political Leaders in Israel*, (Tel Aviv: Sifriat HaPoalim, 1984) in Hebrew; "Political Sociology in Israel: A Critical View," in *Studies of Israeli Society*, vol. 3: *Politics and Society in Israel*, edited by Ernest Krausz, (New Brunswick, N. J.: Transaction Books, 1985); *The Road to Power: Herut Party in Israel*, (Albany: SUNY Press, 1991).

8. Eisenstadt, Shmuel N., *Introduction to the Research of the Sociological Structure of Oriental Jews*, (Jerusalem: The Szold Institute, 1948) in Hebrew; Shafir, Gershon, *Land, Labor and the Origins of the Israeli-Palestinian Conflict, 1882–1914*, (Cambridge: Cambridge University Press, 1989).

9. Shapiro, 1985, op. cit., pp. 6–16.

10. Ben-Eliezer, Uri, "Militarism, Status and Politics," PhD dissertation, Department of Sociology, Tel Aviv University, 1988, (in Hebrew), p. 2.

11. See Mason, Andrew, "Politics and the State," *Political Studies* 1990, 37:4, 575–587.

12. Barzilai, Gad, *A Democracy in Wartime: Conflict and Consensus in Israel*, (Tel Aviv: Sifriat HaPoalim, 1992), in Hebrew.

13. Aronson, Shlomo and Dan Horowitz, "Strategy of Controlled Retaliation: The Israeli Case," *Medina, Memshal v'Yehasim Benleumiyim* 1971, 1: 77–99 (Hebrew).

14. Kimmerling, Baruch, *The Interrupted System*, (New Brunswick, N.J.: Transaction Books, 1985); Kimmerling, Baruch, "The Management of the Jewish-Arab Conflict and Nation-Building Processes During the Mandate," *Medina, Mimshal vi-Yehasim Benleumiyim* 1976, 9: 35–66 (Hebrew).

15. Kimmerling, ibid., 1985.

16. Kimmerling, op. cit., 1992.

17. In this section we rely heavily on Yagil Levy, "The Role of the Military Sphere in the Construction of the Political Order in Israel," Ph.D. dissertation, Department of Political Science, Tel Aviv University, 1993 (in Hebrew).

18. For example, Horton, John, "Order and Conflict: Theories of Social Problems as Competing Ideologies," *The American Journal of Sociology*, 1966, 71:6, 701–713.

19. Tilly, Charles, "War and the Power of Warmakers," in *Global Militarization*, edited by Peter Wallensteen et. al., (Boulder: Westview Press, 1985a); Mann, Michael, "The Autonomous Power of the State," *Archive Européennes de Sociologie* 1985, 24:2, 185–213.

20. Tilly, Charles, "War-Making and State-Making as Organized Crime," in *Bringing the State Back In*, edited by Peter Evans et. al., (Cambridge: Cambridge University Press, 1985b) pp. 169–191.

21. Giddens, Anthony, *The Nation-State and Violence*, (Cambridge: Polity Press, 1985).

22. Shafir, op. cit.

23. Grinberg, Lev. L., "The Israeli Labor Movement in Crisis, 1955–1970." PhD dissertation, Department of Sociology, Tel Aviv University, 1991, (Hebrew).

24. See especially Kimmerling, op. cit., 1976.

25. Kimmerling, Baruch, *Zionism and Territory*, (Berkeley: Institute for International Studies, 1983).

26. Ben-Eliezer, op. cit. 1988.

27. Grinberg, op. cit., pp. 93–173.

28. Ibid., pp. 183–184.

29. Weitzmann, Ezer, *For You the Sky, For You the Land*, (Tel Aviv: Maariv Library, 1975) in Hebrew, p. 23.

30. Ibid., pp. 253–254.

31. Haver, Eytan, *War Will Break Out Today*, (Tel Aviv: Idanim, 1987) in Hebrew, p. 146.

32. Beilin, Yossi, *The Price of Unification: The Labor Party Until the Yom Kippur War*, (No place: Revivim, 1985) in Hebrew, p. 25.

33. Ibid., p. 39.

34. Ibid., p. 44.

35. On the latter, see Shalev, Michael and Lev. L. Grinberg, *Histadrut-Government Relations and the Transition from Likud to a National Unity Government*, (Tel Aviv: Pinhas Sapir Center for Development, 1989).

36. Herzog, Hanna, "Social Construction of Reality in Ethnic Terms: The Case of Political Ethnicity in Israel," *International Review of Modern Sociology* 1985, 15: 45–61.

37. Don-Yehiya, Eliezer, "Religiosity and Ethnicity in Israeli Politics: The Religious Parties and the Elections to the Twelfth Knesset," *Medina, Memshal vi-Yehasim Benleumiyim* 1990, 32: 11–54 (in Hebrew); Peled, Yoav, "Ethnic Exclusionism in the Periphery: The Case of Oriental Jews in Israel's Development Towns," *Ethnic and Racial Studies*, 1990, 13: 345–367; Peled, Yoav, "Explaining Religious Voting Among Oriental Jews in Israel: A Cultural Division of Labor Approach." (Unpublished).

38. Shafir, op. cit.

The Arab-Israeli Conflict and the Victory of Otherness

Ilan Peleg

David K. Shipler, *Arab and Jew: Wounded Spirits in a Promised Land*, London: Penguin Books, 1986.

Ehud Sprinzak, *The Ascendance of Israel's Radical Right*, New York: Oxford University Press, 1991.

I

The Arab-Israeli conflict, one of the most complicated of all conflicts in the contemporary world, has been approached by analysts from numerous angles: broad historical analysis, legal perspectives, personal observations, security dilemmas, attitudinal prisms, and more.[1] The perceptions and attitudes that Jews and Arabs have of and toward each other are among the most interesting aspects of the long-standing dispute; they may very well be the ultimate key to the resolution of the conflict, since political processes and governmental policies are rooted, in the final analysis, in perceptions and attitudes. Both the Shipler and the Sprinzak books are important contributions to the understanding of how Arabs and Jews view each other.

It is the contention of this chapter that the political and societal picture painted by the two volumes, their description of the emerging reality in Greater Israel (Israel and the territories), could best be termed the "victory of *otherness*." It is a reality of growing hostility, estrangement, and hatred that governs the relationships between Arabs and Jews, and although neither Shipler nor Sprinzak uses the concept of *otherness*, their accounts of that reality go a long way toward the substantiation of this chapter's claim.

The Shipler book, winner of the Pulitzer Prize, focuses (despite its broad coverage) on the way in which Arabs and Jews see each other, their thoughts, feelings, and emotions, and particularly their mutual images and stereotypes. The Sprinzak volume, although much narrower in scope and very different in analytical style, also deals with attitudes as determinants of this conflict. It dwells specifically on the Jewish side and, within it, on what the author terms the "radical right."

The strength of the Shipler volume is in vividly describing the reality of *otherness*, in allowing the reader to feel the atmosphere of mutual rejection, in exposing, albeit merely anecdotally, the depth of hatred in Greater Israel. No other book in the market better conveys the estrangement between Arabs and Jews. Shipler dwells on the forces that contribute to Arab-Jewish hostility (forces such as nationalism and "religious absolutism"), devotes considerable space to a description of the images held by the two conflicting groups vis-à-vis each other, and analyzes the interaction between Jews and Arabs and its consequences. Sprinzak, in effect, complements Shipler's journalistic account by covering the material in a more systematic manner, by offering a social science perspective, by carrying the analysis all the way to the early 1990s, and by focusing on the forces responsible in Israel for the negativism toward the Arabs, the radical right.

II

Otherness is the end result, the product and the consequence, of perceiving someone else as the complete negation of oneself, the perceiver. It is a condition in which certain individuals or groups are seen as irreconcilably different when compared to other groups within society. As explained by Albert Memmi in his study of the relationships between groups in a colonial setting,[2] the colonized emerges within such context as the image of everything the colonizer is not. Furthermore, not only is he different, but every negative quality is projected onto him. So much so, that even his humanity is being questioned. Finally, individual *other*s are not even seen as individuals but as part of chaotic, disorganized, and anonymous collectivity.

Although the Arab-Israeli conflict is very different from the colonial situation described by Memmi, Memmi's analysis of *otherness* applies rather well to the long-standing Middle Eastern dispute. The perception of Arabs by Jews as *other*s, and the equivalent perception of Jews by Arabs, is widespread and, in all likelihood, increasing. This perception is often based on complete negation and rejection of the members of the other group, as individuals, and of the group, as a collective. It is a phenomenon which Shipler fully documents, albeit anecdotally.

The treatment given to the subject in *Arab and Jew* could and should lead to an empirical examination of *otherness*, the Arab-Jewish extreme aversion and estrangement. For example, it could be hypothesized (and then examined) that the perception of Arabs as *other*s by Israeli Jews is particularly common among those who are inalterably opposed to any political settlement which requires compromise. Similarly, *otherness* would probably characterize the attitude of Arabs who reject the possibility, as well as the desirability, of a political compromise with the Jews.

Beyond the identification of correlation between a general attitude (the tendency to see the adversary as the "*other*") and a more specific political position (the rejection of a negotiated settlement as a means for bringing the dispute to its conclusion), one may seek a way for understanding and explaining the *otherness* phenomenon within the Arab-Jewish context. From this perspective, the extreme negativism associated with *otherness* seems to be a psychological mechanism designed to sustain the integrity of the belief system of the person committed to such an attitude. If Jews define Arabs entirely negatively, as people with whom one simply cannot "do business," they, in effect, absolve themselves from the duty to seek accommodation with them. The same could be said about Arabs who judge Jews to be entirely negative.

It is clear that those who do not perceive the adversary as the *other* often see a negotiated political compromise as possible and desirable whatever practical problems they may identify on the way toward a political solution. Although cause and effect are particularly difficult to discern when it comes to complex attitudes, those who see the adversary as completely negative and hardly human in the full sense of the word—namely, those who perceive the enemy as a genuine *other*—cannot even entertain the notion of coexistence with that enemy. Those who see the conflict in human terms, rather than metaphysical ones (as the concept of the "*other*" demands), can easily accept coexistence as a highly desirable, if hard to achieve, possibility.

Within the complicated web of the Arab-Israeli relationships, as vividly described by Shipler, *otherness* is the perceptual device through which the conflict is sustained. This does not mean that *otherness* is ordinarily either consciously invented by people of ill will or that it is manipulated by shrewd politicians, although there are numerous cases in which this seems to be the case. In general, it is useful to look at *otherness* as a characteristic of a person's worldview, a dimension of his or her *Weltanschauung* which could very well be subconscious.

When *otherness* becomes an element of a person's worldview, a fixed component, it is likely to be passed to future generations. *Otherness* is so powerful in Greater Israel that children in both groups, Arabs and Jews, have adopted highly negative perceptions of the other group. Shipler quotes studies which conclude that a large majority of children on both sides believe that war with the other group was always necessary (pp. 21–22). A high level of anxiety, focused on and stemming from the *other* group was reported among Jewish and Arab children alike. Fear of and aggression toward the *other* go hand in hand—they are causally linked. If the *other* is genuinely threatening, one wants to make war on him.

The psychological mechanisms operating in the Arab-Israeli conflict, which are competently but only anecdotally described by Shipler, are, of course, not unique to that conflict, but are possibly more profound here because of the unusual high intensity of the confrontation. What might be called the "*otherization*" of one's enemy—turning him into a complete opposite and total negation of oneself—is a perfectly normal, necessary, and in many ways functional, process. In a situation of total conflict (of the type the Arab-Israeli conflict has increasingly become since 1967) not to see the adversary as the *other* is to suffer severe ambiguity, a serious cognitive dissonance. Perceiving the adversary as a totally negative, evil entity is not an unreasonable solution for people locked into conflict. Humanism in a conflictual situation is extremely hard to maintain since it entails a psychological burden which many in society find unbearable.

Otherness is never a static condition, but an ever-changing one. The dynamics of the relationships between Arabs and Jews in Greater Israel is such that each violent or hostile act deepens the hostility and the sense of *otherness*. Moreover, even non-hostile acts by members of one group are likely to be perceived by some members of the opposing group as profoundly threatening. Thus, Shipler documents the story of the arrival of some Israeli Arab families at Upper Nazareth, the perception of this process as "Arab penetration," and the formation of an organization calling itself the "Defenders of Upper Nazareth" (pp. 25–30). Rather than interpreting the process of Arab movement into Jewish neighborhoods as reflecting demographic and economic needs of Arab families in search of appropriate homes, the "Defenders" have seen these families as profoundly threatening their very survival.

Not only is *otherness* a phenomenon given to constant change, but it operates on *different levels of passivity and activity*, forming a dynamic spectrum. On the passive side of the spectrum the *other* is completely ignored, reflecting an attitude of contempt on the part of the perceiver. On the most active side of the spectrum, *otherness* may lead some members of the group to thoughts and even actions designed to eliminate the adversarial group. Between these two extreme options, one can identify such *otherness*-related options as the expression of contempt for the *other* (relatively mild reaction), imposition of legal limitations on the *other* (medium), or expelling it from the conflictual territory (strong reaction). All of these approaches and reactions to the *other* have been in existence for many years among both Arabs and Jews.

In an ethnic conflict, the nationalist right wing in each of the parties is likely to develop a strong, active *otherness* position toward the adversary. A racist, expulsionist, and even annihilationist stance is not unusual in these circumstances. The appearance on the scene of Meir Kahane's Kach movement, extensively documented by Ehud Sprinzak, is a case in point.

Otherness toward an adversary has not only different levels of activity but also different dimensions. Thus, among Arabs and Jews, there is surprisingly little information and knowledge about the other side. Many people are not only entirely ignorant about the other side, but are determined to remain so. Just as prevalent is emotional blockage, ignoring the sufferings, concerns, and aspirations of the *other*. Shipler reports, in this regard, that when Yitzhak Rabin published his memoirs, reporting the details of the forced evacuation of the Arabs from Lod and Ramle, few Israelis reacted. Says Shipler: "Israelis as a whole are so determined to block out this unsavory element of their history that Rabin's revelation had little impact"; it "engendered almost no reaction or debate" (p. 35).

The double blockage of knowledge and emotion toward the *other* prevents a person, a group, or even a nation from dealing with the *other* in a humane way. Thus, the sufferings of Arabs and Jews remains, mutually unrecognized by the other side. The absence of the human dimension from the

The Arab-Israeli Conflict and the Victory of Otherness 233

conflict facilitates the continuation and even intensification of the perception of *otherness*.

The tendency to perceive an adversary as the *other* could easily lead to assigning conspiratorial intentions against the perceiver. Thus, Shipler (p. 42) maintains that Arabs in the occupied territories tend to see the violent deeds of Israeli settlers against them as part of an Israeli grand plan designed to evacuate all of them from Palestine. They have similarly interpreted the incident in which a deranged Australian set fire to Jerusalem's Al-Aqsa mosque, seeing it as a Jewish conspiracy. In general, *otherness* and monolithization go hand in hand; one identifies negative characteristics in the adversary, and then one generalizes to the entire group and each of its members. Traditional anti-Semitism rested on the very same processes.

Although it is clear that *otherness* is often linked to existential, violent conflict among groups of people, usually of different cultural, religious, or ethnic background, it is difficult to precisely identify the process through which *otherness* evolves. Nevertheless, it seems that certain events, fixed forever in the collective minds of the groups involved, could become important symbols, mental benchmarks in the process of the development of full-fledged *otherness*. Undoubtedly, the 1945 and 1967 wars have served in that capacity for the Arabs: they have created a sense of *otherness* toward the Jews and their collective memory has helped in perpetuating this sense. Important events can assume a life of their own, independent of their historical concreteness, when they become focal points for elaborate belief systems. If and when such events become ingrained in the collective consciousness of the group, they are fundamentally indestructible, ineradicable. In this sense, they create a sense of *otherness* which is almost fixed.

Not only can *otherness* become fixed, but it may be used in very different contexts than the one leading to its initial creation. What may be called "*otherness* by displacement" is not unusual in the Arab-Israeli conflict. A good example for this process is the Holocaust, an event mentioned by Shipler on a number on occasions. The Holocaust has influenced, of course, the worldview of all Israelis and Jews, as well as many others. Yet, in the case of many Israelis, particularly those who belong to what Sprinzak calls the "radical right," the Holocaust has become a metahistoric event, symbolizing the *otherness* of *all* adversaries, even those entirely unlinked to the event. The Holocaust has, thus, become an instrument of transferring *otherness* from one context to another context. In the case of the Arab-Israeli conflict, the Holocaust facilitated the transference of the deep sense of estrangement of the Jews in Europe to a Middle Eastern milieu. A generalized *other* can easily be applied to any and all adversaries, regardless of historical circumstances.[3]

An ethnic conflict characterized by *otherness*, such as the Arab-Israeli one, is affected always by a high degree of generalization. Not only are members of the adversarial group perceived most negatively, but there is a strong tendency to see all of them in the same light, with no effort to differentiate among them. Individuals subscribing to a moderate, compromising position toward the adversarial group are usually capable of focusing on the micro-picture and recognize important differences within the adversarial group; not so those who subscribe to a tough, hawkish position.

Radicals on both sides of the Arab-Jewish divide have difficulty recognizing large or small nuances in the *other*'s position or behavioral patterns. They tend to deny *spatial* differentiation, perceiving all individuals belonging to the other group as virtually identical, and they also deny *temporal* differentiation, the possibility that some individual(s) on the other side may change over time. The radical right in Israel has always seen all Arabs as hostile, and its members have refused to recognize any possible change in this Arab position. The same holds for the rejectionists among the Palestinians.

An important psychological mechanism that facilitates the perception of uniformity on the other side of the ethnic divide is that of *denial*. In its extreme form, denial amounts

The Arab-Israeli Conflict and the Victory of Otherness 235

to the negation of the other side's very existence. In a more moderate form, denial spells the questioning of the other side's legitimacy. Both forms are rather common among Arabs and Jews in their relations to each other.

Thus, the Arabs have traditionally made the distinction between "Jews" and "Zionists," emphasizing that while they do not deny the legitimacy of Judaism, they do question the legitimacy of the State of Israel. Many Israelis, particularly on the right but also in the center and in positions of authority, have continuously denied the very existence of a Palestinian nation. Shipler says about what he sees as the typical Israeli approach toward the Palestinians (which could be called an adversary-defined-as-*other*): "It is too threatening for all but a tiny fraction of Israeli Jews to accept the legitimacy of Palestinian national striving" (p. 72). Identically, Shipler believes that Zionism is routinely portrayed by many Arabs as "an artificial nationalism without logical basis" (p. 70). It is clear that somewhat of a mirror-image exists, and that *otherness* and denial go hand in hand.

In fact, denial is an extreme but not illogical form of *otherness*. In arguing that the adversary's cause has no validity whatsoever, *otherness* is brought to its logical conclusion, to its pure form. It is now easier to sustain it, even in the face of evidence that it is distorted and inaccurate, dysfunctional and utterly destructive. In a conflict dominated by *otherness*, such as the Arab-Israeli confrontation, any recognition of the validity of the other's claim, however small, seems to radicals on both sides as detracting from their own legitimate claims.

Moreover, since *otherness* is not only relevant for attitudes but also for policy making, the radical approach which increasingly characterizes the Arab-Israel dispute could be truly disastrous. Put differently, *otherness* could easily become an instrument of control, oppression, and coercion, not only against members of the out-group (the *other*) but also against disloyal members of the in-group. Thus, Israeli Jews who employ Arabs have, on occasion, been attacked, as have individuals accused of sympathy toward the Palestinian cause. *Otherness* requires total conformity; cracks in the wall are considered by the promoters of *otherness*, justifiably, as extremely dangerous. If allowed to exist, they may be widened and this could lead to the quick collapse of the entire *otherness* myth. The murder of Palestinians who are willing to recognize Israel (by other Palestinians), and the ferocious attacks on so-called Ashafists (pro-PLO Israeli Jews) are indicative of the seriousness with which deviations from the controlling *otherness* myth are seen by radicals within the in-group, and often by the majority.

The cause of *otherness*, zealously promoted by radicals on both sides, is routinely helped by violent actions. Violence of any type has a tendency to reinforce the dominance of *otherness*. It "proves," after all, that the adversary, the party that commits the violence, is inhumane. The fact that violence is actually the *result* of *otherness* which is already in existence, is often ignored. Violence breeds and strengthens the *otherness* perception; it causes it to spread and to deepen.

In the Middle Eastern conflict, violence and terrorism are linked organically to the rejection of the *other*. Shipler recognizes, correctly, that "terrorism is not an aberration produced by demented personalities ... [but] an integral part of an existing subculture, encouraged and supported and approved by the mainstream of the society that forms the terrorist's reference points" (108). Put differently and in the language adopted by this chapter, the terrorist is merely the hand that carries out the atrocity; the belief system of *otherness* behind the terrorist, well ingrained in his society, is the fundamental cause for his deed.

Otherness often creates strange reactions. Thus, in the Arab Middle East terrorists are often admired and considered heroes. On the Jewish side, vigilantes, even those committing unprovoked or unproportional acts of violence against civilians, are also highly regarded. The reason for this common approach is easy to find. In acting against the mortal enemies of the group, against the ever-present *other*, those committing acts of violence cannot possibly do wrong.

III

In the final analysis, *otherness* is a *political-cultural phenomenon*, a reflection of the attitudes of a society toward another society or toward certain ethnic, religious, or racial groups within the society. When growing numbers of people in a society adopt not only a negative, but a rejectionist position toward a group which they identify as adversarial, *otherness* prevails.

Within every society there are radicals who are likely to completely reject those they see as the society's unrelenting enemies. Thus, one of Kach's leaders stated that anyone who thinks Jews and Arabs can coexist is a fool. In a society in conflict there is an ongoing struggle over the public's attitude toward the adversarial group. It seems that the last few years have seen the strengthening of the rejectionist position in the Arab-Israeli conflict, the position based on *otherness* and antagonism.

When *otherness* is on the ascendance, it affects modes of thinking and expression on the deepest level. Negative code words come to represent the adversary, the *other*. "Zionist" is the word used now by Arabs in relations to Jews; "terrorist" is often used to denote an Arab, among Jews. Shipler believes that the term "terrorism" has "become almost a catechism in Israeli discussion, a chant that masks the human faces behind the enemy lines" (p. 124). For him it is a "slogan of hatred." The word "Zionist" fulfills a similar role in Arab reaction to and discussion of Jews.

Only over the last few years have Israelis started applying the term "terrorist" to Jews who attacked civilian Arabs, such as members of the Jewish underground in the territories. Nevertheless, the establishment of the underground and the widespread support that its members received even after their conviction in an Israeli court are indications that the powerful subculture of hatred can easily become the dominant culture in society and that zealotry may become the dominant norm of the society. This zealotry is intimately linked with *otherness*.

Moreover, in a situation of *otherness*, not only is the political culture deeply affected but, sooner or later, the legal and governmental structures begin to change in order to accommodate the overwhelming animosity toward the adversarial group in society. In the case of Israel, much of the legal process in the occupied territories has been corrupted as a result of the dominance of *otherness* in the relations between Arabs and Jews in Greater Israel. Thus, the *Karp Report* and other reports have documented numerous violations of due process on the part of the police, the army, and others. Although in Israel itself the political culture and institutions resist such legal corruption, as the *Karp Report* itself demonstrates, its existence in the territories is a testimony to the controlling effect of *otherness*.

Otherness could easily undermine the rule of law in any civil society, especially when violent acts against the *other* are defined as war. Such acts are then being legitimized as necessary rather than condemned as criminal acts which ought to be punished by society's legal institutions. This is exactly what happened in the case of the Jewish underground, when major Israeli politicians came to the defense of the organization and argued for leniency toward its members. Both Shipler and Sprinzak dwell on the case at some length.

Otherness often relies on long-standing, powerful cultural symbols. Shared values are a solid base for the rejection of the out-group. Among members of Israel's radical right, and particularly among religious circles, there is frequent reference to Arabs as Amalek, the ancient tribe that God commanded the Israelites to destroy. This cultural symbol, reflecting *otherness* at its most extreme, is a cultural symbol which can serve as justification for almost any action against the *other*.

Religious symbols in general are often associated with the emergence of *otherness*, and its victory over alternative belief systems. Such symbols tend to be absolutist in nature.

As such they are useful for creating sharp distinctions between in-groups and out-groups, between those who belong to the group and the non-believers. Religions are often exclusionary and rarely pluralistic in outlook. In a situation of ethnic conflict these characteristics are even clearer than might be the case in normal situations. Although religion rarely demands an outlook of *otherness*, it is often compatible with such an outlook and ready to accept it.

Those characteristics are evident in the Arab-Israeli conflict. Although the conflict could be described as essentially secular—a confrontation between two national movements for the control of the same land—religious circles in Israel, as well as some among the Arabs, have insisted on linking it to religious motifs and concepts, especially since 1967. This linkage has helped in absolutizing the conflict and in making it look inevitable and insoluble. *Otherness* reigns supreme under such conditions.

The most dangerous of all conditions is the synthesis of religion and nationalism, since the practical, political needs of nationalism and the fanaticism of religion could justify any act against the *other*. This synthesis, however, is quite common among Arabs and Israelis. Gush Emunim and Hamas are two examples, and the Gush is more dangerous since it is much more powerful.

In a way, *otherness* is inherent both in religions exclusivity and in national uniqueness. Both religion and nationalism routinely identify outsiders and have an inherent *need* to define outsiders. In conflict situations those outsiders are likely to become full-fledged *other*s. Religion adds to nationalism the unshakable conviction and certitude which sustain the integrity and the stability of the belief system. The synthesis of religion and nationalism makes fanaticism and extremism not only acceptable for their supporters; it often makes them reputable, necessary, and natural.

IV

Otherness is based upon, is the result of, and reflects extreme particularism, a phenomenon which both Shipler and

Sprinzak describe but never fully analyze. Yet, in the Jewish tradition and in modern Israel there are also strong universalistic trends. While Zionism started as a nationalist movement, it did so in the name of *joining* the family of nations and becoming "*goy kechol ha'goim*" (a nation like any other nation). The Declaration of Independence for the State of Israel, while committed to Jewish presence in Eretz Israel, is equally committed to universal, humanitarian principles of human and civil rights. Israel's socialist beginnings are equally rooted in a universalistic tradition, and even Judaism as a religious and national tradition is strongly universalistic.

In a way, national particularism and its Siamese twin, a strong sense of *otherness* toward those who do not belong to the national group, are now in a dramatic competition with Israel's long-established universalistic forces. It is clear that the culture of particularism and *otherness* has made major advances over the last generation or so, and particularly since the 1967 and 1973 wars. The philosophy of *am levadad yishkon* (the people shall dwell apart), and its implication—*u'vagoim lo yitchashav* (and pay no attention to other nations)[4]—has gained in importance, not only in religious circles but also among secular Israelis.

Otherness is strongly linked and is even a necessary component of ethnocentrism. If one claims one's nation as the source of all that is good and noble, and inherently superior, the rejection of the outside world follows suit naturally, organically. *Other*ization occurs under such circumstances, especially in a situation of acute conflict. Ethnocentrism *requires* strong differentiation between in- and out-groups, clear boundaries between those who belong and those who do not belong. While universal ideologies emphasize the commonality of the human experience, particularist ideologies emphasize the difference among people. While universalism rejects *otherness* as dehumanizing, particularism—in its nationalist form and other forms—demands it; it places *otherness*, in fact, at its very center as a component of building up the group identity.

Although Sprinzak's book deals with *otherness* in a less direct way than Shipler's, in focusing on Israel's radical right it exposes in minute detail the particularistic ideology of extremist separatism and, by implication, the forces of *otherness* within contemporary Israel. Sprinzak correctly recognizes that the radical right was marginal until 1967 and that its central idea, territorial maximalism, was revived as a result of the war (p. 32).

In analyzing the ideology and the characteristic political behavior of the Israeli radical right, Sprinzak notes the focus on the Arabs by such groups as Kach and Moledet. In this context, it is important to realize that the entire radical right denies the *existence* of a Palestinian people and that all the forces belonging to the right demonstrate extreme insensitivity to the plight of the Palestinians. Thus, forces on the right have supported expulsion of Arabs (by force or "voluntarily") and a policy of long-term discrimination toward the Palestinians. Some in the radical right see all non-Jews as "*other*s," inalterably committed to the destruction of the Jewish people and the State of Israel; only very few in the radical right see even remote possibility for positive Arab-Jewish relations.

The victory of *otherness* among right-wingers can be seen in the fact that they are seeking not merely a solution for the Arab problem in the territories, but they are increasingly dwelling on the future of the Arab minority in Israel proper. The right-wing forces create what Sprinzak sees as an artificial friction between Arabs and Jews over jobs; to his mind there is "a strong *perception* of such competition," a perception which is, in fact, unjustified (p. 87).

The Sprinzak volume is not without some problems, especially in the area of interpretation. The interpretational deficiencies are, possibly, related to the failure of Sprinzak to realize the extent to which "*otherness*"—a concept which he does not use—dominates the inner life of the radical right. Thus, Sprinzak argues that Gush Emunim's resort to terrorism was "completely unexpected" (p. 67). Not so. The core logic of Gush Emunim, its complete rejection of any Arab rights, *had* to lead some of its members to massive terrorism. When someone is defined as the *other*, any actions against him are perceived as legitimate.

Moreover, Sprinzak seems to be all too eager to differentiate between the "moderate members of the nationalist camp who were ready to make compromises for real peace," and the "radicals who believe that no peace is more sacred than the territories" (p. 5). The history of the last few years does not justify this differentiation. The Israeli right as a whole seems to regard the Arabs as foreigners, people with no rights in the land. The only real differentiation between the "moderate" and the "radical" right is in the *methods* they are willing to deploy to achieve their goals: the latter are significantly more violent.

Another problematic (although useful) differentiation offered by Sprinzak is between what he calls the classic or European radical right and the American right. According to Sprinzak, the classic radical right is characterized by: (a) having been born out of repressed national pride such as the one created by humiliating minority status; (b) glorification of the nation; (c) sanctification of ancient borders; (d) preaching of aggressive foreign policy and militarism; and (e) showing an occasional display of fervent religiosity or nationalist neo-religiosity, etc. (p. 10). Even though those characteristics fit the behavior and attitude patterns of large segments of the Israeli radical right rather well, Sprinzak argues that the latter is very different than the classical right. The argument is not entirely convincing.

According to Sprinzak, the Israeli right is much closer to the American right, which he characterizes as being (a) ultranationalist; (b) anti-communist; (c) fundamentalist Christian; (d) militaristic; and (e) supportive of anti-alien sentiment. It is hard to see how the Israeli radical right is closer to the American right than to the European right. At least some elements of the Israeli right are as revolutionary as the classical, European rightists. After all, they are willing to challenge Israel's democratic order in the name of a higher order, a phenomenon documented by Sprinzak himself.

The Arab-Israeli Conflict and the Victory of Otherness   243

Be that as it may, the radical Israeli right, and the right in general, is characterized as subscribing to what this chapter calls "*otherness.*" All of its factions see the Arabs in Israel and in the territories as dangerous aliens who must be dealt with by the harshest means possible.

Notes

1. For broad historical perspective see, for example, Fred J. Khouri, *The Arab-Israeli Dilemma* (Syracuse, N.Y.: Syracuse University Press, 1985); Alvin Z. Rubinstein, ed., *The Arab-Israeli Conflict: Perspectives*, 2nd ed. New York: Harper Collins, 1991); Avi Shlaim, *Collusion Across the Jordan: King Abdullah the Zionist Movement and the Partition of Palestine* (New York: Columbia University Press, 1988). For legal analysis consult, among others, Allan Oerson, *Israel, the West Bank and International Law* (London and Totowa, N.J.: F. Cass, 1978); J. N. Halderman, *The Middle East Crisis: Test of International Law* (Dobbs Ferry: Oceana Publications 1969); J. N. Moore, *The Arab-Israeli Conflict* (Princeton, N.J.: Princeton University Press, 1977). For personal observations, one may want to look at Saul Friedlander and Mahmoud Hussein, *Arabs and Israelis* (London: Holmes and Meier, 1975); Sana Hassan and Amos Elon, *Between Enemies: A Compassionate Dialogue Between an Israeli and an Arab* (New York: Random House, 1974); Amos Oz, *In the Land of Israel* (New York: Vintage Books, 1983), as well as a large number of fictional works.

Security dilemmas were discussed, for example, by Shai Feldman, *Israeli Nuclear Deterrence: A Strategy for the 1980s* (New York: Columbia University Press, 1952), and by Steven J. Rosen, *Military Geography and the Military Balance in the Arab-Israeli Conflict*, Jerusalem Papers on Peace Problems, no. 21, 1977.

Attitudes and perceptions are focused upon in such studies as Yehoshafat Harkabi, *Arab Strategies and Israeli Responses* (New York: Free Press, 1977), and John Edwin Mroz, *Beyond Security: Private Perceptions among Arabs and Israelis* (New York: Pergamon, 1980).

2. Albert Memmi, *The Colonizer and the Colonized.* (Boston: Beacon Press, 1967), p. 82.

3. The idea of the generalized *other* is incorporated into the Passover Haggadah: "In every generation, they rise in order to annihilate us, but the Almighty saves us from their hand." See also Yosef Yerushalmi, *Zakhor, Jewish History and Jewish Memory* (Seattle: University of Washington Press, 1982).

4. Numbers 23:9. This sentence is open to a few alternative translations and interpretations.

The Intercommunal Dimension in the Arab-Israeli Conflict: The Intifada

Efraim Inbar[*]

David McDowall, *Palestine and Israel: The Uprising and Beyond*, London: I. B. Tauris, 1989.

Jamal R. Nassar and Roger Heacock, eds., *Intifada: Palestine at the Crossroads*, New York: Praeger, 1990.

Don Peretz, *Intifada: The Palestinian Uprising*, Boulder: Westview, 1990.

Zeev Schiff and Ehud Yaari, *Intifada*, Tel Aviv: Schocken, 1990. (Hebrew.)

Aryeh Shalev, *The Intifada: Causes and Effects*, Tel Aviv: Papyrus and the Jaffee Center for Strategic Studies, 1990. (Hebrew.)

Introduction

The protracted Arab-Israeli conflict is interstatal, and also contains an intercommunal dimension which gives it a 'compound' quality, i.e., a structure composed of two bordering domains of violence—interstate and communal.[1]

---

[*]This work was conducted under the auspices of the BESA Center for Strategic Studies at Bar-Ilan University and was supported by the Schnitzer Foundation for Research on the Israeli Economy and Society. The chapter was written in 1991.

The communal strife between Jews and Arabs living under British rule, which was dominant before 1948, acquired more prominence after 1967 when the Palestinian inhabitants of Judea, Samaria, and Gaza came under Israeli rule.

The Intifada, which erupted in December 1987, is one expression of the greater weight of the communal dimension of the conflict. At that time riots in several Palestinian refugee camps in the Gaza Strip developed into a popular uprising. The scope, intensity, and duration of the evolving events surprised everybody, including the Palestinians themselves. The Intifada has been characterized by many non-violent methods of struggle such as commercial shutdowns, economic boycotts, labor strikes, and demonstrative funerals, the hoisting of Palestinian flags, the resignation of policemen and tax collectors, and the development of self-reliant educational, economic and political institutions. Such activities were accompanied by low-level violent acts such as throwing stones and petrol bombs, as well as internal terror, in which many accused of cooperation with Israel were murdered. Only about 5 percent of Palestinian activity included the use of firearms.

Toward the end of 1991, after almost four years of Intifada there was much less violence against Israeli targets in the territories and a drastic decline in the participation of the Palestinian masses in such acts of violence. The balance sheet for this period shows that 795 Palestinians were killed by Israeli security forces. A growing number of Palestinian fatalities, over 450, were the result of internal Palestinian terror. On the Israeli side only 69 were killed (22 members of the security forces and 47 civilians).[2] The price tag (direct costs of the Israeli army) for fighting the Intifada for the first three years was approximately $500,000,000. During the summer of 1991 some Palestinians voiced demands for revisions in the patterns of action. Yet, through 1991 it was too early to conclude that the Intifada was over. As a matter of fact, some aspects of the Intifada had become a way of life in the territories for both Palestinians and Israelis.

The Intifada attracted much literary attention. This chapter reviews several items from the burgeoning literature on this subject. The main questions addressed in these works, by Palestinian, Israeli and overseas authors, include the causes of the Intifada; the role of the PLO in the evolving events; the impact of the uprising on Palestinian and Israeli society; and the chances for an Israeli-Palestinian settlement.

The Palestinian View

The collection edited by Nassar and Heacock is a serious attempt by Palestinian scholars and other academics sympathyzing with the Palestinan cause (some spent considerable time in the territories) to analyze the causes of the Intifada and its impact on Palestinian society and on the behavior of outside actors linked to the Israeli-Palestinian dispute. The contributions, written after the first year of the Intifada, lack a historical perspective. This is the main weakness of this volume. All of the essays uncritically accept the need to establish a Palestinian state in the Israeli-ruled territories, and most of them predicted at their time of writing that this goal would be soon realized. This optimistic (and, with the benefit of hindsight, rather unrealistic) vision indicates a somewhat flawed understanding of the social and international factors at work which hinder the realization of Palestinian aspirations. One clear reason for such blurred vision is the flawed conceptual framework of most of the essays.

As early as in the introduction, Abu-Lughod proposes the paradigm of colonial struggle, which inevitably ends with the victory of the oppressed, to understand the reality in Palestine. Such a conceptual framework is very appealing because the situation indeed lends itself to such an interpretation. Yet, it is misleading in respect to at least one of the most important variables in the political equation—Israel, the opponent. A colonial comparison belittles the political power within the Zionist claim to its ancestral homeland. Furthermore, it obscures the acute security concerns, shared by most Israelis, regarding control of the territories. Those two aspects are usually absent in colonial situations. Abu-Lughod's claim that the Intifada does not resort to violence is quite astonishing, particularly since he obviously has no moral qualms about resisting occupation. Similarly disingenuous is his historic review of Palestinian oppression, which ignores the Egyptian role in Gaza and the Jordanian role in Judea and Samaria during the 1948 to 1967 period. Singling out Britain and Israel better fits his colonial scheme, however.

Fortunately, the rest of the volume is less flawed. Actually the readers are presented with an interesting and detailed analysis of different aspects of the Intifada. The fact that many of the authors were not only observers of the events described, but also active participants, gives their writings a clear Palestinian coloration. This is quite valuable for evaluating how the Palestinian intelligentsia in the territories views the Intifada. The collection is usefully divided into three parts: the preconditions; the participants; and the regional and international reactions.

The first part gives a good but partial account of the roots of the Palestinian uprising. Farsoun and Landis critically describe the effects of the Israeli occupation and observe that past Israeli successes in repressing resistance forced the Palestinians to adopt a rather decentralized institutional structure, which proved to be quite effective during the Intifada. The Israeli retreat from Lebanon as a result of determined resistance was indeed an important step in the erosion of Israeli deterrence in the territories. The economic factors behind the outbreak of the Intifada are analyzed in greater depth by Saleh. The development of political and national consciousness among the Arabs in the Israeli-ruled territories is well covered by Taraki, who concentrates on the role of mass organizations, cultural forums, and the Palestinian press. She is honest enough to state that: "Until the late 1950s, the Palestinian cause and national identity were not articulated in distinctively Palestinian forums or organizations" (p. 54), and no claim is made for a thousand years of Palestinian history.

The last chapter in this part of the book, on the health situation, detracts from the quality of the collection. Bargouthi and Giacaman claim that the "colonialism" of military rule was the main impediment to the development of health services, although it is evident that the standard of health services has greatly improved under Israeli rule. It is not clear what the "alternative medicine" suggested by the authors means, nor how it contributed to the Intifada.

The discussion of the roots of the Intifada in the first part of the collection lacks any serious treatment of the disappointment of Palestinians with the Arab countries championing their cause, with the PLO, or with the international community. It focuses almost entirely on Israel as the culprit.

The second part of the volume is devoted to analyzing the roles played by and the changes taking place among the various participants in the uprising: the residents of refugee camps and villages, women, merchants, Islamists, and the PLO. The best article in this part and, indeed, in the whole collection, is that of Tamari, who describes how the petite bourgeoisie—the element most inclined to favor the status quo—was mobilized into the struggle against the occupation. To a great extent, this sector is most important because it usually provides the revolutionary cadres.

Yahya's piece on the refugee camps deserves attention because this element of the Palestinian population is disproportionately active in the Intifada. He is quite correct in stating that the residents of the refugee camps engaged in Intifada-type activities before 1987. His emphasis on nationalistic motives is reasonable, but the evidence offered by Schiff and Yaari—as will be noted later—suggests that such activism stems also from economic and social frustration.

Another interesting piece is that by Hiltermann on the labor movement. He documents the considerate and flexible policy of the Unified National Leadership for the Uprising (UNLU) concerning the working class and the shift of the labor movement from nationalistic concerns to economic interests as the economic pressure grew. Baumgarten's piece on the PLO attempts to prove its important role in the events taking place in the territories. Her tone is representative of most of the articles in the collection, which minimize the tensions between those "inside" (the Palestinians in the territories) and those "outside" (those not living under occupation). Such deference to the PLO also leads to minimizing of the Islamic dimension. Similarly belittled is the role of coercive measures employed by the Palestinians to enforce Intifada rules. The impact of internal terror was not mentioned at all, as at the time of writing the magnitude of this phenomenon was not yet realized.

The third part of the collection, dealing with the international actors, is the most disappointing. It is colored by the temporary successes of the Intifada on the world scene. The claim that the uprising altered the balance between the Arab states and the PLO is no more than wishful thinking. Similarly, the impact of the Intifada on American public opinion is debatable.[3] The piece by Bishara on Israel as the Palestinian rival, which should be one of the most important chapters in the volume, displays ideological rigidity and limited understanding of Israeli society. He is correct in viewing the Intifada as an important input in the ongoing Israeli debate over the future of the territories. Yet, his claim that the strategic debate over the value of territories "nurtures a military mode of thinking" (p. 276) or that the demographic considerations raised by dovish Israelis "contribute to a racist culture" (p. 276) is pathetic. If such an analysis is the best a Palestinian intellectual can offer, then the discrepancy between Israeli scholarship on Palestinian affairs and serious Palestinian writing on Israel provides cause for concern about the future between the two peoples. Another example, symptomatic of the uncritical acceptance of stereotypes about Israel, is the recurrent use throughout the book of the term "Iron Fist," which is supposed to be an Israeli coinage describing its policy in the territories. Such a term is simply non-existent in Israeli parlance.

Despite its shortcomings this book is most useful in learning about how the Palestinians regard themselves. A more careful editing could have prevented some of the overlapping among the chapters.

The Israeli View

One of the best-known works on the Intifada is the book authored by Schiff and Yaari, two Israeli journalist of high calibre and world reputation. Their book is very readable and rich in detailed stories, which gives it an anecdotal flavor. They dwell on why the Israeli government, its intelligence agencies, and the public were totally unprepared for the uprising. This strategic surprise was, in the authors' opinions, the result of a collective mental block. They claim that Israelis preferred to refrain from thinking about the Arabs living under occupation and regarded the Palestinians in the territories as passive subjects. The inclination of the Israeli political elite (Labor and Likud) was to discount the Palestinians as a political factor of little importance. Obviously, the Intifada forced Israelis to pay greater attention to the Palestinians. In this respect, the Intifada was successful. Moreover, public support for continuing the status quo eroded significantly.[4] Yet, the authors realize the limited impact of the Intifada on Israeli society, while noting the increase in threat perception.

As noted, Schiff and Yaari emphasize the socioeconomic factors precipitating the uprising. Indeed, the initial riots by Gaza refugees were directed not only against Israeli targets, but also against the richer Arab neigborhoods. The first stage of the Intifada was depicted by the authors as a rebellion of the *sans-culottes* motivated by poverty and frustration with the socioeconomic environment. Having access to interviews with the first wave of arrestees, Schiff and Yaari were able to convincingly portray the first Intifada activists as being without education and without a developed political and national consciousness. This was a clear sign of the widespread popularity of the struggle against Israel and the changing character of the local leadership. The modus operandi of the "popular committees," in which the representatives of the various outlawed Palestinian terrorist organizations worked together, was based on the cooperation patterns developed in Israeli jails. The Israelis, as noted in the book, had difficulty in eliminating this leadership which was easily replaced by new cadres from below. The increased role of young people in leadership positions, many of them of lower-class origins, was the source of additional strain between the "insiders" and the PLO. The authors stress the fact that when members of this stratum of leadership were expelled, they were not absorbed into the senior ranks of the PLO.

Nevertheless, Schiff and Yaari still see the importance of the PLO for Palestinians in the territories as a symbol of the political struggle for independence. They conclude that the PLO cannot be circumvented in a political process. As an interim step toward an overall agreement, they suggest two options: "Gaza first," namely, establishing a Palestinian entity in Gaza only; or unilateral administrative withdrawal from the territories to allow the Palestinians to run their own municipal affairs. An Israeli-Palestinian-Jordanian confederation is preferred as a permanent settlement instead of a Palestinian state.

Shalev, a senior researcher at the Jaffee Center for Strategic Studies and once the commander of Judea and Samaria (1974 to 1976), wrote a thoughtful book in which the treatment of the Intifada is systematic and detailed. The appendices are also of value. He obviously had access to Israeli policymakers and is well informed. In contrast, his sources from the Palestinian side seem to be rather limited. He begins his book by distinguishing between what he perceives to be the fundamental factors leading to the Intifada and the circumstances that best explain its timing. His analysis of the reasons for Israeli surprise is quite knowledgeable and he distinguishes between cognitive and organizational factors. He attempts to analyze the historical analogies that served the uprising's activists—the 1936 to 1939 Arab Revolt and the Algerian Rebellion, though it is not clear from the book just how those events served as precedents for the Intifada.

A most interesting section of this book is its systematic review of the means of the Palestinian struggle along with Israel's countermeasures. Shalev presents the reader with an array of statistical tables on various aspects of the uprising. By using a limited quantitative approach he can show that there is no reduction in the level of violence following the demolition of homes or the expulsion of activists. Such measures have been considered by Israeli authorities as having great deterrent value.

Shalev is the only author, among those reviewed here, who maintains that the PLO's doctrine of stages has not changed as a result of the Intifada. He quotes PLO official Abu Iyyad in the debate over the Palestinian Declaration of Independence. Probably it is true that many in the Palestinian camp, particularly those who still insist on the "right of return," have not reconciled themselves to the existence of the Jewish state. A systematic review of the Intifada's leaflets, in which none of the works reviewed here engages, also indicates political objectives of a radical nature.[5]

Shalev believes that the Intifada has created a "draw," in which the Israelis cannot eradicate the uprising by the limited measures they are using, while the Palestinians cannot force the Israelis to withdraw. He is probably right, but he fails to see that the asymmetry in resources makes such a "draw" more bearable for Israel. His identification of the political factors that could lead to an exit from this impasse is sound, and his analysis leads him to conclude that the pressures for reaching a settlement are strong and that after an interim stage a Palestinian state will be established in the territories. The realization of his prognosis remains to be seen.

The Overseas View

Despite its name, McDowall's book deals only tangentially with the Intifada. He capitalizes on the uprising to present his analysis of the Arab-Israeli conflict and in particular its intercommunal component. His conceptual framework is sound. Furthermore, at the beginning, he is honest in stating his position as being more sympathetic to the Palestinian view than to the Zionist one. Unfortunately, there is less intellectual honesty as we read on. He attempts to present a balanced analysis of the misperceptions and wrongdoings of both sides. This presumed symmetry is most troubling. In his historic overview, to give just a few examples, the author ignores the Arab predilection for politicide,[6] and the three 'Nos of Khartoum' (1967), and falsely depicts Israel as the only state to reject the 1982 Reagan Plan (so did Jordan and Syria). He deplores the "lack of genuine progress toward peace in the region during the period of 1967–88" (p. 58), totally ignoring the 1978 Camp David Accords and the 1979 Peace Treaty between Israel and Egypt. He is similarly wrong in not admitting that the Israeli recognition of a Palestinian nation preceded the Palestinian perception of a genuine Jewish nationalism by many years.

The author is more concerned with the intercommunal aspect of the conflict than the interstatal one. Yet, he seems little aware of the linkages between the two aspects. He is oblivious to the first partition of Palestine (1920), when Transjordan (75 percent of the territory) was created by British imperial schemes, and to the demographic reality in the political entity situated on the East Bank of the Jordan River, which is mostly Palestinian. This is probably why he rejects any role for Jordan in the quest for a solution for the Palestinians in the territories. It is particularly intriguing because he correctly pays attention to the Palestinians living in Israel as a factor in the intercommunal equation. In treating the Israeli Palestinians he seems to be unaware of what nationalism entails and the fate of national minorities. Such groups, unless assimilated, are never able to become full partners even in an enlightened nation state with a culture different from their own. Therefore, the demands for full equality on the part of Israeli Arabs are sometimes actually, knowingly or not, an attempt to de-Zionize Israel.

McDowall regards the establishment of an independent state in the territories, including East Jerusalem (Judenrein!)

and possibly some Israeli territory within the 1967 borders between Gaza and Hebron (p. 252), as a realistic recipe for peace and stability in the region. Furthermore, a partial return of Palestinian refugees is imperative for McDowall. Though he realizes that the designed contours of his two-state solution are not very palatable to Israel, he believes that the uprising, and the fear of additional uprisings, might move the Israelis in the desired direction. He, like the authors in the first collection reviewed here, suffers from the myopic optimism generated by the evolving events of the first year of the Intifada. McDowall mentions in passing a self-rule arrangement contingent upon elections, but concludes that the Likud as well as Labor reject the idea of elections (p. 246), something which was actually offered in May 1989 by the national unity government.

McDowall, who is less deferent to the PLO than Nassar and Heacock, points out the growing assertiveness of the Palestinians in the territories, though the PLO's role is still considered as indispensable (pp. 119–22). The greater importance of the inside and its successes in the Intifada are the result of the institutionalization of Palestinian nationalism in the territories, a process the PLO nurtured. Observers of Palestinian affairs, including McDowall, point out the significance of the Eighteenth Session of the Palestine National Council in Algiers in April 1987 in which disparate elements within the PLO were reconciled, paving the way for close cooperation during the Intifada. Yet, it is ignored that at that time a militant approach won the day, as the 1985 accord with Jordan was rejected along with the UN Resolution 242. With the exception of Shalev, the more radical goals of the Intifada were ignored by all the authors reviewed. Finally, McDowall is correct in claiming that the Intifada has acquired normalcy (p. 11) and the *status quo ante* cannot be restored.

The book by Peretz is, among those reviewed here, the most comprehensive. It deals systematically with the political, social, and economic aspects of the Intifada on the Palestinian and Israeli sides, as well as its international implications.

His analysis is quite detailed, giving the reader a comprehensive picture of developments. His frequent citations of what the protagonists themselves say about the evolving events is useful in acquiring a better understanding of the differing perspectives.

He could have given less emphasis, however, to the Israeli extremists on the right and on the left. Israeli society is probably less divided than Peretz portrays. Polarization is indeed existent in views about the nature of a future permanent settlement with the Arabs. Yet, there is a large consensus in Israeli society about how to proceed to achieve an interim agreement with the Palestinians. Federal schemes, based on the principle of power sharing, seem to command the support of the political elite as well as of public opinion.[7] This was the cement for the national unity governments (1984 to 1990). Unfortunately, the Palestinians, despite increased moderation, were not ready for a gradual open-ended process with a power-sharing arrangement as the first step until the end of 1991. Therefore, the attempt by Peretz to place the onus of responsibility on Israel for not reaching an agreement with the Palestinians (p. 116) is problematic.

His description of the Likud and of its policies is more appropriate for its first years in power than for the period under discussion. Several Likud leaders indeed attacked Rabin's policies as not "firm enough." The 1988 election campaign bravado or the policy advocacy of backbenchers should be distinguished, however, from policy making. Notably, Shamir defended his defense minister, Rabin. Furthermore, in 1990, Arens, the new defense minister in the right-wing coalition, continued Rabin's line in the territories and even made efforts to eliminate some of the harsher aspects of occupation.[8]

The Israeli reaction to the Intifada indeed contains inherent tensions, but was less "inconsistent" than the author suggests.[9] Actually, in spring 1988 Rabin adopted a comprehensive strategy of attrition against the Palestinians which consisted of a limited use of force, administrative and economic pressure, and judicial measures. The goals were quite clear: to reduce violence to a bearable level, to make clear to the population that the IDF was still in control, and to prevent the establishment of a Palestinian state. Rabin looked for a political avenue to complement the occupation policies, an avenue which materialized with the Israeli peace initiative of May 1989.

Peretz seems to display more understanding toward Palestinian nationalism than to Zionism. Children throwing stones are depicted positively, while Israeli children are "used" (p. 71) by the settlers to make the point that Jews should be able to move freely in Judea and Samaria. Similarly, the "bloody" songs of the Intifada are compared to the Betar pre-state repertoire, ignoring the fact that this Jewish organization was a mere splinter group, while the Intifada art is expressive of Palestinian mainstream nationalism. Nevertheless, Peretz is more attentive than other authors to the emergence of a new culture being created by the Palestinians. Furthermore, he is right on the mark in stressing the formative experience of Israeli jails for Palestinian nationalists.

The Intifada and the Future

All works reviewed concur that the Israeli occupation, which has been a catalyst for the development of national consciousness among the Palestinians, is the main reason for the uprising. There are differences of opinion about the role played by the PLO and how the Intifada has influenced the fortunes of this organization. The short historic perspective prevents all authors from seriously researching more than just the initial impact of the Intifada on the societies of the protagonists. Despite that, the reader is left with the impression that all authors regard an Israeli-Palestinian settlement as closer than before the Intifada started.

Yet, the Intifada, like other intercommunal struggles, is one facet of a protracted conflict, in which each side hopes to bleed the other to defeat. Israelis and Palestinians engage in what Schelling termed "the diplomacy of violence."[10] Therefore, the analysis of the evolving relation between means and goals is a central aspect of the Intifada and Israel's reaction to it. This issue is neglected in the works reviewed, though Shalev pays some attention to it. Israel has gradually developed an attritional strategy and adjusted itself in several ways to meet the new challenge of the Intifada. The Palestinians were successful, for a time, in attracting international attention to their suffering and their demands. As noted, by the summer of 1991 their uprising seemed at a crossroads, seeking a clear direction.

Though the Intifada, as an expression of the dissatisfaction with Israeli occupation, was not over, the evaluation of its political significance is crucial in understanding the dynamics of the Arab-Israeli conflict. The books reviewed convey the feeling that the Palestinians have the upper hand in the intercommunal struggle. From the vantage point of the fall of 1991, "the question who is winning in the contest?" is not as easily answered. The answer to this question depends on the military and political objectives set by the parties. The extent that the goals of the two sides are exclusive is pertinent to what can be termed as a victory. Finally, the price for achieving the goals must be considered.

Initially, Israel attempted to restore the *status quo ante*. This it was unable to do. Later on, "reducing violence to a bearable level" became the goal. It is not clear what "bearable" means. Israeli society, which has succeeded in routinizing the conflict,[11] seems to have adjusted to a certain level of violence in the territories, indicating that the "reasonable" level has been reached. As Israel never really hoped to win the hearts of the Palestinians in the territories, their control would involve a greater military effort. The limit of Israeli society's toleration of greater dosages of force against the Palestinians is not clear. Victory in a conventional sense is not within reach in the immediate future in this protracted conflict.

The Intifada also seemed to be fading away from the Israeli and international consciousness because of the diversion in the focus of international attention to other affairs. Unfortunately for the Palestinians, after a time the world seemed more interested in the hopes and tragedies of other peoples. This could change, of course. In the meantime, the Israeli level of indifference is not conducive to the achievement of Palestinian goals.

Israel also attempted to forestall the challenge to its governing role. As all authors reviewed noted, it was only partially successful as a parallel structure of authority was in operation. In this matter, victory, i.e., the elimination of this communal authority structure, is impossible. Yet, this has never been an Israeli goal. Israel has been ambivalent toward the emergence of a Palestinian leadership in the territories and toward the political institutionalization of the Palestinian national movement, trends which were accelerated by the Intifada. Israeli leaders were happy to observe that since 1987, for the first time, local Palestinians led the struggle. It was hoped that they could be partners to an agreement, particularly after Jordan's King Hussein announced his disengagement from the West Bank (July 1988). Indeed, in May 1989 the government offered an election plan. On the other hand, the activities of the leadership often led them to Israeli jails, which was sometimes needed to authenticate their nationalistic credentials.

Similar Israeli ambivalence can be found with regard to the territories, which confused their inhabitants. Israel did not make up its mind about what to do with the territories in the long run. The lack of clarity was primarily due to the stalemate in Israeli politics. Labor was willing to relinquish part of the territories. Even the Likud leaders spoke about taking the IDF out of the cities in an autonomy arrangement. One inevitable result was the growing Palestinian unrest. It is impossible to secure the cooperation of the population during an uprising if the government states its intention to withdraw.[12] Finally, in the competition to coerce the population into cooperation, Israel has little chance to win vis-à-vis the brutality of the internal terror conducted by the Intifada leaders.

Israeli withdrawal from the territories, one goal of the Intifada, is still far from being imminent. True, polls show a slightly greater inclination on the part of Israelis to part with some of the territories. Yet a Palestinian state, another Intifada goal, is still rejected by most of the Israeli political elite and public. Palestinian behavior in the uprising toward the Jews, or toward themselves for that matter, did not endear them as good neighbors. The support of the Palestinian masses and their leadership for Iraq following its August 1990 invasion of Kuwait, and the stories about Palestinians cheering from their rooftops at incoming Iraqi missiles directed at civilian population centers, further estranged them even from Israelis who had been sympathetic to their cause. The previously noted Israeli adjustment to the new state of affairs did not bring the Palestinians much closer to their goals.

The price paid by Israel in human and material losses is also not exceptional. It parallels the effort invested in combating terror, though the psychological price is higher. An indirect price is interference with preparations for the next conventional war. The troops are chasing children in the territories instead of training, and funds are diverted from research and development and weapons procurement to provide means for effective riot control. Yet an army has to prepare for the most likely encounter. Nowadays, in the aftermath of the Gulf War, it seems that the main threats to Israel are in the sub-conventional and non-conventional areas in the spectrum of violence. The Intifada and chemical weapons on-board missiles are more of a problem in the near future than the conventional armies of Israel's Arab rivals. It is also not clear that possible failures in a future conventional war are more potentially damaging to Israel than a setback in the struggle against the Intifada. Taking into consideration that the Intifada could influence the drawing of Israel's future eastern border, this confrontation probably constitutes the most critical front. Low-intensity conflict could well be the decisive form of warfare in the near future.

The price paid by the Palestinians for having an Intifada is quite high. As the occupation became harsher, they experienced massive disruption of their daily lives. Over one thousand were killed and thousands were wounded. Tens of thousands spent some time in Israeli jails. The strikes, curfews, and Israeli economic pressures, in conjunction with economic developments in the Gulf and in Jordan, caused a drastic drop in the standard of living. Security has deteriorated. The education system was paralyzed and only recently has the Intifada leadership realized the importance of leaving this sector outside of uprising activities.

Israelis were quite impressed with the ability of Palestinian society to sustain such heavy costs. Nevertheless, Israeli policies toward the territories remain basically unchanged. The acceptance of the Palestinians of the Israeli preference for a Camp David–based formula for negotiations at Madrid (October 1991) seems also to indicate Intifada's limited successes. Similarly, the curtailed PLO role and the higher profile of the "insiders" is closer to Israeli preferences. The erosion in the power of the PLO, however, also pleases some Palestinian elements and points out that this intercommunal conflict is not necessarily a zero-sum game—areas of mutual interest do exist. This does not mean of course that the two sides will discontinue causing suffering to the other.

The reviewer's evaluation is that Israelis are probably better equipped in the competition to exact costs on the other side. Possibly, the suffering on both sides will have an educational value in lowering expectations and redefining goals and the meaning of victory. Protracted compound conflicts in other places in the world seem to indicate, however, that collectives are not fast learners and that collective aspirations legitimize the heavy societal costs.

This chapter has covered several books in the first wave of literature on the Intifada. A second wave with a longer historic perspective will undoubtedly emerge. Attempts at answering the question of who won the contest will be definitely offered. The research agenda should include evaluation of the long-range effects of the Intifada on both sides. The high degree of social mobilization among the Palestinians during the uprising will leave a lasting imprint on the development of Palestinian nationalism and policies vis-à-vis the Israelis. As the Palestinians are extremely politicized, the Intifada has had an impact on social, economic, and cultural trends. Israelis, though veterans of protracted conflict and to a limited extent insulated from the small war waged in the territories, cannot really escape the dispute with the Palestinians. Their responses in the sociopolitical and cultural spheres will be assessed with a longer perspective.

There is little doubt that Israeli and Palestinian societies will regard the Intifada as an event of great historic importance. Its significance will be measured not only in sociopolitical terms, but also according to the prevailing historical interpretations future authors will offer to the Intifada. The mythology emerging from the events started in December 1987 will affect the future of the Arab-Israeli conflict.

Notes

1. For the term "compound conflict" see Shmuel Sandler, "The Protracted Arab-Israeli Conflict: A Temporal-Spatial Analysis," *Jerusalem Journal of International Relations* 10 (December 1988): 55; see also Edward E. Azar, Paul Jureidini and Robert McLaurin, "Protracted Social Conflict: Theory and Practice in the Middle East," *Journal of Palestine Studies* 6 (Autumn 1978): 41-60. For a review of the types of Israeli-Palestinian exchanges of violence see Stuart A. Cohen and Efraim Inbar, "Varieties of Counter-insurgency Activities: Israel's Military Operations against the Palestinians, 1948-90," *Small Wars and Insurgencies* 2 (April 1991): 41-59.

2. The figures are taken from the 1 October, 1991, B'tzelem report.

3. See Eytan Gilboa, "The Palestinian Uprising: Has It Turned American Public Opinion?" *Orbis* 33 (Winter 1989): 21-37.

4. See Giora Goldberg, Gad Barzilai and Efraim Inbar, *The Impact of Intercommunal Conflict: The Intifada and Israeli Public Opinion*, Policy Study No. 44 (Jerusalem: Leonard Davis Institute for International Relations, Hebrew University, February 1991), pp. 11-15.

5. For such an analysis see Shaul Mishal with Reuben Aharoni, *Speaking Stones: The Words Behind the Palestinian Intifada* (Tel Aviv: Hakibbutz Hameuchad Publishing House and Avivim, 1989), Hebrew.

6. For this term and the Arab positions toward Israel see Yehoshafat Harkabi, *Arab Strategies and Israel's Response* (New York: The Free Press, 1977), pp. 1-77.

7. Gad Barzilai, Giora Goldberg, and Efraim Inbar, "Attitudes of the Israeli Leadership and Public Toward Federal Solutions for the Arab-Israeli Conflict," *Publius* 21 (Summer 1991): 191-209.

8. For an argument that the Likud has over time moderated its positions see Efraim Inbar and Giora Goldberg, "Is Israel's Political Elite Becoming More Hawkish?" *International Journal* 45 (Summer 1990): 643–60.

9. For an analysis of the Israeli strategic and military response, see Efraim Inbar, "Israel's Small War: The Military Response to the Intifada," *Armed Forces and Society* 18 (Fall 1991): 29–50.

10. Thomas C. Schelling, *Arms and Influence* (New Haven: Yale University Press, 1976), pp. 1–34.

11. Baruch Kimmerling, *The Interrupted System* (New Brunswick: Transaction, 1985).

12. Frank Kitson, *Low Intensity Operations* (London: Faber and Faber, 1971), p. 50.

LIST OF CONTRIBUTORS

James Armstrong is Associate Professor and chair of the Department of Anthropology at SUNY Plattsburgh. He is co-editor of *Distant Mirrors: America as a Foreign Culture*.

Efraim Ben-Zadok is Associate Professor of Public Administration at Florida Atlantic University. He was a faculty member at the State University of New York and Tel Aviv University. His fields of interest are public policy analysis, and urban politics and policy. His recent book is entitled *Local Communities and the Israeli Polity* (1993).

Shmuel Bolozky is Professor of Hebrew in the Department of Judaic and Near Eastern Studies at the University of Massachusetts, Amherst. Formerly he taught in the Department of Linguistics at Tel Aviv University. He holds a B.A. from the Hebrew University of Jerusalem, an M.A. from the University of London, and a Ph.D. in Linguistics from the University of Illinois. His research specialization is in Hebrew and general phonology and morphology.

Giora Goldberg is Senior Lecturer in Political Studies at Bar-Ilan University. He has written numerous journal articles and book chapters about Israeli politics, society, elections, and parties. He is also the author of several books in Hebrew, including *Political Parties in Israel: From Mass Parties to Electoral Parties* (1992).

Efraim Inbar is Associate Professor in Political Studies at Bar-Ilan University and the Director of its BESA Center for Strategic Studies. He has published extensively on Israeli national security problems and his latest book is *War and Peace in Israeli Politics: Labor Party Positions on National Security*. He is currently engaged in a study of the Israeli use of force.

Yagil Levy is an Instructor in the Department of Political Science at Tel Aviv University. He recently received his Ph.D. from Tel Aviv University, with the dissertation "The Role of the Military Sphere in the Construction of the Social-Political Order in Israel: The Conduct of the Arab-Israeli Conflict as a Statist Control Strategy." He is the author of a number of forthcoming articles on military-society relations in Israel and elsewhere.

Abraham Marthan is Professor at Gratz College, near Philadelphia, where he teaches Hebrew literature and the literature of the golden age in Spain. He holds a Ph.D. from Dropsie University, and is author of a volume of Hebrew poems *Shavot Hasirot im Erev*, and numerous essays and critical studies in the field of Hebrew literature.

Yoav Peled is a Senior Lecturer in the Department of Political Science at Tel Aviv University. He is the author of *Class and Ethnicity in the Pale: The Political Economy of Jewish Workers' Nationalism in Late Imperial Russia* (1989) and of several articles on Israeli society and politics.

Ilan Peleg is the Charles A. Dana Professor of Government and Law at Lafayette College in Easton, Pennsylvania. Among his books are *Begin's Foreign Policy 1977–83: Israel's Turn to the Right* (1987); *The Emergence of a Bi-National State: The Second Republic in the Making* (1989); and most recently, *Patterns of Censorship Around the World* (1993). He specializes in Israeli foreign policy, the peace process, and the Israeli right.

Uri Ram is an Instructor in the Department of Sociology at Haifa University. His Ph.D. is from the New School for Social Research. He is the Editor of *Israeli Society: Critical Perspectives* (Breirot, 1993, Hebrew). His book *The Changing Agenda* of *Israeli Sociology: Theory, Ideology & Identity* is forthcoming (SUNY Press).

Aviad E. Raz is a teaching assistant and Ph.D. candidate in the Department of Sociology and Anthropology, and the Interdisciplinary Program at Tel Aviv University. While serving in the Israel Defense Forces he has written extensively on Israeli literature in various literary supplements. His most recent research work, concerning personal narratives in old age, is in *Studies in Symbolic Interaction* (1993). He is currently interested in Israeli youth delegations to Auschwitz as forms of initiation rites in collective memory.

Jerome Slater is Professor of Political Science at SUNY Buffalo. He is the author of a number of books and articles on American foreign policy, international security, and the Arab-Israeli conflict.

Russell A. Stone is Professor of Sociology and Associate Dean for Graduate Affairs in the College of Arts and Sciences, The American University, Washington, D.C. His research interests include Israel, the Middle East and Third World societies, the application of social indicators models to the study of social change, and environmental sociology. He has done field research in Tunisia and Afghanistan as well as Israel, is author of *Social Change in Israel: Attitudes and Events*, and has several other publications on development in Middle East societies. He is editor of the SUNY Press series on Israel Studies.

Madeleine Tress is a Program Associate at the Hebrew Immigrant Aid Society. Her research focuses on the resettlement of Jewish immigrants and refugees in North America, Western Europe and Israel. She is currently conducting a comparative study of the resettlement of Jews from the former Soviet Union in the U.S., Israel, and Germany.

Walter F. Weiker is Professor of Political Science at Rutgers University, Newark, New Jersey. He has written extensively on modern Turkey, and is author of *The Unseen Israelis: Jews from Turkey in Israel*, and *Ottomans, Turks and the Jewish Polity: A History of the Jews of Turkey*. He is at work on further studies of ethnicity in Israel and elsewhere.

Walter P. Zenner is Professor of Anthropology at the University at Albany, SUNY. He has specialized in the study of Jewish ethnic identity, with special regard to the history of Syrian Sephardim. His works include *Persistence and Flexibility: Anthropological Perspectives on the American Jewish Experience*; and *Minorities in the Middle: A Cross-Cultural Analysis*. He co-edited *Jewish Societies in the Middle East*. He is editor of the SUNY Press Series in Anthropology and Judaic Studies.